W9-DBW-734

Globalization and Global Governance

Globalization and Global Governance

Edited by
Raimo Väyrynen

ROWMAN & LITTLEFIELD PUBLISHERS, INC.
Lanham • Boulder • New York • Oxford

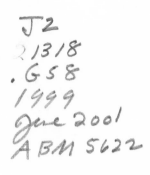

ROWMAN & LITTLEFIELD PUBLISHERS, INC.

Published in the United States of America
by Rowman & Littlefield Publishers, Inc.
4720 Boston Way, Lanham, Maryland 20706

12 Hid's Copse Road
Cumnor Hill, Oxford OX2 9JJ, England

British Library Cataloguing in Publication Information Available

Library of Congress Cataloging-in-Publication Data

Globalization and global governance / edited by Raimo V. Väyrynen.
    p. cm.
   Revision of papers originally presented at the Canadian-U.S.
Conference on Global Governance held May 8–10, 1997 at the
University of Notre Dame.
   Includes bibliographical references and index.
   ISBN 0-8476-9154-3 (cloth : alk. paper). — ISBN 0-8476-9155-1
(pbk. : alk. paper)
   1. International cooperation.   2. International economic
relations.   I. Väyrynen, Raimo.   II. Canadian-U.S. Conference on
Global Governance (1997 : University of Notre Dame).
JZ1318.G58   1999
337—dc21   98-48273
                                                       CIP

Printed in the United States of America

♾ ™ The paper used in this publication meets the minimum requirements of
American National Standard for Information Sciences—Permanence of Paper for
Printed Library Materials, ANSI Z39.48–1992.

Contents

Tables

Figures

.

Preface

Global governance has become a key challenge in the conduct of international relations. It calls for national and multilateral actions to respond collectively to the fragmentation of economic and political systems and the transnational threats permeating through borders. The growing need for global governance is in part the product of various forces of globalization that reduce the relevance and efficiency of national governments. Increasingly, states can thwart financial instabilities, political crises, and environmental deterioration only by acting in concert.

Globalization is not, of course, a single process but rather a bundle of different economic, technological, political, and ecological processes. Because of differences in actors, issues, policy instruments, and structural contexts, their management requires quite different approaches. Moreover, it would be misleading to think that the need for global governance arises only from the spread of globalization.

In fact, most international problems today have domestic roots which spill over borders and thus threaten the security of other people; refugee flows are a case in point. Therefore, global governance cannot replace the need for good governance in national societies; in fact, in the absence of quality local governance, global and regional arrangements are bound to fail or will have only limited effectiveness. In a way, global governance has to be built from the ground up and then linked back to the local conditions.

There is in the present international society an enforcement gap that needs to be filled if global governance is to be effective at all. Norms of security, democracy, and human rights cannot be upheld in the absence of international institutions and other capabilities by which to address the problems of compliance. The United Nations obviously has done better than many of its critics acknowledge in coping with security and monetary relations and international public "bads." Yet, the United Nations as an institution is only a partial answer to the contemporary challenge of global governance.

Enforcement faces the task of mustering adequate collective capability to make sure that most actors in the international system heed its basic norms reasonably well. Maximal thinking about enforcement is dangerous; it too easily leads to ambitious efforts to impose a specific and partial solution on a complex issue. Instead, enforcement should be considered a limited strategy by which acceptable compliance with principal international norms can be attained; it should be a flexible instrument to achieve specific goals. Enforcement needs to be tailored to the requirements of each particular situation or problem. It should rely on facilitation and persuasion rather than coercion and its threats.

Economic sanctions have turned out to be too blunt an instrument to reach specific political goals; even if some success has been attained their humanitarian costs may have been excessive. General sanctions seem to work only when the political system of the target is relatively open and vulnerable to pressure by the sanctioner. However, democratic governments are today the least likely targets of sanctions, which are generally directed at recalcitrant, authoritarian states. This suggests that the recent sanctions era in international relations is over, not the least for the reason that both transnational corporations and popular movements tend to be opposed to sanctions.

There has been an effort to rescue sanctions as a method of enforcement by advocating more targeted and specific sanctions that would punish the wrongdoers rather than the people. Targeted sanctions, such as the freezing of bank accounts, are, indeed, an instrument of enforcement that deserves closer scrutiny. However, the ability of those in power to shield themselves from the punishment and switch the costs again to the people should not be underestimated.

Material sanctions alone are unlikely to fill the enforcement gap in international relations. They may work primarily as a political lever in situations in which the targeted leadership is already contemplating the opportunity costs of alternative strategies. The exposure to sanctions increases the potential future costs of noncompliant behavior and thus decreases its attractiveness. The use of incentives to reward compliance with international norms will probably increase the appeal of the change in political course.

Sanctions are imposed from outside and thus rely on a hands-off approach. Peacekeeping, on the other hand, requires presence in the conflict theater and therefore involves contacts with the parties to the conflict. Peacekeeping, like all methods of international enforcement, is an instrument of politics. As politics has changed in the post–cold war era, so has peacekeeping been transformed. To be effective, peacekeeping must promote long-term cooperative solutions to internal violence. Such peace building is increasingly expected to be a tool of political and social transformation.

Military peacekeeping is needed to prevent the parties from using force against one another and to protect humanitarian deliveries. Troops alone are not enough, however, especially if they rely on the traditional capabilities and doctrines of military force. For the enforcement of norms to be effective, peace building needs stronger police units, lawyers to build up judicial systems, experts in economic reconstruction, and, first of all, local mobilization to strengthen civil society.

Canadian and U.S. views on the preferred world order and ways to attain it are obviously quite different. In the United States there is a strong tendency to consider U.S. political and moral standards superior to those of others. They provide, by definition, international benchmarks with which the performance of other states should be compared even if the United States itself does not necessarily comply with these standards.

The presumed superiority of U.S. normative standards means that others are not permitted to judge the United States by their own criteria; in fact, the United States expects to be exempted from such international scrutiny. The process leading to the establishment of the international criminal court provides ample evidence of U.S. exceptionalism in global governance.

The strong stress on U.S. sovereignty illustrates how state's normative standards are domestically determined. The Canadian case initially appears to be quite different. Canada is often regarded as a "like-minded" middle power that advocates multilateralism and international collective good rather than its own specific interests. Although Canadians emphasize the sovereignty of their country, they do so mainly as a defense against U.S. economic and cultural predominance. However, it can also be argued that for Canada, multilateralism and global governance are perfectly rational instruments to pursue its own interests.

Thus, both the United States and Canada, like most other countries, have made their approach to global governance contingent on domestic politics. The difference is that whereas Washington limits global cooperation by opting out from many collective efforts for its own peculiar reasons, Ottawa is juxtaposing domestic and global policies in a manner that does not create major frictions.

These and many other issues of global governance and enforcement were explored at the "Canadian–U.S. Conference on Global Governance" on May 8–10, 1997, which was organized by the Joan B. Kroc Institute for International Peace Studies at the University of Notre Dame. Since then, most of the papers presented at the conference have been heavily revised to provide timely and coordinated contributions to this volume.

The organization of the conference was greatly facilitated by a grant provided by the Canadian Department of Foreign Affairs and International Trade to the Kroc Institute, to cover the expenses of the Canadian participants. Paul Heinbecker, assistant deputy minister for global and security policy, gave a profound and witty keynote address to the conference. In addition, we would also like to warmly thank Donald T. Wismer, the consul general in the Canadian Consulate in Detroit, and George Costaris, its director for political and economic relations. Paul Frazer, minister at the Canadian Embassy in Washington, D.C., deserves special credit for proposing at an early date closer cooperation between Canadian scholars and Notre Dame.

In the Kroc Institute, Colonel Thomas Moe(USAF, ret.) was superbly in charge of the early preparation and coordination of the conference. With his departure, the role of Clare White became increasingly pivotal. She made sure that everything in the conference went smoothly and effectively. Hal Culbertson helped in a significant way in the editing of the present volume. Elizabeth (Suzy) Grandin and Diane Hagens provided excellent technical assistance in preparing the manuscript.

—Raimo Väyrynen

I

Globalization and the Need for Global Institutions and Norms

1

Three Types of Globalization: Communication, Market, and Direct

Robert T. Kudrle

Globalization has become one of the words most frequently employed concepts to characterize the dynamics of the present era, yet most dictionaries tell us that the word does not exist. The term must therefore be considered carefully in light of the intent of those using it. I have discerned three foci of attention and associated literatures; each has rather different implications for governance, and therefore they should be treated separately.

Perhaps the largest part of writing in political science and international relations concerns what I have termed *market globalization*, and this is probably the dominant popular usage as well. There is much dispute about whether the volume of certain economic measures relative to national and world economic products exceed some past levels, but few dispute that the character of these modern exchanges is different.

Improvements in transportation and particularly in communication make many international trade and investment linkages more organic than was possible in previous periods, resulting in an unprecedented degree of "functional integration between internationally dispersed activities" (Dicken 1992, 1). A much smaller part of international exchange now takes place through arm's-length transactions than previously, and much more takes place within a single firm or through bargains struck, revised, and monitored at the firm level.

Global warming and the destruction of the rain forest suggest another widely recognized phenomenon. The term *direct globalization* can be used to describe what economists would call international externalities: nonmarketed actions that palpably affect persons across borders. The idea of externality can be extended to issues that go beyond physical interaction. For example, outsiders may view environmental matters in another country with disfavor even though the outsiders are not physically affected by them. Some literature refers to such effects as negative "psychological" externalities (Esty 1994, 107; Aaron et al. 1995, xxvi).

The element that provides the key qualitative difference from earlier times and most justifies the claim that we live in an "age of globalization" resides in yet a third use of the term: *communication globalization,* a phenomenon that provides a critical weft for the warp of market and direct globalization. The organic connection within multinational corporations, the speed, volume, and accuracy of the financial information that binds world capital markets, and the vividness with which both tangible and intangible externalities are perceived internationally turn on dramatic changes in both the quality and the quantity of international communication. These staggering changes have resulted not only from technological discovery— satellite broadcasting, fiber-optic cables, and the internet—but from a rapid drop in the real price of the services of these technologies as they are more widely used and understood.

Communication globalization has facilitated market globalization and intensified direct globalization. In addition, much of the international transmission of information, ideas, and styles can be linked to either externality or commerce and could be subsumed under the first two categories of globalization. Nevertheless, communication globalization does more than highlight the qualitative difference between earlier periods and the present in those two dimensions. It stands as a major force in its own right. The ability of a concerned citizen in one country to capture both the facts and the "texture" of events unfolding in another part of the world provides just one example.

This chapter makes three claims. First, most of the writing on globalization can be related to one of the three meanings just outlined. This claim can be tested by the reader but will not be documented here.[1] Second, and far more important, each of the three types of globalization poses challenges for governance. Third, those challenges differ quite sharply from each other. I consider the problems posed for national governments, the problems that are raised for a state's relations with others, and the prospects that those problems can be dealt with satisfactorily through international cooperation.

COMMUNICATION GLOBALIZATION

Communication globalization poses challenges that differ sharply among the developed countries and also presents problems for the governance of poorer countries. It may be useful to distinguish the significance of communication globalization on the basis of three broad impacts: the economic effect, the cultural effect, and the comparison effect.

The Economic Effect

The technical essence of communication globalization lies in ongoing technological discoveries and commercial applications that may provide a more vivid example of what Joseph Schumpeter has called the "gale of creative destruction" (1943, 84) than anything the great economist saw in his lifetime. The cost of voice communication has dropped by a factor of ten in the two decades before 1996, and the cost of data communication fell by a factor of one thousand (Petrazzini 1996, 2). The associated innovations have changed the character of commercial life in virtually every country.

Characteristically, the first reaction of most developed states to the formidable combination of computers and telecommunications was to try to protect their own manufacturing and service industries. The United States was relatively slow to act against this new form of protectionism (Spero 1982), although it had by far the most to gain from open access. It did succeed in getting the relevant issues discussed in the Uruguay Round of the GATT (General Agreement on Tariffs and Trade) negotiations, although the first major agreement was struck only in early 1997.

One interpretation of the speed with which rampant protectionism gave way to an evolving but fairly open regime stresses the danger of falling behind in the availability of the latest technologies. At a given exchange rate, all protectionism raises the domestic costs of commercial users and makes their international sales success less likely. Telecommunications simply presents the problem more vividly, because the product is such a universal input. Every day that passes without accommodation to the advantages offered by the newest technologies, whatever their national provenance, hurts domestic firms in myriad industries in terms of their ability to compete with foreign counterparts. Recognition of this reality has led the governments of both rich and poor countries to privatize previously public facilities and to allow the import of the highest-performance equipment. In addition, although some countries with acceptable domestic purveyors maintain protection, many states are providing unprecedented openness to new competitors, both foreign and domestic. In many poor countries, the low cost of the new technologies is permitting wide-scale voice communication for the first time. The new technologies are also expanding the scope of international trade, especially in services. Accountants in Bombay can now serve clients in Seattle.

The Cultural Effect

The second major impact brought about by communications globalization is the cultural effect. Whereas authoritarian states may want to control information for its own sake, many democratic governments aspire to protect national cultural integrity against the threats posed by global commerce in entertainment and information. The consumption of this material from foreign sources is believed to erode the collective sense of national uniqueness.

Canada has declined to bargain with foreigners (especially the United States, in their bilateral Free Trade Agreement or in the subsequent trilateral agreement with Mexico) on foreign ownership of its "cultural industries," including broadcasting, sound and visual recording, filmmaking and film distribution, and all forms of publishing. (As many critics have pointed out, however, restrictions on foreign ownership are neither necessary nor sufficient to control content in the way that would preserve a distinctly national viewpoint [Globerman and Vining 1983].) France pushed successfully in the Uruguay Round to prevent coverage of trade in cultural products. Despite these temporary victories, protection of nationally sourced broadcasting through quotas, rather than by offering more appealing programming, appears doomed. Some past policies have successfully pushed content in a nationalist direction, but this was far more feasible when there were only a few radio and television outlets. Cable and satellite technologies have now multiplied the number of choices so dramatically that, for example, even if every channel (or package of channels) were obliged to offer the 50 percent European content agreed on by the European Union, all viewers would, at any given time, face a plethora of non-European options (however the latter is defined).

It seems reasonable to assume that, under current and future conditions, the only successful attempts to control national exposure to a large volume of compelling foreign communication will be mounted by distinctly non-democratic governments. A typical citizen is simply unwilling to forgo very much choice in entertainment to serve the goal of cultural autonomy—even when that goal is accepted as very important.

A simple view of the cultural impact of communication globalization portrays it as a vehicle for increasing American dominance of world styles and attitudes. But careful students of the media see a more complicated picture. First, most would point out that misleading generalizations are often drawn when attention is focused on Canada and France. Despite considerable cultural differences between the United States and Canada (Kudrle and Marmor 1980), the English-speaking parts of both countries are similar in international perspective. One country, however, is ten times the size of the other. A worldwide pattern reveals that most smaller countries import much more media than larger ones and, although the small import from the large, the large do not import much from each other. Much of this can be explained by the extraordinary economies of scale in broadcasting and films combined with an attraction for national material in the national language. Both sets of states also import a considerable amount, especially of high-fixed-cost entertainment material, from the common denominator source, Hollywood. Canada is unusual in being so heavily dominated by imports from one foreign country.

Second, the failure of the large European countries to import much "cultural production" from each other raises serious doubts about the potential of a genuinely European industry to compete globally with the Americans. Third, non-Western markets, particularly large ones, are not easily dominated from outside the culture. Japan, for example, consumes more than 95 percent of its electronic information and entertainment from domestic sources (Tunstall 1995, 12–13). The Middle East draws heavily on Cairo's products, and South Asia on Bombay's. Fourth, although much U.S. material is used to fill up the many channels of entertainment in Europe, only a few U.S. programs typically make the top fifty programs in most markets. The U.S. dominates in Europe only in major films, a market segment in which it continues to rule the world. This dominance causes consternation in France, the only European country with a major domestic film industry. Finally, production taking place in the United States is increasingly owned in Australia, Japan, and Europe, so the meaning of "foreign influence" becomes complex.

None of the above denies that foreign influence of various kinds is at a higher level in most countries than ever before and that it is growing—largely because of communication globalization. But the U.S. role in that influence may well be falling rather than rising. As long ago as the 1970s, many developing countries concluded that the superior resources of the developed world, including its technology, and its dedication to "a free flow of information" posed a threat to the development of a national consciousness and the global presentation of their points of view. The ensuing wrangle over what was called the New International Information Order (NIIO) took place largely in UNESCO (United Nations Educational, Scientific, and Cultural Organization) and provided a major reason for the U.S. withdrawal in 1984 (Graubart 1989, 630). The NIIO seems to have faded with a generally more outward-looking posture by many poorer countries, along with the end of the cold war, and was largely gone before the full potential of the new technologies was fully understood.

The British media commentator Anthony Smith has written, "Perhaps we are moving into an era in which the 'identity' and 'heritage' of most individuals will lie somewhere between the local or regional or national and the international—a kind of global creole?" (1995, 3). But for most of the world's population, even in the richer countries, this era appears some distance in the future, and the complex process will involve far more than "Americanization."

The Comparison Effect

A third and extremely important result of communication globalization, the comparison effect, has important but still poorly understood implications for governance. Professional international benchmarking in nearly all fields (Rose 1991, 1993) depends to some extent on improvements in transportation and communication; however, its more informal popular counterpart, what I call simply "the comparison effect," is greatly amplified by continuous, vivid, instantaneous communication. That communication greatly increases the apparent relevance of the nominally foreign, not just in the style of daily life but also in social relations and the demands made on governments. Whereas the cultural effect deals with general attitudes, the comparison effect draws attention to specific practices with direct political implications. Such issues as environmental degradation, gender relations, and social deference—each of which has serious implications for governance—now appear to be strongly and continuously influenced from outside the polity (unless perhaps that polity is the United States). Experts believe that the urge to migrate from poor countries has also been heightened by the vivid portrayal of superior material conditions abroad (Weiner 1995).

In many places communication globalization will increase the demand for democracy, and the intrinsically borderless world of telecommunications technology therefore represents a threat for some states. China, for example, has attempted to develop an internet system that controls domestic access and monitors incoming material. Most experts believe that the system cannot work. Offending material may be identified only long after it has entered the country, if at all. This implies, among other problems, that the number of persons who can ultimately gain access to such material is essentially impossible to control.

International Implications

What continuing international relations issues do varying national postures toward communication globalization suggest? Among the developed countries, problems linger in the two broad areas of telecommunications and cultural industries. Anxiety about economywide effects of lagging in the former sector has yielded a recent international agreement that promises almost complete openness within a few years among the industrialized countries and the most successful economies of the Far East. Many developing countries maintain restrictions, but restricted access, even by such technologically competent states as India and Brazil, appears to owe more to reflexive nationalism and special interests than to national economic strategy. Present resistance to openness may well collapse in the face of demands from domestic users, and, in the meantime, the holdouts have not delayed agreement by others.

Protection of cultural industries may generate additional conflict, but it appears largely self-limiting. Technological change means all states will increasingly attract audiences to national fare only by making it competitive rather than by eliminating competition, and this poses no impossible challenge. National audiences generally prefer national entertainment in the national language (Tunstall 1995, 12). This still leaves a considerable market for imports, and the U.S. now dominates this market. Non-U.S. industries, especially in Europe, may try to establish stronger global competitors through subsidy. If they do, U.S. firms selling against them will undoubtedly protest, but the dispute is unlikely to be unprecedentedly important, even as a trade dispute, and scarcely threatens to seriously damage overall relations among the affected countries (Van Harpen 1995).

MARKET GLOBALIZATION

Market globalization encompasses the increased mobility of goods and services, capital, and labor. It has been powerfully buttressed by communication globalization. Each of these three major categories of mobility has created alarm and demands for tighter governance at both the national and international level.[2]

Trade

Many regard the increase in international trade as responsible for both a decline in the standard of living in the industrial countries and a deterioration of the distribution of income. There are important theoretical reasons for believing that unskilled labor might be hurt by an expansion of manufactured exports from countries with lower per capita incomes, and recent research suggests that somewhere between a negligible amount and as much as 30 percent of the change in income distribution in industrial countries income distributions since the early 1970s may be attributable to increased trade (Rodrik 1997a). Virtually no economist believes, however, that the solution involves greater protectionism. Generations of policy elites in Europe, Japan, and the United States have absorbed the implications of the doctrine of comparative advantage—what Paul Samuelson has called the most important nonobvious proposition in the social sciences.

High levels of unemployment in Europe and low rates of growth in nearly all rich countries make bargaining for greater openness with trading partners difficult; but most of the industrial countries are continuing to make substantial progress in opening their markets to one another. Even more significantly, as part of the worldwide "rediscovery of the market" in the 1980s, poorer countries began using the price system far more extensively than had been the case since the end of the colonial period.

Although enormous variations exist, what Anne Krueger (1997) has called "outer" policies now solidly prevail over "inner" policies in the developing world, producing astounding results. A clear majority of the population of the developing countries now lives in states in which the per capita income is growing faster than in the developed countries. The bottom 20 percent, much of it in Africa, has yet to see much progress.

The enormous increase in economic activity in the nonindustrial world did not come at the expense of the overall income of the richer countries. The newcomers certainly hastened the decline of certain sectors in the industrial countries, but they have also provided important new sources of demand for developed country exports. There is no theoretical or empirical reason for believing that their ascent as a group has significantly affected the overall welfare of the previously industrialized states. Increased economic activity anywhere may pose a challenge to the global environment, of course, but that is a different argument.

The deteriorating income distribution in the rich countries is paralleled by similar deterioration in at least some developing countries, and the chief culprit appears to be technology (Krugman 1995). Technical changes across a broad range of industries are increasing the value of skills relative to pure labor power. The major solution for the distributional problem also appears to be the most promising path of overall economic advance for each state taken alone: an increase in human capital formation through more successful education and training, leading to an increase in labor productivity.

Capital Mobility

Capital mobility has also been widely blamed for the increase in income inequality on grounds that capital cannot be successfully taxed when it can easily escape any national jurisdiction. This is an argument that simply does not stand up to the facts, however much cover it may give to some politicians. Most commentary fails to distinguish between gross capital flows based on speculation about exchange rates and sustained net capital flows based on real differences in private capital yield among countries.

Capital will try to abandon states temporarily when the future exchange rate is expected to be lower, but this is very different from the continuous loss of capital from a country because it refuses to reward its owners at the level available elsewhere. The latter possibility has not been an important cause of international capital flows among politically stable countries. In the 1980s, for example, no OECD (Organization for Economic Cooperation and Development) country financed more than 15 percent of its investment from foreign borrowing, and no country sent more than 10 percent of its savings abroad, despite widely varying rates of return (Feldstein 1992). Most economists believe that the principal barrier to greater capital mobility lies in the very movement of exchange rates that accompanies the massive movements of short-term speculative capital (Frankel 1992, 200).

A closely related claim suggests that governments are incapable of taxing firms because of their international mobility. Doubters can take comfort from the experience of the United States. Although the total state tax burden on business dropped moderately over the past several decades, the states as a group were estimated to have collected 70 percent more in taxes on business in 1992 than the estimated value of the services provided by the states to business (ACIR 1981; Oakland and Testa 1996).

Overall, the claim that the international mobility of capital is constraining the ability of states to maintain taxes should be viewed with great skepticism. Moreover, it should be remembered that the increasing inequality of income distribution is not between conventional capital and labor but between *human* capital and relatively unskilled labor, and most of that human capital has no practical jurisdictional recourse in the face of government taxation. This implies that earnings inequality can be combated not only by more effective education of the presently unskilled but also by fiscal redistribution, if the polity chooses to implement it.

Despite the fact that capital mobility provides no excuse for growing income inequalities in the industrial countries, international tax matters do matter. In particular, the prior tax claim of host governments on the corporate income of multinational corporations disadvantaged the United States over most of the post-war period. A U.S. firm may be indifferent about whether it pays taxes to the Argentine government or the U.S. government, but the United States as a whole is not. This element of taxation now matters relatively little to the United States, however, because there is as much direct investment in the United States as there is U.S. investment abroad.

Two other tax issues are now important with respect to capital. The failure of the United States and some other developed countries to tax the portfolio (nonownership) investments owned by rich residents of developing countries means that those earnings go entirely untaxed. Many experts think that a withholding tax should be introduced, to be forgiven only when the taxpayer proves that the tax was paid in the person's home country. Another big tax problem concerns so-called tax havens. These are countries that essentially serve as switching stations for international capital, offering little except secrecy and low tax rates. Nearly all developed and developing countries alike would benefit from having such tax shelter arrangements eliminated. Policies to do so are available. Profits assigned there could be subject to double taxation (Slemrod 1990), or the tax havens could be attacked with revised "unfair trade" laws that are now used mainly to penalize legitimate foreign competition (Hufbauer 1992, 155).

Labor Mobility

The final mobility about which one hears much these days, and which many U.S. commentators apparently regard as an intrinsic element of globalization, is labor mobility (Sassen 1996). Americans may not understand how unique their situation is, however. They find in an apparently uncontrollable international human mobility a parallel to the international mobility of goods, services, and capital. Most of the rest of the world sees the issue very differently. Japan's foreign population remains well under 1 percent of its total citizenry, and postwar immigration in the European Union countries stems almost entirely from two causes: an unsuccessful attempt to engage in labor service trade without permanent migration, in the 1960s, and various humanitarian crises. In general, immigration to Europe has not been regarded as a success, and European immigration policies in future years can be expected to refine restriction. Interestingly, stringent attitudes toward immigration are at their peak at just the time when the European Union makes possible free internal migration by citizens of the cooperating states.

For the United States, Canada, and Australia, immigration is linked to nationhood itself and is generally viewed with favor. In modern welfare states, however, citizens are tempted to view each new migrant (and progeny) on the basis of net fiscal benefit or burden. The most careful recent scholarship suggests that unskilled immigration to the United States does not pass that test (Borjas 1987) and also contributes significantly to income inequality (Chiswick 1991). Only the United States has continued to allow substantial legal immigration of the unskilled and has, until very recently, taken a relaxed view of illegal immigration, most of which is also unskilled.

The issue of refugees and asylees—about 15 percent of U.S. legal immigration—is, of course, indissolubly bound to a respect for human rights. Nonetheless, there is increased pressure to develop options for refugees that would allow them to escape persecution without gaining admission to the richer countries (Weiner 1995, 214).

The future appears to hold little chance that unskilled migration from the poorer to the richer countries will be allowed to increase, and it will probably diminish. But the other end of the skill spectrum may become an increasingly important international issue. Because of a general resistance to immigration, even highly skilled foreigners are rejected by Japan and usually accepted by Europe only from within the EU. Nonetheless, two developments suggest a possible future need for coordination of personal tax rates: the increasing interstate competition for talent within Europe and, as U.S. immigration policy shifts to an emphasis on human capital, increased migration of the highly skilled from the rest of the world to America. The European Commission may need to consider both this issue and the coordination of corporate tax rates, and there could even be some pressure for the United States to increase its top personal tax rates to decrease its competitiveness with the rest of the industrial world.[3]

The poorer countries understandably resent the rejection of immigrants by the richer on grounds that smack of racial or ethnic discrimination. They realize, however, that with few exceptions their national fate turns overwhelmingly on their own performance and not on using the rest of the world as a vent for their surplus population. Moreover, the leaders of many developing countries now take a more relaxed view of the out-migration of their highly skilled citizens, viewing them as a source of remittances, technology transfers, business contacts, and political influence abroad. Instead of demanding compensation for the "brain drain," more views are expressed such as that of former prime minister Rajiv Gandhi of India some years ago who regarded Indians overseas as a bank "from which one could make withdrawals from time to time" (Weiner 1996, 133).

Opting Out

There is always the possibility that some states will drop out of the international race for increasing income and wealth. Reducing capital and labor mobility may be part of that strategy. As such mobility increases, some countries may decide that national preferences do not permit the inequalities among their citizens that result from a tax and expenditure structure even approximately matching that of less egalitarian industrial countries. They might then accept a slide down the table of per capita income, not only as a result of reduced domestic effort, but also because some of their most capable citizens would emigrate, and part of the national savings would flow abroad. Some of this could be damped by heavily taxing emigration and introducing capital controls. Nevertheless, the increasingly common ideological socialization brought in part by communication globalization makes this an unlikely outcome. (If skepticism about the central importance of aggregate growth becomes general rather than differential, the competitive problem disappears.)

Assessment

Some commentators on market globalization claim that the economic power of the nation-state in the global economy is rapidly being reduced to little more than that of a state within the American union. This argument ignores the much lower level of capital mobility internationally than within the United States. Far more importantly, however, the analogy fails in the sphere of human mobility. The nation-state has two powerful tools that can be exercised on behalf of the collective welfare that a subnational state lacks. First, it can tax its citizens, whose only complete escape is through the major act of abandoning their citizenship. This is not yet a significant problem, although future developments may require tax coordination and greater fiscal penalties for emigrants. On the other hand, the state can avoid immigration to virtually any extent it chooses. The failure to control immigration is mainly a *domestic* political issue, not a technical issue.

The problems of market globalization are to a large extent soluble at the national level. The General Agreement on Tariffs and Trade and its successor institution, the World Trade Organization, along with other major international bodies such as the Organization for Economic Cooperation and Development and the International Monetary Fund, have moved steadily to facilitate the removal of barriers to the mobility of goods, services and capital, which would generally be in each state's interest even if the state acted alone. The future may present the advisability of the harmonization of some taxes, but the failure to do so hitherto is an indication of the lack of urgency of the problem more than the difficulty of solution.

DIRECT GLOBALIZATION

The previous sections imply that, however far-reaching the unknown implications of communication globalization may be, the challenges to domestic governance—except for the alteration of ownership and regulation necessary to accommodate the technological revolution itself—appear to be mainly indirect. Moreover, the international relations tensions resulting from the telecommunications revolution, including its implications for the control of information and entertainment, appear to have yielded to satisfactory accommodation, whatever their long-run implications. Similarly, the unilateral efficacy of trade and investment openness for the promotion of national prosperity leaves for international bargaining the politically supportive role of overcoming established import-competing interests with those who aspire to export, while each state gains access abroad by extending offers of its own. Direct globalization presents a far more difficult set of challenges. These, in turn, differ in their implications depending on whether they are palpable or "psychological."

Communication globalization has increased awareness of common international problems in general and environmental problems in particular.

Behind the increased awareness lie worsening problems. In particular, we now have the increased scientific understanding of the global interconnectedness of many environmental problems (Hahn and Richards 1989).

Saving the Commons

The international policy problems of cross-border spillovers differ radically from those spawned by the communication revolution and market mobility. In both of the other spheres, states must mainly decide how open they wish to be to incoming and outgoing flows of information, goods, services, labor, and capital. International cooperation plays a role distinctly secondary to national policy. In the case of international externalities, however, the problem is definitionally one of international relations: either, as in the case of acid rain, because one nation is damaging another (and very likely itself as well) or, as in the case of global warming, because all nations are making at least some contribution to a generally destructive outcome. Because our interest is globalization, the discussion focuses on the second type of problem.

Coping with international environmental problems implies meeting challenges similar to those for domestic environmental issues with the inevitable additional enforcement problems. First, there must be an acceptable characterization of damage caused by the externality. Such valuations often employ complex and controversial methodologies. This is true even when the physical causation involved is well understood, as in the case of acid rain. Where it is not, as in the case of global warming, that uncertainty powerfully magnifies uncertainly about valuation and makes the entire enterprise far more difficult (Skolnikoff 1990).

Second, the methods of effecting a solution must be developed. Environmental problems in most countries have historically been confronted with what is known as the "command and control" approach. Some simple rule, such as a certain percentage reduction of a pollutant by every manufacturing plant producing a certain product or the adoption of the latest approved technology of amelioration, has frequently been employed. Economists have strenuously resisted this approach and have estimated that its employment typically increases the cost of amelioration manyfold. Instead, they have insisted that any environmental standard can be most efficiently met by treating the total allowable amount of the pollutant as a scarce resource and essentially allocating it like any other scarce resource such as labor. The right to a certain amount of pollution may be gained for a fixed fee per unit, through auctioning, or by the assignment of tradable rights. This way of thinking initially offended environmentalists, but as Daniel Esty (1994) has explained, it has now become increasingly accepted by defenders of the environment in many countries, including the United States.

It might be thought that international environmental amelioration could avoid such complications because each country could solve its share of the problem in the way it deems most appropriate. Unfortunately, where all states make some contribution to the problem (and suffer some share of the negative consequences), the same efficiency problem that arises among plants within a state also looms among states.

Global warming illustrates how an efficient and equitable solution generally requires a compatible and cooperative international approach. Carbon emissions are most efficiently deterred by taxing the use of carbon, but if the only innovation is a carbon tax at the production level, the result is an enormous shift of revenue to the producing countries. If it is placed at the consumption level, the revenue piles up in the coffers of the consuming states. Both could cut use, but with dramatically different distributional consequences. The most appealing theoretical solution lies in the assignment of internationally tradable rights for carbon emissions. These could be assigned internationally by formula, for example, on a per capita basis, or inversely in relation to the estimated total past cumulated emissions of the state.

Although it is efficient, the emission rights approach would cause a dramatic flow of resources toward many poor countries; and the stakes surrounding the assigned property rights are huge. One estimate (Whalley and Wigle 1991) suggests that reducing carbon emissions by 50 percent would involve collecting revenues of up to one-tenth of gross world product. (These revenues, collected for allocative purposes, could be used in lieu of other taxes.)

Global warming provides a prime example of the most difficult kind of environmental problem. The entire world economy is involved, physical damage estimates vary widely, as do attempts to evaluate them, and the estimated cost of amelioration is staggering. The *efficient* lowering of emissions by 50 percent over what they would otherwise be is estimated to cost 3 percent of world product (for a discussion of various estimates, see Winters 1992). In theory, large state actors still have an incentive for some independent amelioration (Olson 1965), but internal politics may greatly delay any (still suboptional) initiatives.

What if national resources provide international benefits? For example, does Brazil have an obligation to the world to preserve its rain forest, or does the country have a right to demand payment from the world for its preservation? One obvious solution would be for Brazil to bear no more of the share of the costs of the amelioration than it does of the benefits, but the valuation problems are clearly enormous.

As Richard Blackhurst and Arvind Subramanian (1992) have stressed, the three problems outlined here are not only difficult but, in real settings, they are also interdependent. The accepted valuation of environmental improvement by a state's representatives will not be independent of the proposed remedial measures and their distributional consequences for that state. Furthermore, a country may fail fully to comply with an agreement if it believes that it was ill served in its distributional aspect.

Beyond the Commons

Despite the formidable difficulties, the establishment of a goal for common action in response to negative externalities appears most clearly in the case of an environmental problem that directly affects the physical living standards of human beings. But globalization has generated or magnified myriad concerns about the environment and beyond for which "damage" becomes almost notional.

Economists have long recognized a category of public good called "existence value": for example, people take pleasure from knowing that blue whales are out there somewhere, even if they never experience one directly. But what if the cost of such a pleasure is very high, and the benefit differs greatly in intensity among individuals? Unsurprisingly, some of the greatest environmental controversies *within* countries have resulted from costly attempts to preserve threatened flora and fauna. Moreover, the valuation of species preservation by an average citizen could be expected to be much lower in poorer countries than in richer ones because, in general, concern for the environment has high income elasticity. When concern for animals goes beyond their existence as a species to their general welfare, as in the U.S. law concerning the netting of dolphins, much of the world sees little more than anthropomorphism.

Some have argued that there is a "race to the bottom" argument for an international agreement on environmental standards independent of the direct environmental spillovers because countries will compete with one another for investment with lax environmental standards, making them harder to defend elsewhere. Like the argument about tax competition discussed earlier, however, this is a theoretical possibility with little empirical support for its current importance (Wilson 1996, Klevorik 1996, and Levinson 1996).

Labor Rights

Although the term "psychological externality" appears often in the literature to refer to environmental concerns in which no measurable stake can be demonstrated by the evaluator, communication globalization appears to have greatly increased a parallel concern: the continuing interest of persons in one country for the welfare of those in another. Without putting the welfare of human beings in the same category as the well-being of dolphins, there are some similarities between the two sets of concerns in the way communication globalization has increased international awareness, in the kinds of political pressures that are visited upon national governments, and in the recommended policy remedies.

Two major concerns have dominated recent discussions. Throughout the Uruguay Round of the GATT negotiations, many voices demanded a "social clause" providing grounds for retaliation against states that trade goods produced by labor forces not enjoying certain minimal rights. One frequently cited list included the right to organize and bargain collectively; a minimum age for employment and other protections connected with child labor; freedom from employment discrimination on the basis of race, sex, religion, and political opinion; and freedom from forced labor (*BNA International Business and Financial Daily*, editorial, Apr. 12, 1995).

In general, developing countries have resisted the inclusion of such concerns in trade agreements, expressing their fear that protectionist forces in the richer countries will attempt to manipulate any agreed language to raise the production costs of poorer states. (Their fears are given credence by the role of organized labor in rich countries in promoting such causes.) Moreover, most proposed language is inherently ambiguous. The efficacy of bargaining, for example, depends on the level of effective monopoly power over the labor supply that a given collective bargaining unit exercises. This, in turn, depends on the size of the bargaining unit relative to the firm or industry and the legal ease with which workers can be replaced—dimensions in which interstate practice differs widely. These issues will continue to be discussed by international bodies, including the International Labor Organization and the World Trade Organization, (WTO) although sharp differences, particularly between richer and poorer countries, suggest that adoption of many definite labor standards beyond some minimal child labor restrictions is most unlikely for the foreseeable future.

Human Rights

The broader area of human rights can also be construed in terms of globalism-enhanced psychological externality. One need only think of the impact of television pictures of the massacre at Tiananmen Square to conclude that communication globalization not only intensifies immediate world reaction but also encourages ongoing concern.

The postwar period is replete with declarations and other largely hortatory expressions of concern for fundamental human rights. Many critics, however, believe that such expressions involve claims that are too political—for democratic government, for example—to gain the near universal acceptance necessary for success. A recent proposal by Patricia Stirling

(1996) takes a different tack. She distinguishes "core human rights" (drawn from the Second Geneva Protocol and section 702 of the Restatement [Third] of Foreign Relations): freedom from torture, collective punishments, prolonged arbitrary detention, genocide, slavery, and threats to commit them (1996, 39). She proposes to establish a Human Rights Body (HRB) as part of the World Trade Organization, which would administer a defined retaliatory mechanism against violators.

Enforcement

The enforcement of established standards presents a problem for all the globalism-enhanced externality problems. As Oran Young has argued, some environmental agreements provide examples of governance without government (1989; 1994); but examples of success illustrate the limiting conditions. The CFC (chlorofluorocarbon) problem, so quickly and effectively attacked by the Montreal Protocol, had many characteristics that contrast sharply with the issues surrounding global warming. The science was clearer, the number of critical states was small, the aggregate amelioration cost was modest, and the offending production system had a simple structure (Enders and Porges 1992).

International success typically depends to a large extent on selective incentives, either side payments or sanctions (Olson 1965). Most writing on international compliance stresses the greater efficacy of positive over negative incentives (Chayes and Chayes 1991). Nevertheless, the demand for negative sanctions for a range of externalities provides the basis for many recent disputes. There is a call both for the formal development of sanctions in international agreements and for single-state retaliation for some of the same provocations. And there is little doubt that communication globalization has been responsible for part of the dramatic increase in the call for sanctions in recent years. In the United States, President Bill Clinton and the Congress have either imposed or threatened to impose economic sanctions sixty times against thirty-five countries between 1993 and early 1997, about the same number as for the first four decades after World War II ("Converting the Dollar into a Bludgeon," *New York Times*, April 20, 1997, sec. 4, p. 5).

The literature on the efficacy of sanctions stresses that they work best when (*inter alia*) they are comprehensively multilateral, the cost to the imposers is small, the target is small and weak, and the target desires the general cooperation of its opponents (Hufbauer, Schott, and Elliott 1990, 12–13). What kind of sanctions are available? Once various avenues of persuasion, including positive incentives, have been exhausted, impeding trade and finance often appears to be the most efficacious response short of military action (and the latter has seldom been considered for the kinds of issues discussed here [Stirling 1996, 11]). Concessionary resources, if any, can be denied, and assets can be frozen. Finance on commercial terms is nothing more than a form of trade, the blockage of which, like the extreme measure of an embargo, will usually draw the hostility of export interests.

Given the limitations of alternative instruments, much attention is drawn to penalizing imports from the offending country. But such sanctions are likely to violate the rules of the World Trade Organization. Currently, as under the GATT, there is no mechanism for blocking imports on the basis of the environmental impacts of production processes employed in their manufacture. The only arguably social concern legitimating retaliation deals with goods made by prison labor. (Even this clause in the original GATT appears to have been derived not from human rights concerns but from the same rationale by which domestic prison labor is attacked by firms within a state: as "unfair" competition.)

Many regard the trading rules developed under the GATT/WTO as essential ingredients in the prosperity of the postwar world, including the huge increase in the income of the poorer countries as a group. They are understandably loathe to condition trade access on environmental, human rights, or other concerns, which they fear will be manipulated by protectionists working in league with environmental and human rights groups to damage global prosperity severely. Nonetheless, those seeking effective international enforcement in the area of externalities will inevitably continue to focus on the world trading system: retaliation for misdeeds is an accepted and elaborated behavior there, and the comprehensiveness of the group seems to offer the greatest probability of success. (For a variety of views, see Esty 1994; "The Cost of Clean Living," *Economist*, July 9, 1994, 67; and Anderson 1995, 389–92.)

Esty (1994) has proposed the establishment of an independent international body for environmental issues (the Global Environmental Organization, or GEO) partly to protect the trading system from being burdened and perhaps weakened by other issues, although he accepts an "enhanced GATT" as second best. At the very least, it may be unwise to incorporate additional spheres of authority before the newly strengthened trading system finds its feet.[4]

CONCLUSION

The three varieties of globalization differ sharply in terms of Robert Keohane's (1984, 51–55) trichotomous delineation of harmony, cooperation, and discord, and hence they suggest quite different implications for governance. The previous arguments are summarized in table 1.1, in which each

Table 1.1　Key Elements of the Three Globalizations

	Communication Globalization	Market Globalization	Direct Globalization	
			Palpable externality	Psychological externality
Driving forces	Communication technology	Communication and transportation technology	Physical production and improved communication	Improved communication
Principal effects	Prosperity enhancement; cultural interpretation; external comparison for domestic practices	Prosperity enhancement; reduced efficiency of some traditional policy instruments	Environmental deterioration	Crossborder value disputes
Main policy challenges	Preserving national uniqueness	Assuring a fair share of global taxes and appropriate after-tax domestic income equality	Assigning international responsibilities and producing amelioration efficiency	Controlling international conflict
Central governance arena	National	National, with limited international, cooperation	International cooperation	International cooperation

of the three globalizations is tracked by source of change, effects, policy implications, and the necessary level of effective public action. (Only a few of the main considerations have been mapped.)

Open societies that are also concerned about economic progress embrace communication globalization almost automatically. Nationalistic opportunism continues to impede cooperation, but not critically. Communication globalization challenges all states in some respects. It presents a growing and possibly fatal challenge to authoritarian states. Moreover, for open democracies at various levels of economic development, the availability of international comparisons may influence national government policy in ways that we do not yet fully understand. An increasing internationalization of styles, attitudes, and tastes clearly poses a long-run threat to the uniqueness of national traditions. Nonetheless, although distinctions preserved by communication monopoly have become technically obsolete, the national uniqueness of most states will erode slowly rather than collapsing.

Market globalization has revolutionized the material character of the world and has led to the decreased efficacy of some traditional devices of economic management. This chapter has argued, however, that much confusion results from mistaking constraints on stabilization instruments for the inability of the state to pursue its own growth and distribution policies. Indeed, both logic and evidence suggest that the most powerful overall economic growth policy continues to be openness, despite the fact that some short-run gains may sometimes be possible at the expense of others through selective closure. This implies that international rules will need to be continually refined to prevent behavior regarded by others as unfair, possibly leading to destructive retaliation. It is sometimes said that those who engage in protection are "free riding" on the larger open system and that therefore this problem looks much like the cooperation problem involved in meeting the challenge of direct globalization. This is misleading, however. Economic closure does usually damage the trading partners of those practicing it, but the principal losers have typically been the citizens of the state practicing the economic nationalism.

Market globalization poses the governance challenge of taking the fullest advantage of international economic opportunities while assuring that both the international and domestic gains are shared equitably. Internationally, this means increasing attention to tax issues; domestically, it implies the use of the state's fiscal power for selective redistribution. It also implies maximum attention to training and education as well as to increasing flexibility in the labor market, so that economic change no longer yields either high unemployment, as it has in Europe, or sharply deteriorating income equality, as it has in the United States. The inadequate responses by national governments to these globalization-related domestic policy challenges suggest not market failure but government failure (for the distinction, see Krugman 1997). Overall, the challenges and opportunities of market globalization for state action in the service of its own people suggest trade and investment openness with restrictions on international labor mobility.

Unlike the challenge of both communication and market globalization, where much basic harmony can be enhanced by fairly loose cooperation, direct globalization demands a far greater ratio of agreed and monitored international action. In theory, large states have some incentive to act on global environmental problems. But independent action on some critical environmental issues is likely to be grossly suboptimal. When this reality is combined with the difficulties of negotiation outlined earlier, effective governance challenges appear greatly to exceed those presented by communication and market globalization. Many fear that only some environmental shock, whether a genuine harbinger or not, will galvanize collective action. That action may still yield highly inefficient measures cobbled together with little systematic concern for equity.

This chapter also has briefly explored two categories of psychological externality, labor standards and general human rights, because both are currently making demands on institutions closely bound to the world trading system. Much of the future of international relations doubtless lies in this direction. By its very nature, however, increased activity in this sphere will generate high levels of discord, because they involve claims against state sovereignty. Most of the issues treated here pose challenges to Westphalian states but not to the system itself. States must respond to their own citizens and interact with other states to face problems requiring varying levels of interstate cooperation. Disputes may range from trivial to profound as states seek solutions to commonly (if not unanimously) perceived problems. Psychological externalities, however, definitionally deal with judgments by the citizens of one state about conditions or practices in another state that do not physically affect outsiders. Such concerns have never been absent from international relations, but an increase in the range of issues that are widely accepted as legitimate targets for remedy by both public and private action threatens traditional sovereignty and hence the very foundations of the present state system.[5]

NOTES

The research for this chapter was sponsored by the Air Force Office of Scientific Research, Air Force Material Command, USAF, under grant number F49620–94–1–0461. The views expressed herein are those of the chapter author and not necessarily thoses of the Air Force Office of Scientific Research or of the U.S. government.

1. This chapter does not consider one important phenomenon fueled by market globalization: international crime. Much of the increase in such crime can be regarded as a negative externality of increased volumes of international physical trade, trade in personal services, and tourism. In this sphere, too, communication globalization plays a critical supporting role.

2. This section draws heavily on Kudrle 1999.

3. Looking even farther into the future, the coordination of state and inheritance taxes might be necessary to avoid emigration for tax avoidance. Even today, some states attempt to penalize persons moving to escape estate as well as personal income taxes.

4. For example, the insistence by the United States that the Helms-Burton Act deals with security matters and thus cannot be challenged in the WTO is a far more serious issue with the new dispute resolution mechanism than it would have been earlier, when a challenged country could simply reject unwelcome decisions.

5. Paul Krugman's recent comparison of the "purist principle[s]" (1997, 119–20) of free trade with the Westphalian state may confuse more than it clarifies. Free trade is a doctrine about what states should do (with minor exceptions) unilaterally to maximize national wealth. The "hard shell" Westphalian state seems a more pragmatically derived and contestable concept. In particular, it appears to deny the legitimacy of much of the internationalization of concern that this chapter explores.

2

Norms, Compliance, and Enforcement in Global Governance

Raimo Väyrynen

Global governance refers to collective actions to establish international institutions and norms to cope with the causes and consequences of adverse supranational, transnational, or national problems. It is a broad definition, but not as broad as that suggested by the Commission on Global Governance: "Governance is the sum of the many ways individuals and institutions, public and private, manage their common affairs." The commission sees global governance as "broad, constantly evolving and responding to changing circumstances" (Commission on Global Governance 1995, 2, 4). Such a concept is, however, too broad and makes it virtually meaningless both for theory construction and social action.

The demand for global governance is partly a result of the globalization process. As Robert Kudrle explains in the previous chapter, the nature of governance depends on the type of globalization; being supranational in scope, direct globalization demands more engaged cooperation for governance than do communication and market globalizations. Market globalization may lead to failures owing to the inability of the market operations to take care of a variety of economic, political, ecological, and cultural needs of the human societies. As Todd Sandler (1997, 9–12) notes, market failures can result from negative externalities, problems in the production of public goods, or undefined property rights.

The concept of globalization is all too often used in a loose manner. It is important to make a distinction between *interdependence* and *globalization*; the former refers to the relations of mutual dependence between states, the latter is economically a corporate-level phenomenon. Thus, *globalization* means, as Wolfgang Reinicke points out, the "spatial reorganization of corporate activity" through the "reach of corporate industrial networks and their financial relationships." An interesting corollary of this distinction is that interdependence constrains the external sovereignty of states, but globalization, by penetrating into domestic systems, limits also their internal sovereignty. Thus, "globalization differs from interdependence in that it . . . internalizes into its own institutional structure economic activities that previously took place between national markets, that is between distinct economic *and* political units" (Reinicke 1998, 7–8, 52–74).

As becomes clear from above, interdependence is characteristic of a state-centric and globalization of a multicentric world (Rosenau 1990). Following a similar systemic distinction, Oran Young (1997, 283–84) suggests that there are two "pure types of regimes": international regimes have states as members, and transnational ones are composed of nonstate actors. Of course, there can also be mixed international and transnational regimes. In the state-centric international system, governance calls primarily for the management of market failures and their consequences in interstate relations. It has even been suggested that only interstate arrangements which cope with market failures should qualify as regimes (Eden & Hampson 1997). Typical examples of such a governance include arms-control and free-trade regimes to cope with the risks of arms races and protectionism.

However, the globalized world is multicentric; in addition to governments, important actors include transnational corporations and international nongovernmental organizations (NGOs). In such an international system, challenges to governance are both horizontal and vertical; that is, they may manifest between actors on both the same and different levels. Thus, subnational problems may require intergovernmental cooperation, which may, in turn, prompt international NGOs to react to its consequences. Various global issues, such as the volatility of the international financial system or adverse environmental changes, call for mixed intergovernmental and transnational management.

Global governance cannot work without power to produce desirable outcomes. Power in the state-centric and multicentric world is, however, different. In the state-centric world the main elements of power are the national capabilities of the participants, their distribution, and their management. Regime formation in the state-centric world can be approached from both the institutional and the power-oriented perspectives, which are united around the primacy of the states as key actors in international relations (for a systematic review of research on interest- and power-based approaches to international regimes, see Hasenclever, Mayer, and Rittberger 1997).

The state-centric approaches adopt a contractarian or rationalistic view that assumes the prior existence of actors, their interests, and their identities. On the other hand, the constitutive or constuctivist perspective assumes that institutions play an important role in defining the interests and identities of the actors involved. Contractarian and constitutive perspectives do not, however, need to be opposed to each other: they can be combined (Young 1997, 276–77; Checkel 1997).

In the multicentric world, power not only is dispersed, but it also assumes more forms than the traditional power analysis suggests. For instance, power can also be symbolic and reputational, as well as material, and it may reflect conventions and narratives. The fluidity of "soft" power means that it is difficult to capture and use for specific purposes. One implication of this state of affairs is that, in the multicentric world, traditional power resources alone cannot assure stability and progress; the management of power must be based also on norms and institutions. Power is embedded in transnational institutional networks. Such a comprehensive and pluralistic approach to international governance has been called "complex global governance" which operates simultaneously in multiple issue areas and on multiple levels (Zürn 1998).

I have introduced these distinctions to justify my choice of perspective. The international system is moving from the state-centric toward the multicentric, in which transnational regimes assume increasing significance over time. Constitutive approaches to the definition of interests and identities provide a better understanding of the society than do contractarian views. These developments increasingly challenge the internal aspects of sovereignty, in addition to the external ones.

FROM NATIONAL POWER TO INTERNATIONAL NORMS

Recent changes in international relations have created a situation in which their conduct relies less on the distribution of power and more on rules and institutions. In fact, compliance with them has become a new standard of legitimacy in international relations, which has a tendency to spread and attract new adherents. Legitimacy requires a "rule-making institution which itself exerts a pull towards compliance on those addressed normatively" (Franck 1990a, 16–19).

According to realist thinking, order can be best maintained by the balance of power and deterrence between states. Realists admit the existence of institutions; however, they claim that they do not have independent influence on the outcomes but rather reflect only the distribution of material power in the world (Mearsheimer 1995, 7–9). As the degree of international institutionalization is low, rules have to be enforced primarily by threatening to use coercion against the noncomplying state. This calls for either unilateral or multilateral political or military intervention into another state; however, such intervention is difficult to mount due to multiple political obstacles.

An important distinction, to be elaborated later on, is whether the compliance with rules is embedded in the institutional practices or whether it has to be reached by external incentives and measures of enforcement. Internal sources of compliance are rooted in domestic structures and belief systems of the participating actors; that is, compliance is "habit driven." Compliance is driven externally when the other actors and the environment so change the incentives that it is rational for the actor to abide by the rules. If an actor fails to comply, and especially if noncompliance is serious, other actors may resort to punitive measures to restore the situation *ex ante* (Duffield 1992, 836–38).

The stabilizing mechanisms of the cold war, such as military alliances and deterrence strategies, have become progressively weaker in their original tasks since the 1980s. Therefore, other mechanisms are needed to maintain stability in the emerging multicentric world. The search for a new basis of international stability has resulted in an emphasis on the norms and institutions and compliance with them. During the cold war, norms were mostly embedded in the strategic interactions between major powers and formal agreements or tacit understandings they negotiated. In the post–cold war world, norms have multiplied and have become more explicit, and even their international enforcement has been put on the agenda.

The gradual shift to a system based more on rules and institutions engenders tensions with the traditional international system whose structure is defined primarily by the distribution of national capabilities. In the traditional interstate contest, the amount of capabilities, their relational symmetry, and the effectiveness of their use matter most. However, in the emerging system of interstate relations, power has to be interpreted more broadly, as the ability to control political outcomes. With this transformation, power is becoming more complex and diversified, but it is also being restrained.

Unilateral military power, built on the national resource base, may have been efficient in a state-centric system but is now less usable than before. The unilateral use of force is gradually replaced by multilateral institutional power, applied through the medium of international norms that actors are expected to comply with. National power is primarily used in international institutional networks rather than unilaterally in interstate relations. As states are important actors in networks, national power and international institutions are not necessarily opposed to each other. Rather, there are two types of power, institutionalized and noninstitutionalized, of which the former is gaining ground at the expense of the latter.

The institutionalization of power is a response to the growing complexity, disjuncture, and diffusion in international relations, which, as a result, cannot be managed effectively by unilateral national means. Complexity is due, among other things, to the global redistribution and differentiation of economic and military power and the growing cultural diversity. Traditional power resources are facing a crisis of relevance as most new problems cannot be managed by coercive means. The dismantling of the ideological cold-war overlay has further increased complexity. During the cold war, unilateral means may have helped to safeguard national security, but now they are insufficient to address new types of security problems such as refugee flows, humanitarian emergencies, and environmental crises.

In a word, increasing complexity, disjuncture, and diffusion of issues and structures is a hallmark of the present transitional era. The emerging international system has more layers, issue areas, and functions than its predecessor; it is "plurilateral" by nature (Cerny 1993). Both conflict and cooperation between states naturally continue, but increasingly they also involve subnational and transnational actors and focus on new issues. As conflicts do not disappear in the "plurilateral world," new means and strategies are needed for their management and resolution to prevent eruptions into violence.

As mentioned, the management of "new" international relations is increasingly based on norms and institutions. An interesting aspect of this change is the "domestication" of the international norms of peace: they can now be enforced by legal and police actions rather than by the use of military force. It has been noted that domestic and international normative standards have approached each other, but the means of their enforcement have not yet been domesticated and still rely predominantly on selective state actions. To improve the methods of enforcement, international institutions should be empowered and should use primarily noncoercive instruments (Johansen 1996).

Charles Kegley and Gregory Raymond (1994) make a helpful distinction between permissive and restrictive international normative orders. In a permissive order, norms give national leaders considerable latitude of action; in a restrictive order, the behavior of leaders is more effectively controlled and specific actions prohibited by the prevailing normative constraints. After discussing trends in several issue areas, the authors conclude that the restrictiveness of the international legal order is on the increase, unlike the situation in previous transitions from bipolar to multipolar international systems in which it became more permissive.

To this one can add that on a general level all international orders are restrictive in the sense that states much more often comply with rules than violate them. Thus, the normal behavior of states involves cooperation, regulation, and sharing rather than the use of coercion. This has led Stephen A. Kocs (1994) to suggest that political realism explains exceptions rather than rules which can be better accounted for by a law-based model of international relations. In the realist model, the behavior of states is constrained primarily by external factors, such as the preponderance of power and deterrence; in the law-based models, constraints are both external and internal.

The essential point here is that a major normative change seems to be under way in interstate relations. Previously, the use of force and its threats were a common phenomenon; now the need to prevent and limit interstate violence and settle disputes peacefully are assuming the normative force that also guides state actions. This normative transformation of international relations from interstate war to interstate peace has been compared with the replacement of colonialism by the principle of self-determination. Both of these historical breakthroughs are "marked by change of principled beliefs and the institutions that embody them" (Jackson 1993, 111–38; the quotation is on p. 114).[1]

To take another example, international humanitarian intervention in domestic crises, previously limited to some exceptional situations, has now become largely permitted. The norm of intervention is not, however, universally accepted and in no case is it mandatory, even if standards of acceptable behavior are grossly violated in the target state. The more permissive attitude stresses humanitarian concerns more than before. To address these concerns, a third-party intervention, especially if carried out by a multilateral coalition and using proportionate force, has become rather widely accepted (Arend and Beck 1993, 80–92; Finnemore 1996).

NORMS AND RULES IN INTERNATIONAL RELATIONS

Global (or regional) governance is conducted by actors through prerequisite institutions and norms without which governance cannot be effective (unless, of course, the system is hegemonic). Norms, which can create both rights and obligations, are "collective expectations about a proper behavior for a given identity." They can be either regulative (when they prescribe or proscribe standards of appropriate behavior by positive or negative feedback) or constitutive (when a particular identity is recognized and validated by others) (Jepperson, Wendt, and Katzenstein 1996, 54). Norms are a part of a social system rather than the property of its individual members.

Norms and institutions are constitutive of global governance if they strengthen identities and interests of states and thereby encourage states to behave in a manner that is consistent with the need of cooperation and regulation. Global governance is not a result of political "engineering" of international institutions or of an "architectural design" by individual actors but is, rather, a result of fundamental social transformation. In that sense global governance can be considered an institutional fact constituted by acting in accord with the norms that stress coordination and cooperation over unilateral actions (Searle 1995, 27–28).

This point of departure suggests that norms and institutions should be scrutinized not in isolation but as interrelated elements of a larger system called global governance. The analysis must pay attention to the interdependence of norms, which thus cluster and contextually influence individual actions. James S. Coleman speaks in this context of a dual movement between micro and macro levels. Normative social systems start from individual actions, but once the norms are institutionalized, and possibly internalized by the actors, they affect subsequent individual actions (Coleman 1990, 243–45).

This conclusion takes sides in a central debate in the current study of international norms. It leans more on the constructivist interpretation which assumes that decision makers internalize norms through learning and adaptation and by enacting domestic laws in which norms are embedded. The rationalist interpretation suggests that decision makers follow norms either because they are imposed on them by domestic and international pressures or because compliance is advantageous to them. The commitment to norms is given up when the pressures ease or the advantages fade away. Although I believe that norms are often fundamental and cannot be changed like clothes, it is also clear that constructivist and rationalist accounts do not need to be mutually exclusive; their validity depends, for instance, on the nature of the domestic political system (Cortell and Davis 1996; Checkel 1997).

To take a concrete example of the normative system as an institutional fact, the ban on chemical weapons is not confined only to the specific norms and institutions that the Chemical Weapons Convention (CWC) creates; it is a part of the broader movement toward controlling the weapons of mass destruction and, ultimately, war in international relations. Using Thomas M. Franck's terminology, one can say that specific norms have a "pedigree" if their rights and obligations can be linked to previous or more comprehensive norms. A norm can be symbolically validated by its pedigree, which also increases the likelihood of compliance with it (Franck 1990a, 94–97). For instance, the CWC has a pedigree starting from World War I and extending through the 1925 convention to the present date.

To qualify as an institutional fact, the global governance of a particular problem, such as war and its means, requires collective intentionality by the actors. Thus, the attachment of a general disarmament function to the CWC means that it acquires a normative status beyond the specific norms included in the convention (constitutive rules are discussed in Searle 1995, 43–51). Similarly, norms banning nuclear testing or specific types of nuclear weapons become constitutive if they are linked to efforts at comprehensive nuclear disarmament. In that case, general norms proscribing nuclear weapons should be diluted neither by developing low-yield or nonlethal nuclear weapons nor by placing them in the same category with chemical and biological weapons, as such redefinitions could adversely change the beliefs and expectations of decision makers (Kier and Mercer 1996, 100–105).

The definition of global governance as an institutional fact has a direct bearing on the way in which norms in international relations are defined. A common approach is to define norms as relatively uniform behavior due to fear of punishment or to the imitation of the actions of others (Axelrod 1986). In my approach, however, norms cannot be understood merely as observed regularity and consistency of behavior, as they can also result from factors other than the compliance of actors with norms. Neither is it adequate to contend that norms exist only if there is an external sanction mechanism to punish noncompliance. Instead, we must separate the issue of enforcement from the definition of norms. This means that norms have primarily to be defined by the moral rights and obligations they embody. They create standards of behavior that are widely regarded as legitimate and thus give rise to stable expectations (Goertz and Diehl 1992, 636–39; also Thomson 1993, 79–81).

Thus the question is, are there global standards of action which states regularly comply with? And if so, to what extent are they internalized? The answer is simply yes; there are several sets of norms that prescribe states to act to curtail causes and consequences of adverse supranational, transnational, and national problems and proscribe particular kinds of behavior. In other words, the sovereign state is situated in an "increasingly dense normative web that constrains its foreign policy in general and its use of military force in particular" (Barnett 1995, 50).

A similar conclusion can also be extended to norms on human rights and democracy. At least in selected situations they can become independent bases of action as happened in the case of the norm of racial equality, including the rejection of apartheid. Its transnational dissemination pushed states to apply economic sanctions against South Africa even when doing so hurt their own material interests. Although it is not entirely clear to what extent sanctions were responsible for the change in the policy of the South African whites, it is obvious that they signaled the commitment of the international community to work systematically for the abolition of apartheid (Klotz 1995b).

There are, of course, exceptions to the compliance with the global normative order; for instance, norms of global governance are only partially institutionalized. This is natural because the institutionalization of norms is always a result of a historical process, a process that has not, in the case of global governance, yet matured (on the institutionalization of norms, see Katzenstein 1996a, 21–22). The strength of the international normative individual order concerning global governance can be assessed by focusing on actors and their actions.

Some state actors have a reputation of consistently subsuming their national identities and interests in a larger, collective context by supporting, for example, global human rights, environmental protection, and collective security. Canada, Denmark, and the Netherlands are examples of countries having an identity that leads others to expect them to promote and comply with the standards of global governance. It has been noted, though, that the current scholarship has rather little to say about the process of identity construction among the states (Kowert and Legro 1996, 469). Both the Swedish foreign policy during the cold war and the Canadian policy in the 1990s would provide ample and interesting material for such a study.

Indeed, more research along these lines is needed. There is no obvious reason that Canada, Denmark, and the Netherlands should have converging identities as the supporters of global governance. Of course, no government acts always in precisely the same manner or supports all global norms. Rather, one should speak, in a Rawlsian mode, of "partial compliance theory" as it describes most real-world situations. Such a theory helps us to understand that compliance is not a binary choice (Young 1979, 9–10, 105).

Norms are directed at what James S. Coleman calls "focal actions" and "focal actors." Proscriptive norms damp out such actions; prescriptive norms expand them. In our example, global governance is the focal action whose norms most states usually comply with. It can be assumed that the compliance by focal actors and in focal actions with the norms of global governance is more likely than in more peripheral cases. Coleman makes a further distinction of relevance between conjoint and disjoint norms. Norms are conjoint if the beneficiaries and targets are the same actors and disjoint if they are separate (Coleman 1990, 246–48).

It can be argued that norms of global governance are conjoint in the case of small or middle-sized industrialized countries as they observe norms and benefit from them. The norms of nuclear non-proliferation provide, in turn, examples of disjoint norms. Many nuclear-weapon powers emphasize the importance of such norms, but routinely violate them by exporting nuclear materials, equipment, and expertise. Clearly, they benefit from the norm of non-proliferation because it keeps the nuclear-weapon club small; at the same time they stress how the nuclear-weapon policies of India, Pakistan, and various threshold countries are, politically speaking, illegitimate.

It has been suggested that the strength of a norm is increased by the existence of metanorms. They prescribe that the enforcement of the norm should be directed not only to its violator, but also to those who refuse to punish the defector. Thus, metanorms broaden the domain of the norm and try to make it self-policing (Axelrod 1986). However, the existence of few metanorms in international relations suggests that their normative basis is not yet very robust. In counteracting terrorism and nuclear proliferation, the United States has made major efforts to persuade other countries to punish those states that have supported "rogue" states. The U.S. success has been limited, however; U.S. allies have not started policing among themselves the metanorm that China, Cuba, and Iran should be collectively punished by economic or other sanctions for their potential violation of international norms. The U.S. has also been criticized for unilateralism and the extraterritorial extension of its national jurisdiction.

The proliferation of nuclear weapons illustrates another important aspect of international norms as a response to external actions. If particular actions produce externalities, the actors affected by them have a common interest in creating and enforcing a norm that bans or mitigates the original action. The overconsumption of common property resources produces probably the most serious negative externalities which have to be addressed by public action. Obviously, the establishment of a norm is not the only possible reaction to externalities, but they can be addressed also by individualistic measures or market arrangements (Coleman 1990, 249–55; Eden & Hampson 1997, 369–71).

Most externalities have visible effects on other actors, who deal with them by means of taxes, subsidies, quotas, and other similar arrangements. Being largely a binary phenomenon—that is, a government either has or does not have nuclear weapons—nuclear proliferation calls for different remedies. The limited number of nuclear-weapon powers means that their actions have "unidirectional" rather than "reciprocal" external effects (Sandler 1997, 39–43). This makes the establishment and enforcement of robust nonproliferation norms a difficult task, in particular because the legitimacy of nuclear weapons and their oligopolistic ownership is increasingly challenged.

Focal actions are not selected arbitrarily but are supposed to address the key issues of global governance. The support of global governance may lead to collective action problems and moral hazards in that responsible actors may also reward the irresponsible ones and they may have to carry an unfair share of the burden. On the other hand, the whole notion of responsibility has been questioned on the grounds that those who stress a norm may do so in pure self-interest. The supporters of free trade and nonproliferation often argue that their actions produce a public good that benefits everybody through the international economic division of labor and international stability but usually they also benefit from those goods individually. This suggests that norms are purposively created to serve both the individual and possibly the common good.

This is, however, only one answer to the problem of how international rights and obligations emerge. Other answers may suggest that new norms and identities are responses to critical changes in the international environment, including externalities. Another possibility is that norms are diffused among states as a result of imitation or emulation, which leads to a sort of normative consensus. New norms and identities can also be created through internal processes stimulated by subnational groups (Kowert and Legro 1996, 470–83).

It seems that the norms of global governance do not arise, in the first place, out of internal processes. Thus, norms are not constituted and internalized by the innate needs of actors. They may spread, of course, but it is more likely that norms and identities associated with global governance are responses to globalized crises in the international economy, polity, and environment. It may sound overly functionalist, but norms and institutions of global governance are responses to real and perceived needs of actors in a larger international contest.

Another approach to international normative change suggests that it is evolutionary; that is, norms are contested, transmitted, and selected for application in much the same way as genes. To emerge as the winner, a norm must be initially prominent, thanks to the actions of a "norm entrepreneur," and coherent with other norms in the system, and they must grow in an advantageous international environment (Florini 1996; Axelrod 1986). Such an approach is potentially compatible with the explanation that the emergence of new norms and identities is a response to changes in the environment with which the actors try to cope by prescribing or proscribing new standards of behavior.

ENDOGENOUS AND EXOGENOUS ENFORCEMENT

The view that norms are upheld only because there is a threat of external sanctions comes close to the contractarian view that actors are not moral beings but only calculate the costs and benefits in deciding their courses of action. This approach postulates that only norms that are exogenously enforced by a combination of punishments and incentives have any explanatory and predictive value. However, such an instrumentalist view of actors leaves out the possibility that there is a common morality that obliges people to behave in a reasonable manner. Such a Kantian, nonreligious theory of morality is based on "a system of laws or precepts, binding upon rational creatures as such, the content of which is ascertainable by human reason" (Donagan 1977, 6–9, 26–29). Such a theory of morality permits also the endogenous enforcement of norms, not on religious but on rational grounds.

As pointed out, compliance by governments with international norms is high, and their violation is an exception, not the rule, (see also Chayes and

Chayes 1993, 185–87). The high degree of compliance with norms can be a result of either endogenous or exogenous enforcement. Endogenous enforcement refers to normative or rational constraints that have been internalized by the actors either in their values and standards of assessment or in their mutual relations.

Exogenous enforcement is carried out by other parties through punishments and incentives. Such a mode of enforcement is possible only if the state is developed as a coercive apparatus to serve in the process of enforcement the particular interests of those who control it (North 1990, 58–60). Endogenous enforcement is favored by the institutionalist-constructivist approach; the liberal-rational perspective recommends exogenous enforcement. However, as the Kantian idea of common morality suggests (Donagan 1977), these two approaches do not need to exclude each other. There can be rational grounds for both externally and internally induced compliance.

The internalization of norms can occur in at least two different ways: either they are embedded in the structure of world politics or they are internalized by the actors (or both). In the former case, international relations have, in and of themselves, a normative structure that shapes, independently of material power relations, the behavior of actors. In the latter case, norms are internalized and complied with by actors either because they hold ethical concerns important or because it is advantageous to them.

Hedley Bull has adopted a systemic normative view in which informal agreements of commonly held values figure prominently. Bull points out that in international society, order is dependent on "a sense of common interests in the elementary goals of social life; rules prescribing behavior that sustains these goals; and institutions that help to make these rules effective." In this view there are three main types of rules in international society: rules on the fundamental normative principles of world politics, such as national sovereignty; rules pertaining to the ways in which states pursue specific objectives; and rules that regulate cooperation in the functional fields of technology, environment, and culture (Bull 1977, 65–71).

The internalization of norms by actors can result from either moral and habitual commitments or utility calculations. In the former case, the compliance with the norm is based on such nonutilitarian factors as obligations, habits, and practices (Young 1979, 23–25). Obviously, moral commitments and obligations make compliance with a norm more sustained and predictable, because their violation would undermine the identity and value structure of the actor. If compliance is based on utility calculations, it can change as soon as the structure of the actor's incentives changes.

The theory of self-enforcing agreements is premised on utility calculations under conditions of relatively perfect information. Parties comply with norms and agreements as long as it is beneficial for them to do so, and they are autonomous to decide whether they want to continue cooperation or not. Therefore, "a self-enforcing agreement between two parties remains in force as long as each party believes himself to be better off by continuing the agreement than he would be by ending it." In more concrete terms, "a party to a self-enforcing agreement calculates whether his gain from violating the agreement is greater or less than the loss of future net benefits that he would incur as a result of defection of his violation and the consequent termination of the agreement by the other party" (Telser 1980; see also Schelling 1980, 134–37; North 1990, 55–56).

The formulation of self-enforcing agreements in terms of public choice theory leaves only limited room to norms. Such agreements are also inherently unstable, because parties can terminate them if they consider it to be in their interest to do so. The instability of agreements fosters, in turn, efforts to increase their durability and robustness. This aim can be accomplished, for instance, by investing actors' own resources in cooperation, forging linkages, or creating new interdependencies and thus "economic hostages." One may also add normative elements to cooperation, for example, by creating and observing the norm of reciprocity, which enhances mutual benefits. Defection becomes also less likely if the agreement has an uncertain termination date because in this case the costs of defection are more difficult to calculate.[2]

The theory of self-enforcing agreements departs from the premise that the third-party enforcement of norms in international relations is difficult and costly, and sometimes impossible. Therefore, agreement is feasible only when it can be designated to impose automatic costs on any noncomplying party, for instance, by building a threat of retaliation in the mutual relationship (Yarborough and Yarborough 1992, 84). Self-enforcing agreements are considered a potential solution to the dilemma of "cooperation under anarchy," especially if states pursue absolute rather than relative gains.

The institutionalist focus on absolute gains facilitates cooperation even in the absence of exogenous mechanisms of enforcement. On the other hand, the focus on relative gains, stressed by the neorealists, makes cooperation difficult and, at best, temporary. If opportunities exist to increase relative gains by violating the norm of cooperation, the actor will do so unless there is a mechanism of exogenous enforcement in place (for a summary of theoretical debates and an effort at integration, see Powell 1993). Self-enforcing agreements appear to be more common in international economic relations than in security cooperation, in which equilibrium is more difficult to achieve. This may be due to the fact that in economic relations hostages and interdependencies can be created without giving rise to excessive suspicions and feelings of insecurity. Such reactions are more likely in security cooperation, in which self-enforcement is based mostly on deterrence. Deterrence is explicitly based on taking hostages and can, if it fails, jeopardize the very survival of nations. Cooperative security is obviously possible without external enforcement. It is, however, difficult to achieve on a sustainable basis, and therefore the need for external enforcement arises, for instance, by means of collective security (Niou and Ordeshook 1994).[3]

As pointed out, enforcement can be either endogenous or exogenous. Endogenous enforcement is embedded either in bilateral relations between the parties, in domestic institutions, or in the internalized norms and morality. Endogenous enforcement obviously has an external dimension, as it can be made more robust by outside support and reinforcement. Compliance with the norms starts, however, not from outside but rather from the internal values and practices of the actor.

This facilitative approach to compliance assumes that violations of norms are not always intentional but may result from the ambiguity of the norm, lack of information, or inadequate state capacity. Moreover, compliance (or noncompliance) is not a binary event; there is a range of acceptable behavior and a grey area where the opinions on compliance differ (Chayes and Chayes 1995, 9–22). The assessment on the level of compliance also depends on the amount and nature of information available and whether it is based on self-reporting or other-reporting (Mitchell 1998, 116–20). In general, the facilitative approach aims to enhance the norm and compliance with it by persuasion, counseling, and incentives.

On the other hand, exogenous enforcement is more often based on punishment on the assumption that the target is intentionally violating the norm and should be brought back in line. Such exogenous enforcement actions can be carried out both by other governments (unilateral enforcement) or by a coalition of states and international organizations (multilateral enforcement). Such a third party should have competence, interest, and resources to enforce international norms either by noncoercive (e.g., third-party mediation) or coercive (e.g., military intervention) measures.

It can be suggested that unilateral enforcement actions, at least the coercive ones, have become less common. This may be due to the erosion of the integrated national power base and changing legal conditions that have reduced the efficiency and legitimacy of unilateral actions and increased their costs. As a result, the importance of endogenous enforcement may be on the increase. Yet, some norms and decisions require exogenous enforcement if international stability and standards of civility are to be maintained. For this purpose institutions are needed as a medium through which states can pursue their goals. At the same time institutions shape state strategies and become an important link between their interests and the outcomes of international political processes.

In the study of enforcement, a similar view of the role of institutions as intermediaries in international relations can be adopted. The choice must be made, however, whether to stress state-driven or institutional actions. If the state has the priority, international institutions have only limited autonomy and are, in the first place, arenas rather than actors of enforcement. If the emphasis is on institutions, a claim can be made that their involvement is a necessary condition for enforcing norms. They mobilize political and material support, make decisions, and implement enforcement actions. On the other hand, institutions are also forums for bargaining about the norms that need to be enforced (Fearon 1998).

Although a claim on the primacy of institutions is obviously too strong, it can be argued that there is a transition taking place from state-based to institution-based enforcement of norms. This conclusion relies on a broad definition of enforcement as "carrying out effectively." In the case of institution-based enforcement, economic and military coercion are only a part of the enforcement process, which also includes monitoring, persuasion, and negotiation. Such actions are seldom carried out unilaterally but rather through multilateral institutions.

In other words, power is not opposed to the institutional approach, but it is a built-in element of institutions. In part, institutional power can be traced back to the states, but there are also contextual power resources that cannot be divided between them. Power can be both intrainstitutional and extrainstitutional; the importance of the former is increasing at the expense of the latter.

This view can be criticized for adopting too benign an interpretation of the capabilities and consequences of international institutions and regimes. In reality, they may fail to solve complex issues, reduce the interests of states to work for long-term solutions, and otherwise worsen the situation (Gallarotti 1991; Eden & Hampson 1997, 362–63). This criticism is partly misleading, however, as it does not consider in counterfactual terms the failures that would appear if international institutions did not exist at all.

TYPES OF NORMS AND RULES

The focus on rules and rule-guided behavior in international relations is important because it helps to divert attention from simplified presumptions of anarchy and power politics. Despite frequent claims to the contrary, anarchy is not a primal condition of international relations. Therefore, compliance of states and other actors is not based, in the first place, on threats and punishments by the other actors. There are certainly incidents of anarchy; but in general, normative, regulatory mechanisms maintain order by affecting the reasoning of decision makers and their tendency to utilize institutions.

The problem of order in international relations is closely related to their governance, that is, efforts to maintain stability and predictability. Governance in international relations is needed because of the absence of a centralized political authority. The term *governance* depicts the lack of centralized authority and suggests that, despite uncertainties, there is always a fair amount of order in international relations. The efficiency of governance depends on the capacity of international institutions to establish a consensus on the contents of norms and enforce them when actors fail to comply (Rosenau 1992, 3–8).

Rules and norms are not, however, all similar: their strength varies. Friedrich Kratochwil (1989, 54–56, 72–81) notes that rules in international relations can be divided into several categories, depending on the degree of commitment they entail and the way they are expressed. Both commitments and expressions can be explicit or tacit. Rules may be derived from treaties and contracts in which they are explicitly formulated, but they may also be contained in more vague customs and conventions. Yet rules in both of these categories are strong in terms of their degree of commitment, whereas rules in various casual agreements and, even more so, in unspoken understandings are weaker in character.

In international law, norms are usually explicit; in strategic interaction, often described in game-theoretical terms, they tend to be tacit and informal, conditioned by the interests of actors and their ability to adjust them to each other. The main difference is, thus, between norms that are formally codified for application and those that are created by adjusting, through interaction, actors and their interests to one another. A related distinction can be made between conceptions in which "norms are sovereign" and those in which they are manipulated for strategic purposes. In the former approach norms are supposed to provide for the consistency, regularity, and continuity of cooperation; in the latter, strategic interests often overshadow social rules (Edgerton 1985, 7–16).

There are basically two approaches to the study and application of norms in international relations. The weaker version is based on the assumption that actors are interested in accommodating their behavior to common norms. In such cases, only limited exogenous enforcement is needed. Governments observe one anothers' actions; if the variance of such actions falls within acceptable limits, they exchange commitments not to alter their behavior in the future. Compliance is not based on any overarching institutional or contractual arrangement but on continuing adjustment of one government's actions to those of another.

This perspective has been echoed by Stanley Hoffmann (1981, 194–95) who writes that "world order is nothing other than the set of processes and procedures, the global regime, that makes ethical foreign policy action possible." In this view, world order can be maintained by a combination of unilateral restraints and mutual cooperation, neither of which, however, cannot be imposed from above. As the sanctioning power in such a system is diffused, it is appropriate to speak of decentralized norms, which, especially if they become essential, shape the behavior of actors.[4]

Nicholas G. Onuf suggests that the realist conception of norms relies primarily on instruction rules and less often on commitment rules and directive rules. Instruction rules are based on experiences gained from everyday life and thus provide common-sense guidelines for action. Commitment rules formalize promises into rights and duties. In international relations, instructive experiences and commitments on future behavior may be exchanged, but the nature of sanctions cannot be easily determined. The violation of instruction norms can lead to denigration and ostracism; noncompliance with the commitment norms tends to result in punishment.

The directive rules presume the existence of a permanent arrangement to monitor the behavior of actors and apply sanctions against the deviant ones. Such an arrangement does not exist, in any systematic form, in an "anarchical" system. That is why compliance with the directive rules can be assured only in hierarchical or hegemonical systems in which directives are issued, supervised, and enforced from above, even by the use of military force, if needed (Onuf 1989; Onuf and Klink 1989).

Means for a more restrictive policy of enforcement are also available. They include peacekeeping, limited coercive diplomacy, and humanitarian intervention, which all involve at least some use of force. Force should, however, be complemented and even replaced by nonmilitary instruments of enforcement, which have both practical and symbolic implications (Johansen 1996, 313–16). Enforcement mechanisms obviously vary by the types of norms. For instruction rules, the mechanism is usually normative criticism; for commitment rules, defection from cooperation; and for directive rules, the resort to coercive measures.

Punishments can be conveniently grouped under the concept of "coercive diplomacy," which Alexander L. George (1991, 4–14) has defined as an effort to "persuade an opponent to stop and/or undo an action he is already embarked upon." Coercive diplomacy uses limited force and utilizes a mixture of threats and persuasion. If coercive measures are used, the violation of norms and commitments has already taken place. These measures are used to communicate, both by words and actions, that it is in the interest of the target to backtrack from this violation.

Coercive diplomacy is a process; once the explicit demand is made to alter the target's policy, the next step is to define its time frame and the instruments by which the goal is to be achieved. The process nature of coercion is reflected in Alan Wertheimer's distinction between coercive proposals and coercion itself. According to him, a coercive proposal is a necessary but not a sufficient condition of being coerced. The sufficient condition is achieved only when the target has no acceptable alternative but to succumb to a coercive proposal (Wertheimer 1987, 267–69).

Thus, the coerciveness of state actions is defined not only by the instruments of threats and punishments used, but also by the autonomy and available options of the target. This means that even incentives, if they are exploitative and unreasonable, are coercive in the case in which the target is dependent and vulnerable (ibid., 222–33).

Coercive diplomacy comes close to the definition of enforcement by negative means, which are even more pronounced in the strategy of compellence. However, coercive diplomacy and compellence have a common feature in that both try to limit costs and risks of conflict in the effort to avoid its future escalation (Schelling 1980, 195–99). Coercive diplomacy is primarily a nonviolent strategy; in addition to threats and punishments, it also relies on incentives and various methods of persuasion. It tries to combine effective influence with limitations on political and economic costs.

Enforcement actions are triggered by noncompliance with the relevant norm. As pointed out, the probability and nature of enforcement depends on the type of norms but also on the degree of noncompliance. Compliance with a norm is rarely complete; that is, it is not a binary choice. Therefore, for noncompliance to occur, the departure of actual behavior from the prescribed behavior must be significant. Decisions to launch enforcement actions must define the standard of acceptable compliance and define the instruments accordingly (Young 1979, 104–10; Chayes and Chayes 1995, 17–22).

ENFORCEMENT AND ITS LIMITS

The Gulf war and its aftermath popularized a specific type of punitive, collective enforcement by which not only is the aggressor punished but also democratic and humanitarian standards are upheld. Such enforcement actions are supposed to be carried out exogenously, by an international organization or other coalition of states. The focus on negative, exogenous enforcement alone is, however, too restrictive and needs to be expanded to cover incentives and various cooperative ways to ensure compliance with essential norms.

Negative enforcement builds on the assumption that compliance can be obtained by raising the costs of noncompliance (defined ultimately by the target itself). The fear of costs is not, of course, the only factor motivating human beings, whose behavior can also be altered by using promises and rewards to raise the expected value of compliance. There are moral arguments against rewarding noncompliant actors. However, they can, at least in part, be overruled by noting that negative enforcement can be cheap when it works but especially costly and risky if it fails; and inducements cost when they succeed but are cheap when they fail (Young 1979, 20–22; see also Kratochwil 1989, 70–71). To pay for success, however, seems to be preferable to failure. This speaks in favor of relying on incentives rather than punishments in enforcement.

The problem of limits in enforcement actions can be approached in two different ways; first, by asking why enforcement can fail and second, by asking what alternatives to negative, coercive enforcement are available. The failure of international enforcement may be caused by the intransigence of the targeted leaders. If stubborn, evasive, and smart enough, leaders can resist the enforcement efforts so effectively that they are delayed and possibly even given up. The UN resolutions aimed at the elimination of weapons of mass destruction in Iraq have been partially enforced, but the government of Saddam Hussein continues to have a capacity to produce biological and chemical weapons. It has also been able to harass the work of UN inspectors and thereby delay the process of enforcement.

In Haiti, the military chiefs were able to defy the international enforcement of democratic rule for years, before an agreement was reached in 1994 to restore Jean-Bertrand Aristide to power by an international military operation. In Somalia, the clan leaders retained their power position in spite of the international intervention and carved the country into spheres of influence. In Myanmar, the ruling junta has repressed its democratic opposition and maintained business contacts, the limited economic sanctions notwithstanding. Iran and Libya have also been subjected to economic boycotts, but there are no major internal political changes in sight.

Another type of limitation on enforcement concerns the willingness of states and international organizations to undertake them. In the early 1990s it was widely thought that the international community was entering a new era of enforcement. However, the realization of major political obstacles to modifying the behavior of targeted countries soon weakened this trend. Major powers realized that the very complexity and uncertainty of the situation in failing states raised the threshold of success. Because of the sensitivity of domestic public opinion to any losses in a humanitarian intervention, the leaders of major powers have become increasingly reluctant to provide resources for military enforcement actions. Instead, sanctions, as a simpler and less demanding action, have been increasingly used to signal political dissatisfaction with the situation in the target country.

The limits of enforcement are not solely determined by the inadequate political will to comply with the international norms; they may also result from the lack of capabilities to ensure compliance with them. If the state is weak and volatile, other states may be reluctant to conclude agreements with it because the enforcement of its provisions is uncertain and would, in all likelihood, be costly. Therefore, agreements whose norms are strongly enforced are more likely to be concluded between coherent and capable states because the costs of compliance are lower between them (Downs and Rocke 1995, 136–37).

Any analysis arguing that international norms have become more central and that their enforcement is now more feasible should take seriously various costs of enforcement. These costs have several components; for example, the compliance with the rules has to be verified and significant noncompliance with them has to be punished if international order is to be maintained. In fact, one can make a distinction between verification costs and implementation costs. Recent experiences with enforcement suggest that both the public opinion and policy makers of leading powers have become more sensitive to implementation costs, which have been further multiplied by negative images attached to enforcement in mass media.

An interesting contrast to the present situation is provided by the violation of arms-control agreements during the cold war. The fact that the costs of verification and implementation were higher than in today's enforcement actions in local conflicts did not prevent the United States from stressing politically the Soviet violations. On the other hand, Washington did not undertake any major actions to punish Moscow for its alleged violations of agreements in the 1970s and the 1980s. This means that verification costs were high but implementation costs, including potential political costs, remained low.

Another limit on enforcement concerns the inefficiency of international institutions. The main reason for passive enforcement is the lack of willingness on the part of governments to resort to action, but there may also be institutional inertia and even resistance if they decide to act. Ineffectiveness of international institutions reflects their limited capabilities or interests either to realize the initiatives made by the member states or, even if they are implemented, to secure that enforcement produces an adequate impact on the outcomes (conditions of institutional effectiveness are discussed in Young 1992).

An international organization may also drag its feet in defending its own coherence and organizational culture. Thus, it has been argued that the UN reactions to humanitarian crises have become in the 1990s more cautious and bureaucratic, even indifferent. Its decisions are increasingly shaped by the effort to protect the organization against potential failures (Barnett 1996).

The costs of enforcement may also be dependent on the types of norms to be enforced. If the question is of norms to which there are formally no exceptions, such as the *jus cogens* norms in international law, the costs of verification can be relatively low, whereas the costs of implementation may be high. Obviously both costs are lower in the enforcement of norms, with certain exceptions. When norms become more flexible and manipulable, their verification costs increase and the enforcement of violations becomes more complex. In real life, exceptions to rules are needed to keep the system in operation, but one has to recognize that allowing exceptions increases enforcement costs (for further analysis of norms with exceptions, see Edgerton 1985).

The general conclusion seems to be that both the unintended and adverse consequences of negative enforcement actions and their relatively high costs cast serious doubt on their feasibility and efficiency. Therefore, one has to think of alternatives. In recent debates, it has been increasingly suggested that a "strategic management of compliance" is preferable to negative, exogenous enforcement. Such cooperative compliance strategies, applied in a normative treaty framework, "seek to remove obstacles, clarify issues, and convince parties to change their behavior." In general, an active, noncontroversial management of compliance calls for capacity building, increasing transparency, dispute settlement, and possibly adaptation of the agreement (Chayes and Chayes 1995, 109).

The potential success of the cooperative, persuasive approach to enforcement does not necessarily mean that actors have internalized norms so deeply or that institutions are so influential that compliance has become habitual. It has been rightly observed that unenforced, compliant behavior may also be the result of the undemanding nature of the norms or the lack of deep cooperation in the negotiation and implementation of agreements (Downs, Rocke, and Barsoon 1996).

CONCLUSION

International relations are undergoing a sea change in which the role of national power is diminishing and the impact of international institutions and norms increasing. As a result of this change, the issues of compliance and enforcement are becoming more central. In fact, they are becoming building blocks of a new emerging system of global governance. These issues should not be approached, however, in legalistic and mechanical terms, and norms and their scope of application should not be defined narrowly. One must also avoid the view that the violation of norms should almost automatically lead to the imposition of punitive measures.

Attention should be paid to various persuasive and facilitative solutions to the problems of compliance, rather than a coercive enforcement of norms. The targeted actors should be assisted by technical and political support to comply with international standards of behavior. Coercive enforcement should be retained for those cases in which the violation of norms is intentional and based on strategies to obtain unilateral gains. In promoting global governance, monitoring, sharing, and support are more important than the use of deterrence and punishment.

NOTES

1. On the norm of decolonization, see also Goertz and Diehl 1992, 646–55. This norm has created a global prohibition regime forbidding the involvement of state and nonstate actors in specific activities such as colonization; see Nadelman (1990). Nadelman points out that global prohibition regimes tend to focus on transnational activities that are declared illegal in the criminal laws of dominant countries. In addition, there is a growing consensus, as Richard Price shows in this volume (chap. 11), that absolute bans should be imposed on particularly destructive and inhumane weapons.

2. For more detailed analyses of various liberal–rational strategies to enhance compliance, see Axelrod and Keohane 1986, and Yarborough and Yarborough 1986, 1992.

3. The essential institutional difference between security and economic cooperation has been also stressed by Lipson 1984.

4. On decentralized norms, see Goertz and Diehl 1992, 640–41. For a discussion of cooperative, decentralized, and hegemonic norms concerning risky states, see Väyrynen 1997b.

3

Uniting Nations: Global Regimes and the United Nations System

Mark W. Zacher

The United Nations system provides many diplomatic settings in which states are involved in varied and often intense conflicts, but its diplomatic forums also provide opportunities in which states are able to gain an understanding of their mutual interests. From these understandings there emerge some important international regimes. Despite what many observers might think, some remarkable movements toward international governance have occurred within the multifaceted UN system, which comprises the United Nations centered in New York, thirteen autonomous specialized agencies, and many other bodies. From the cacophony of the United Nations' approximately 185 voices, there have emerged some strands of governance that together make the world quite a different place from what it was in the past. The international political world is fraught with conflicts; but over the past half-century there has been significant progress as states seek to adapt to broader and deeper forms of interdependence—what many refer to as globalization.

This chapter reflects on what has evolved in a number of the major issue areas in which different parts of the UN system have been involved and on what types of regimes have emerged from these global forums. In particular it looks at the global regimes pertaining to security, monetary relations, international transportation and communications networks, health and the environment, and international trade.

In this survey of UN generated global regimes, key points are highlighted: First, the development of international regimes within the UN system has significantly enlarged the number and breadth of international issue areas governed by norms and rules. Second, not all global regimes are strong or have increased in strength over the past half-century. Some are basically modifications of those that existed before World War II, and parts of some regimes have collapsed. These "collapses" of the rule systems for particular international issues have, for the most part, concerned the rejection of restrictions on commercial competition—often because of understandings that the traditional regulatory arrangements are not conducive to international welfare. Third, the regimes provide greater protection for the basic jurisdictional parameters of states (particularly their territorial control), but at the same time they weaken their effective control over economic and social interactions across and within their borders. Fourth, the large majority of UN-generated regimes have reduced barriers to the movement of international goods and services; in other words, they have opened the arteries of the global commercial system. They have done this by

- establishing jurisdictional rights to traverse global commons (oceans and the airspace above them) and states' territories;
- reducing the possibilities of damages to goods and information in transit between states;
- assuring technical interconnection; and
- preventing international commercial transactions from leading to transborder damages such as the spread of diseases or environmental harm.

Fifth, global regimes are increasingly the product of negotiations among state and nonstate actors. At the same time, when crises over the basic structures of political and economic order arise, interstate and often UN-affiliated institutions are still central to their management.

Before reviewing the major global regimes it is important to make several points. First, it is difficult to separate the United Nations *per se* from the society of states operating within a variety of international forums. It is, however, a fact that most international organizations that legitimate global regimes are affiliated with the UN system. Second, in a presentation of this length it is impossible to incorporate the variety of conflicts that have shaped these multifaceted regimes. This does not imply, however, that divergent interests and power machinations did not have significant impacts on them.

SECURITY

Among the regimes that the global community of states has fashioned, it is important to focus first on the fundamental issue area of security or the use of force. Many observers wrongly judge that there has not been any significant global security cooperation or that the UN system has been quite marginal to significant forms of international security cooperation. Evidence to which such observers point is the fact that the UN has passed resolutions calling for withdrawals or cease-fires in only a small percentage of all wars since 1945, and states have failed to comply with a number of these directives. What such a focus on wars overlooks is the significant changes in international norms that proscribe and influence the international use of military force.

In evaluating the scope of developments since World War II it is valuable to begin with the international security order prior to 1945. At the heart of the Westphalian security order there was an acceptance that states would not eliminate other states (the late eighteenth century division of Poland being an exception). On the other hand, from 1648 through 1945 territorial aggrandizement was a common and tolerated dimension of international politics. In fact, wars of territorial conquest provided the dominant motif of international relations. Territorial gain was an important feature of most wars, and 80 percent of all wars involving disputes over territory led to some exchange of territory. In the two decades between the two world wars of the twentieth century there were important international proclamations against territorial aggression, such as the League of Nations Covenant and the Kellogg-Briand Pact, but the sad history of those times indicates that the proscription against territorial aggrandizement was not accepted in practice.

Something quite striking occurred after 1945: states appear to have accepted the proscription that they should not practice or tolerate wars for territorial gain. Related to the development of this injunction, states have legitimated the principle of self-determination for the juridical state—as opposed to the principle of self-determination for the national grouping. This norm proscribing the use of force to alter boundaries was embodied in Article 2(4) of the UN Charter, but there were few statesmen or observers in 1945 who anticipated a marked change in state practices. One of the first signs of a change in states' attitudes was the acceptance of the principle of decolonization (most definitively in the 1960 United Nations Declaration on Granting Independence to Colonial Territories and Countries), which prescribes that states should not be allowed to rule lands and peoples far from their home territories. There was, however, a broader delegitimation of coercive territorial aggrandizement in both the 1960 declaration and the 1970 United Nations Declaration of Principles of International Law concerning Friendly Relations and Cooperation among States. Both documents stipulate that the juridical state and the territorially delimited colony are the legitimate entities to which the principle of self-determination should apply and that coercive territorial revisionism against them is illegitimate. This norm is reiterated in pronouncements of the Organization of African Unity (OAU) of 1963 and 1964 and in the 1975

Helsinki Accords (the Final Act of the Conference for Security and Cooperation in Europe). The society of states may tolerate the occasional breakup of states into two or more states, but it does not tolerate external armed intervention to detach a piece of territory from another state.

Beyond what appeared in various declarations and treaties in the postwar decades, there were important changes in state practices in international conflicts, which were influenced by the growing consensus among UN member states against territorial revisionism. In order to grasp the change in the postwar era it is important to understand that in the three preceding centuries most wars concerned territorial revisionism in some way, and 80 percent of these territorial revisionist wars ended in some exchange of territory. Between 1946 and 1996, only 23 percent of territorial revisionist wars (eight of thirty-four) eventuated in exchanges of territory. Of the eight cases in which territory was transferred, six were postcolonial disputes between Asian states, and the other two involved Israel and its Arab neighbors. In most of the thirty-four conflicts, the UN, a regional body, or the great powers took a stand against territorial revision. The most notable recent cases are the UN—great power stands with regard to the Gulf war and the Yugoslav–Serbian attempts to carve pieces of territory out of the new states of Croatia and Bosnia. The UN stands against Iraq's attempt to absorb Kuwait, and Yugoslavia's attempts to absorb parts of Croatia and Bosnia were tremendously important in legitimating the sanctity of juridical borders. Also relevant to the strengthening of this norm in the 1990s was the mutual respect of the fifteen successor states from the former Soviet Union for each other's territorial boundaries. Prior to our contemporary era, states would almost certainly have embarked on territorial revisionist wars after such a momentous dissolution of an empire (Zacher 1979; Holsti 1991; Jackson and Zacher 1997).

Apart from the marked strengthening of the norm of antiterritorial revisionism, other remarkable developments in security cooperation are the consensus against the use of nuclear weapons and the related *de facto* proscription against wars between the great powers both resulting from the potential for nuclear war. It is quite remarkable that there has been neither a nuclear nor a great-power war over the past half-century; and global normative trends are central to these phenomenon. While the anti-nuclear war consensus emerged first and foremost from the great-power club, the entire UN membership has been brought into the process of norm consolidation through the Non-Proliferation Treaty (NPT). It is notable that almost all countries have signed the NPT and that the proliferation of nuclear weapons in the Third World has been limited to China, India, and Pakistan. Whether the line can be held against proliferation of nuclear weapons is certainly problematic; but the strength of sentiment against the acquisition of nuclear weapons by a large majority of the world's states, and particularly by the great powers may be adequate to uphold the norm. Among the UN membership there is a growing consensus that war, for whatever purpose, does not generally have the legitimacy that it once did and that nuclear war in particular must be avoided. We are clearly seeing a security order distinctly different from that which existed in the past centuries of the Westphalian system (Gaddis 1987; Jervis 1989; Mueller 1989; Holsti 1991; UN 1995; Simpson and Howlett 1995).

There are several key points to make about the developments in the global security order mentioned above. First, the key contributions of international society to the security of states have been in the realm of gradual norm development more than in the realm of responses to specific conflicts. At the same time, collective international responses to specific conflicts such as the UN's stand in the Gulf war and the response to the breakup of Yugoslavia, do have crucial effects in consolidating the legitimacy of norms. In fact, until norms are actually tested in situations of intense conflict, it is difficult to evaluate their strength. Furthermore, when it comes to international security norms, the authoritative responses must come from the United Nations and the great powers. Both the larger international society and the most powerful countries must support such rules of conduct.

Second, security regime developments within the United Nations have provided significant support for the fundamental jurisdictional parameter of the state—namely, the legitimacy of state boundaries. Strong opposition to nuclear war and consequently great-power war have also given the great powers a degree of security with regard to their basic territorial parameters, and the great powers' heightened sense of security has consequently provided a less violent international environment, which has enhanced the security of most countries. Lastly, UN security politics indicates that some international prescriptions and proscriptions strongly depend on global support for their effective implementation—namely, those injunctions that touch on the states' basic jurisdictional parameters or most fundamental values. This is certainly the case with regard to the sanctity of borders and the control of nuclear warfare and nonproliferation. Strategies for bilateral and regional cooperation with regard to these problems are important, but ultimately a global sanctification within a UN context is necessary.

MONETARY RELATIONS

Most UN bodies are concerned with economic cooperation, and at the center of the evolution of international economic regimes have been six UN specialized agencies. The two most important institutions are the International Monetary Fund (IMF) and the World Trade Organization (WTO);[1]

the other four institutions, which are concerned with international transportation and communications, are the International Maritime Organization (IMO), the International Civil Aviation Organization (ICAO), the International Telecommunications Union (ITU), and the Universal Postal Union (UPU). The IMF, the IMO, the ICAO, the ITU, and the UPU are all concerned, *inter alia,* with the facilitation of international trade, and they are therefore addressed before the activities of the WTO in promoting a reduction of tariff and nontariff barriers. In fact, most of the obstructions to the flow of commerce that are addressed by the above five organizations are types of nontariff barriers, some of which are similar to ones that are regulated by the WTO.

From a certain perspective the history of postwar monetary cooperation after 1970 looks like a sad tale. In the pre-1971 era the IMF, with strong U.S. backing, made some important contributions to currency convertibility among the industrialized states (an underestimated accomplishment), exchange-rate stability, and the regaining of financial viability for states with large debt burdens. All of these accomplishments were aimed at promoting commercial openness. Changes in the economic fortunes of states, as well as changes in financial flows, during the 1960s caused some political eruptions in the early 1970s that ruined the Bretton Woods edifice for multilateral control of exchange rates and the control of the debt problem. The story of the 1970s is not as disastrous as it might appear at first, because the Bretton Woods architects erred on a number of critical issues in 1944 and because the evolution of the international financial system after 1960 altered what could and should be done in managing international monetary relations. The Bretton Woods architects miscalculated in their acceptance of two key beliefs: first, that exchange rates could be regulated at a global level, given changes in states' economic fortunes in the evolving global economy, and, second, that floating rates would be disastrous for international trade and security relations. What they failed to anticipate was the dramatic growth in capital movements starting in the 1960s. These errors in judgment and inadequacies in forecasting led to the demise of the pegged-exchange-rate regime after its operation from 1958 to 1973 as well as the virtual collapse of the IMF's control over balance-of-payments financing and debtor states' adjustment policies from the mid-1970s through 1982. During this time the banks tried to manage the debt problem independently, and they failed miserably.

The failure of the private banks to manage states' debt problems and the sidelining of the IMF with regard to international debt management for close to a decade did, however, lead to a new kind of debt regime starting in 1982, one in which the IMF (led by the United States and a few other major powers) developed a new cooperative relationship with the international banks. The Mexican debt crisis of 1982 was the wake-up call that led the major financial powers, private bank officials, and IMF officials to re-structure international arrangements for steering debtor states back to fi-nancial viability. In fact, in a certain sense the new debt regime has given the IMF more control over the economic policies of debtor states than it used to have—if only because private banking and industry circles as well as governments look to the IMF for judgments as to whether states are good risks for lending and investments. The IMF may now control only 5–10 percent of international lending to debtor states, but its evaluations have profound effects on the behavior of banks, firms, and states. One need only look at the central role of the IMF in the Asian economic crises in 1997 and 1998 to recognize the central role that it plays in the manage-ment of international financial crises that involve the need for countries to borrow and restructure their economies. The IMF is looked to as the most legitimate organization for developing a plan for putting the troubled countries in question, as well as the global economy, back on track (Dam 1982; Walter 1991; Bordo and Eichengreen 1993; Cline 1995; Cohen 1998).

Looking broadly at the monetary regime, the collapse of the pegged-ex-change-rate system was not a bad thing, and in fact it was probably a good thing. Certainly more coordination among the G-5 countries with regard to periodic misalignments would strengthen the international monetary system. Over all, however, the demise of pegged rates has not had negative consequences for trade. In the case of the debt management regime, states and the banks have refashioned the regime for the era of massive capital flows and a growing acceptance of neoliberal economic orthodoxies, and the result has not been a bad one, as the flow of private capital back into many Third World countries during the 1990s indicates. A hybrid regime based on international governmental organizations and private banks has achieved a reasonable degree of stability on the balance-of-payments front (the recent Asian problems notwithstanding), and the overall effect seems to entail much greater IMF influence over states' macroeconomic and reg-ulatory policies than existed before the debt crisis.

The IMF is looked upon as the central body for laying out ground rules for a number of reasons. A key reason is that the wealthiest states do not want to bear the criticism of debtor states for imposing certain conditions on them as a price for new loans or loan forgiveness. Countries like the United States, Japan, and Germany are willing to give up a measure of con-trol over financial recovery packages in exchange for escaping at least some resentment from the financially troubled states. At the same time, the close integration of these wealthy states in the formal deliberations to resolve such crises is crucial, because they possess the resources that are required to resolve the problems. As IMF members, these financial powers are brought formally into the international deliberations. The role of the

United States within IMF structures was, of course, particularly crucial throughout the difficult debt crisis of the 1980s—culminating in the Brady Plan of 1989. Nonetheless, the United States was always anxious to work significantly through the IMF rather than unilaterally. The debtor states from the Third World have also seen the advantages of working through the IMF, because they do not want to assume an inferior status by being dictated to by the major industrialized powers. Their *amour propre* is not as offended by a conditionality package from an international organization as one from the financial powers of the First World. Also, these states have some leverage in UN-affiliated bodies—even ones, such as the IMF, with a weighted voting formula. Of course, as noted above, private banks are unable to manage these problems on their own because they do not have the ability to monitor the financial policies of states or to impose effective sanctions.

INFRASTRUCTURE INDUSTRIES: TRANSPORTATION AND COMMUNICATIONS

Moving from the monetary front to the major international infrastructure industries of shipping, air transport, telecommunications, and postal services, there have been a number of developments that parallel what has occurred in the monetary field. Certain parts of the traditional transportation and communications regimes have collapsed as a result of some states' and firms' support for competitive markets and "deregulation," and private commercial actors are much more prominent in the crafting of the intergovernmental accords that constitute the regimes. Also, the four regimes are designed first and foremost to reduce obstacles to the flow of commerce.

In the four infrastructure industries there are four subissue areas in which norms and rules have developed—namely, jurisdictional rights, damage control, technical interconnection, and prices and market shares. In the case of the first three there has been consistent cooperation around the central principle of international commercial openness over the past century, but the scope of the cooperation has mushroomed since 1945. Norms relating to (1) the freedom of the high seas and adjacent airspace and (2) innocent passage for carriers and information through foreign territories and airspace run through all four communications and transportation industries. There are also extensive international treaties and agreements promoting the reduction of damages and the assurance of technical interconnection. It is important to stress that rules relating to minimization of damages, compensation for damages, and technical interconnection are usually quite contentious, because the accords generally favor particular national manufacturers and industries. Nevertheless, agreements do emerge from such "coordination games," because the global industrial complex demands that interconnection is assured (Zacher 1996).

In the case of shipping, the United Nations Law of the Sea Conferences have approved jurisdictional norms and rules relating to the freedom of the high seas and innocent passage through territorial seas. In so doing they have opened the avenues for maritime transport to move goods throughout the world's oceans and have continued a tradition of the law of the sea that goes back several centuries. (Ninety percent of world trade by weight moves by ship.) It is the International Maritime Organization that formulates conventions concerning the prevention of damage to ships and goods, the prevention of pollution, and compensation for damages. The two central treaties, which are regularly revised, are the International Convention for the Safety of Life at Sea (SOLAS) and the International Convention for the Prevention of Pollution from Ships (MARPOL). Universal rules for the shipping industry are necessary because ships enter harbors throughout the world and because shipowners generally want rules that impose equal costs on all shipping firms. Universal rules both open the lines of maritime transport and assure a level playing field for international shipping firms (M'Gonigle and Zacher 1979; Gold 1981; Farthing 1987).

With regard to air transport, both jurisdictional and technical norms and rules are prescribed by the International Civil Aviation Organization. The freedom of overflight over the world's oceans has always been a bedrock of international air transport; another very important norm, to which most states subscribe, is the right of overflight over countries' territories. This right of overflight has greatly facilitated the movement of international air traffic. The technical rules facilitating international air transport are included in annexes to the International Civil Aviation Organization (ICAO) Convention. Some technical issues (especially concerning the coordination of trips using different airlines and the facilitation of traffic in airports) are handled significantly by the International Association of Transport Airlines (IATA). In fact, there is a close relationship between ICAO and IATA, especially on technical matters, because the control of air piracy by means of cooperation among governments and airlines is central to the smooth operation of the international industry (Matte 1981; Jonsson 1987; Dempsey 1994).

Telecommunications is one of the most important industries in the world today, and many aspects of it are regulated by the relevant UN specialized agency—the International Telecommunications Union. In fact, the present ITU is the successor to the first international public union—the International Telegraph Union created in 1865. The ITU has never formally stated that the frequency spectrum is an international commons to which all states have access; but it has implicitly backed this stance in prescribing that states can only use certain frequency bands for specific purposes and that states have a right to broadcast on a particular frequency once they have registered it with the ITU. Despite considerable conflict over the uses of the airwaves and the geostationary orbit (where communications satellites circle the earth), ITU members have been able to work out rules of the road for the frequency spectrum and outer space.

Most work in the ITU is devoted to developing technical standards that assure the movement of messages and information through the spectrum and over wires. The setting of technical standards was previously confined to a few radio standards and switching equipment at borders. Now ITU standards cover equipment throughout the physical telecommunications networks—right down to the computers on desks. The financial implications of ITU standards for different national firms such as AT&T, Northern Telecom, Siemens, and Sony are very high; nevertheless, accords are reached to assure technical interconnection because the international commercial world demands it. The issue generally faced by public and private representatives to ITU and other standard-setting bodies is not whether standards for international interconnection will be set but rather what those standards will be. As a result of the speed of technological change a great deal of international standard setting in recent years has taken place through coordination among U.S., European, and Japanese bodies and their major telecommunications firms, and the ITU tends to register accords that have been concluded elsewhere. This does not, however, detract from the fact that firms and governments manage to craft standards that assure interconnectivity (Codding and Rutkowski 1982; Savage 1989; Aronson and Cowhey 1989; Drake 1995; Zacher 1996).

International postal services do not quite have the same status as the other international infrastructure industries, but they are an important element in the global economy. The Universal Postal Union (created in 1874) prescribes technical standards that assure the movement of the mails and a right of transit passage. This right establishes the obligation of states not to interfere with mail going through their territory while in transit between two other states. The proscription is sometimes violated for political reasons, but on the whole it is a relatively strong norm (Codding 1964).

Among these four international infrastructure industries, the one area in which there has been a real decrease in cooperation concerns prices and market shares. From the late nineteenth century through the 1970s the international markets for these industries were basically controlled by cartels of state-owned firms, in the case of air transport, telecommunications, and postal services, and a network of cartels of private firms, in the case of shipping. The oft-stated rationales for the cartels were, first, that there were economies of scale in these industries and, second, that higher rates were necessary to assure reliability of service. A less publicly trumpeted rationale was that governments believed that any self-respecting state had to control the most important national infrastructure industries, including their international interconnections.

Both the economic and political rationales for cartels began to attract strong criticism in the 1970s. "Deregulation" became the battle cry of many economists and private business interests in Western states, who increasingly believed that states should give up the kinds of economic controls they had traditionally possessed. In other words, they thought that both businesses and states had to become "leaner and meaner." The demise of the cartels cannot be explored in depth in this chapter; suffice it to say they have all either disintegrated or been so badly weakened that they can in no way be viewed as governing prices and market shares. Competitive markets have assumed a preeminence for most of the international industry in the sense that there is quite simply no intergovernmental consensus on the desirability of either cartels or international antitrust laws; and a hybrid competitive-managed international market is a kind of default position in such circumstances. Again, it has to be stressed that this situation does not threaten disruptions in service, and without such threats the present competitive scene is quite acceptable to most states, or at least to the most powerful ones (Zacher 1996; Cafruny 1987; Doganis 1991; Drake 1995).

It is critical to account for the role of particular states and technology in the demise of the intergovernmental cartels. It is often said that the United States was the central force behind international deregulation, but its influence is probably overstated. In the case of shipping it was the East Asian lines and containerization that brought down the network of shipping cartels. In the case of air transport, the first very successful challengers to the IATA cartel were the Asian lines, and although the United States exerted a great deal of effective pressure toward deregulation starting in the late 1970s, the increase in plane carrying capacity and the dramatic increase in economy-minded tourists were likely to promote international commercial competition in the long run. With regard to telecommunications, there is no doubt that the United States was tremendously important in pushing for deregulation in the early 1980s, but large firms had been getting special competitive deals long before then. Furthermore, the increase in modes of communication would probably have brought down the old intergovernmental telecommunications cartel in the long run. In the case of postal services, the advent of courier services in the 1970s and e-mail in the 1980s marginalized state postal administrations, and it is only a matter of time before many states open up to competition for door-to-door service among private firms.

What has pressured states and firms to liberalize the traditional market controls are, first, the opportunities for enhanced commerce presented by technological change (in particular, the diversity of telecommunications services and modes of transmitting information) and, second, the transformation in many economists' and governments' ideological and policy perspectives that often go under the labels of neoliberal economic thought and deregulation. States and firms have brought these perspectives into the councils of UN-affiliated organizations and, as a result, have brought about some dramatic changes in global regimes—or at least the demise of old cartel arrangements. The UN system is no more immune to technological and ideological forces of change than other political and economic institutions in the world.

TRANSBORDER DAMAGES: HEALTH AND ENVIRONMENT

Two interesting issue areas in which there are global regimes are the international spread of diseases and the transmission of environmental damages across state boundaries. Failures to deal with these transborder damages often lead to reactions against or curtailments of international economic exchanges. The scope of cooperation in the health sphere has actually been quite modest, for very good reasons, but the recent development of international environmental regimes exceeds popular impressions. In both spheres, UN-affiliated organizations have been and are still central actors, although nongovernmental actors have been quite instrumental in the development of international cooperation.

The earliest conferences to craft a global regime to control the international spread of diseases occurred in the mid-nineteenth century. Finally, in 1903, the International Sanitary Regulations were accepted, and their rules were subsequently revised at regular intervals (Cooper 1989). Responsibility for the regulations fell to the World Health Organization (WHO) after World War II, and they were retitled the International Health Regulations. The regulations prescribed international reporting requirements with regard to occurrences of certain diseases (cholera, plague, yellow fever, smallpox, typhus, and relapsing fever) and the measures that states and international carriers (ships and planes) should adopt to control the spread of diseases and avoid unnecessary delays to carriers. The goals of the regulations hence encompassed not only the control of infectious diseases but also the prevention of unnecessary interventions with respect to the maritime transport. Throughout the twentieth century the regulations have had only a modest impact on the international spread of the designated diseases and the free flow of commerce, because the international spread of these diseases decreased markedly over the twentieth century. Also, the rapidity and scale of international travel have made it and still make it extremely difficult to detect people with diseases at borders. Hence the central strategy of the regulations of preventing peoples with diseases from crossing borders was increasingly questioned. (The other main strategy was monitoring diseases throughout the world.) Increasingly, international health experts and governments realized that the best strategies for controlling the international spread of diseases are monitoring disease outbreaks and reducing the incidence of diseases within countries through aid programs. International health assistance was and still is largely transferred through national aid programs, although there have always been some rather modest financial contributions and coordination efforts under the auspices of the WHO, the World Bank, and other organizations.

Some interesting changes in the international health regime have been evolving in the last decade. First, outbreaks of the so-called emerging and reemerging diseases (dramatized in *The Coming Plague*, [Garrett 1994]) have led to a recognition that a much broader group of diseases should be covered under the International Health Regulations and that international reporting should be quicker and more thorough. Proposals on these matters will be accepted in revised regulations in 1999 or 2000 (WHO 1998). Second, some important institutional developments have occurred. Several national health centers (especially the U.S. Centers for Disease Control [CDC]) have taken over most serious emergency responses to disease outbreaks (often at the behest of the WHO), and they are at the forefront in designing preventive strategies and emergency measures in many parts of the world. Third, an internet disease information website called Promed, which relies on reporting by private medical personnel, has become a more important vehicle for disease reporting throughout the world than the long-standing WHO system for surveillance and reporting. Promed, along with expanded health reporting by the media and a new WHO Rumor Outbreak Page on the internet, have dramatically altered international disease surveillance. Finally, within the world of international governmental institutions the World Bank—not the WHO—is now at the cutting edge in the development of public health strategies that control diseases at their source. It is, however, important to recall that the World Bank is one of the thirteen UN specialized agencies.

Overall, the network of international health cooperation is rather fractured, with the central UN-affiliated body (WHO) performing rather limited roles. The World Bank and the CDC are probably more important than WHO in controlling the international spread of diseases although the role of the WHO is likely to increase in the next decade. Independent medical groups are also significant participants in international health cooperation, and they are being assisted by modern information technology. This organizational patchwork quilt is, however, not a disaster. In fact, this cooperative network which draws on different bodies and groups for varied skills and capabilities, has been reasonably effective in addressing the problems associated with the international spread of infectious diseases. The health regime is the epitome of some modern regimes that draw increasingly on nongovernmental groups for building international cooperation and making the world safe for international commerce (Goodman 1971; Leive 1976; Fidler 1997).

One of the most remarkable areas of progress in international cooperation in recent decades concerns international environmental damages or transborder damages caused by national industrial activities. Given the fact that international environmental issues did not achieve significant status on the global agenda until the 1970s, it is amazing that so much has been done in a couple decades—largely through UN-affiliated organizations. In the case of five specific issues of transborder damage (ship-generated marine pollution, dumping at sea, acid rain, ozone depletion, and the export of hazardous wastes), significant progress has occurred. In the case of another (nuclear reactor accidents and emissions), an accurate evaluation of significant progress is somewhat more problematic. Nevertheless, some important strides have been made. The two areas where there has been less success in controlling the damages are land-based marine pollution and climate change, and the reason is quite obvious: the costs involved are significantly higher than in the previously mentioned issue areas. However, even in these two issue areas there have been modest strides forward, and gradual progress is likely in future decades. It is important to stress that most of these environmental regimes emerged from UN bodies because of the need to include all states in the cooperative arrangements.

There are three major sources of marine pollution for which regulations have been developed. International control of ship-generated pollution by the International Maritime Organization dates back to the 1950s, but effective control really started with the acceptance of the International Convention for the Prevention of Pollution from Ships in 1973. This treaty has been remarkably successful because it relies on construction and equipment standards that can easily be inspected. Also, because international maritime interests do not want any excuses for states to delay vessels in ports, they have cooperated in promoting a relatively effective regime. The control of dumping of wastes at sea dates back to the acceptance of the London Dumping Convention of 1972, soon after the conclusion of the 1972 United Nations Conference on the Human Environment in Stockholm. There was a strong feeling that states should not be allowed to deliberately dump hazardous wastes near the shores of other states; and this sentiment has sustained quite a strong regime. United Nations bodies have enunciated general principles against the discharge of wastes from land into the oceans, but serious action has been confined to regional settings, basically around Europe. It is only wealthy countries (e.g., those bordering the North Sea) that are willing to pay for an effective regime; and therefore global action through the UN is not practical—especially because the costs of reducing land-source discharges are quite high.

Air pollution constitutes another important transborder damage problem, and perhaps the best-known form of air pollution in the industrialized world is acid rain. The negotiations to control its international manifestations in Europe have occurred within the context of the United Nations Economic Commission for Europe, because it was an organization to which both Western and socialist states belonged in the 1970s and 1980s. Both the European and North American acid rain accords have been conducted in relatively isolated regional settings; and they both entail significant progress in pollution abatement. An even more striking air pollution accord concerns ozone depletion. The negotiations for the 1985 treaty and subsequent protocols were concluded under the auspices of the United Nations Environment Program (UNEP) because it involved damage to a common property resource and it was important that all states agree to curtail the use of certain chemicals. Also, most major chemical firms were concerned that foreign firms not be allowed to manufacture the chemicals in question and thus achieve a competitive advantage in world markets. Another form of air pollution is the emission of the greenhouse gases that cause global warming and climate change. The rationales for UN involvement are similar to those applicable to ozone depletion, but the costs are so much higher than in the case of ozone depletion that little headway in regime development has occurred. The 1996 Kyoto Protocol to the 1992 Climate Change Convention is an important step, but states are not ready presently to pay the costs of meaningful abatement of greenhouse gases.

Two somewhat unique problems of transborder damage concern pollution from nuclear reactor accidents and the export of hazardous wastes. Most cooperation to prevent nuclear reactor accidents occurred for many years in the OECD because the major users of nuclear energy were Western industrialized states. However, it later became important to integrate the Eastern European states into cooperative arrangements on safety standards, and as a result greater collaboration on safety issues developed within the relevant UN specialized agency, the International Atomic Energy Agency. Although concern about nuclear accidents tends to be focused on Eastern Europe, all national nuclear industries realize that accidents anywhere in the world harm their local political situations. Therefore global approaches are quite attractive to them. In the case of the export of hazardous wastes from developed to developing countries there was relatively strong support for a global approach for the 1989 Basel Convention on the Export of Hazardous Wastes because such disposal policies were seen as immoral. Also, major chemical companies did not want their foreign rivals to benefit from cheaper disposal opportunities if they had to accept tough controls, and therefore most of them supported the convention. The regime is now a strong regulatory arrangement.

As is clear from the above discussion, the reasons for the centrality of UN or global institutions in the formation of environmental regimes vary. First, a problem can touch on a strongly held value among countries, a value that goes beyond the prevention of transborder damages. One such value seems to be opposition to the deliberate disposal of wastes in other countries' territories or territorial seas, particularly if they do not have the capabilities to treat them properly. This seems to have had a marked influence on the conclusion of the London Dumping Convention of 1972 and the Basel Convention of 1989. Second, when pollution is caused by international carriers such as ships that travel among different national ports throughout the world, it seems only sensible that the problem be regulated within a UN-affiliated body such as the International Maritime Organization. It would be very inefficient if ships could only service certain ports because states had different construction and equipment standards. This is perhaps the central reason for the IMO's responsibility for the International Convention for the Prevention of Pollution from Ships. Third, a reason for the success of the UN–global management of environmental interdependencies is that firms are generally willing to be regulated as long as all of their competitors in the global marketplace are regulated in the same manner. They do not want to have to bear costs that rival firms do not have to bear. This consideration has definitely influenced the management of dumping at sea, the export of hazardous wastes, ship-generated marine pollution, acid rain, and ozone depletion. It is, of course, also central to progress on climate change or global warming.

Fourth, the wider the geographic impact of pollutants, the greater the support for global management. It is particularly the contributions of pollutants to "global damages" (such as ozone depletion and climate change) that evoke demands for UN management. The ozone depletion regime is probably the most impressive example of a global response to international environmental damage, and the global scope of the damages certainly was an important factor in the regime's development. Lastly, there is a further consideration that comes into play in many environmental negotiations: there is fear that if transborder damages are allowed to continue, there will be strong public reactions against the international industries that caused them. Transnational economic interests are well predisposed to regimes that avoid hostile feelings toward transnational economic forces.

There is yet another interesting feature of the evolution of international environmental regimes, and that is the role of transnational, as well as national, environmental groups in regime developments. Environmental NGOs have played a unique role in mobilizing domestic political support in many countries for environmental controls and in mobilizing particular states behind their political initiatives. Third World countries in particular have at times been drawn into effective environmentalist coalitions because of the initiatives of organizations such as Greenpeace and Friends of the Earth. In very few areas can one say that public interest groups have had a major impact in shaping international regimes, but this is certainly one of them. Some governments literally fear environmental NGOs because of their influence with domestic constituencies; at the same time, others rely on them for understanding environmental damages and proposals.

TRADE

The previously discussed global regimes are significantly concerned with the facilitation of international trade, but tariff and nontariff trade barriers, of course, are also regulated directly by the World Trade Organization (and prior to 1995 by the GATT). It is a daunting task to review the outcomes of global trade negotiations—and even more daunting to comment briefly on the driving forces. The key elements of progress are

- a decrease in tariffs on manufactures, from around 40 to 5 percent between 1947 and 1995;
- application of the norm of nondiscrimination to a wide variety of trade relationships (the major compromise concerning regional common markets and free trade areas);
- significant expansions in the rules for nontariff barriers (e.g., health and technical standards and state subsidies to firms) in the GATT accords at the end of the Tokyo and Uruguay Rounds (1979 and 1995);
- a gradual increase in the strength of dispute settlement procedures culminating in the binding force of panel decisions since the end of the Uruguay Round in 1995;
- the growing integration of developing countries and former socialist states into the trade regime; and
- very importantly, an increase of trade as a proportion of global GNP from around 4 to 20 percent between 1947 and 1998.

The birth of the postwar era of trade liberalization was influenced by liberal trade theory, but it was affected even more by the United States's views on the ties between growing trade and peace. The U.S. backing for the norm of nondiscrimination was tied clearly to a desire to discourage the development of trade blocs along the lines of what occurred in the 1930s. Support for a global trade organization was a logical strategy for the United States in the immediate postwar years. (The GATT was treated as a *de facto* specialized agency within the UN system.) With the onset of the cold war, the United States and its European allies saw the GATT primarily as an organization for developing close economic ties and prosperity among the Western alliance states. The socialist states were outside of the GATT system, and the developing countries were rather marginal because of their commitment to protectionism. The developing countries began to become full-fledged members of the GATT system in the 1980s as they increasingly recognized the costs of their past policies. The conclusion of the Uruguay Round in 1995 marked a decisive step toward their acceptance of WTO trade disciplines. The former socialist states, of course, have moved slowly toward integration into the Western trading system in the 1990s. They still have some way to go before they accept the tariffs and nontariff barriers binding on the Western nations, but they are moving toward integration into the WTO trade system.

Perhaps the most remarkable fact about the international trade regime is that the Western powers have accepted increasing liberalization over the past half century—even with the end of the cold war. They constitute the central pillar of the global trade order, and it is their trading system for all intents and purposes that the developing and former socialist states want to join. As noted, the Western trading system benefited tremendously from U.S. political support during the cold war throughout most of the last half of the twentieth century; but at the same time industries and important political forces everywhere in the Western world have increasingly recognized that all countries benefit from trade liberalization. Strong vested interests in a liberal trading order have grown over recent decades (Finlayson and Zacher 1981; Milner 1988; Jackson 1989; Schott 1994; Hoekman and Kostecki 1995).

The reasons for a global trade regime and UN-affiliated trade organization are many. An important one is that a good number of political leaders accept the relationship between economic interdependence and peace, and therefore it makes sense to support a global regime that promotes complex trade ties among all states. During the 1990s, although the major economic powers have been interested in reaping gains from regional trade arrangements, they are wary of allowing the world to evolve into exclusionist trade blocs for fear that such blocs could nurture security competition. Regarding economic considerations, it is important to recognize that trade theory in economics, despite a recognition of imperfect markets, focuses on the mutual gains from multilateral trade liberalization. Theoretical knowledge does penetrate international decision making. Finally, important industries in many countries have developed strong vested interests in trade and a continued decline in trade barriers. Globalization has influenced important elites in the international economy.

CONCLUSION

In reflecting on this tour through the major global or UN-generated regimes we can ask, What is interesting and surprising? First, there has been a lot more global cooperation within the UN system than most observers have attributed to it. Perhaps the growth of the global security order constitutes the most surprising development for many people. Both developed and developing countries have their own particular reasons for supporting self-determination for the juridical state and the delegitimation of territorial revisionism as central pillars of global society, and these two norms are central to what can be called "the territorial covenant." Both groupings also oppose the spread of nuclear weapons, and this has enormous implications for international stability. John Gaddis (1987) spoke of nuclear weaponry's promotion of "the long peace" because of nuclear deterrence, but over the past half-century there have also been other forces working for a longer and broader peace.

Second, a remarkable group of UN-generated regimes have promoted greater openness in the global economy. Global regimes for service industries have mandated that jurisdictional rights, threats of physical and financial damages, and technical standards should not stand in the way of commerce. They have also sought to control unintended damages to human health and environmental quality from the operations of the global economy, hence reducing the fears of private parties of engaging in international commerce. The monetary regime has, of course, provided a basis of international financial stability by its contribution to the management of the balance-of-payments problem, and the management of this problem has given the IMF the basis for extensive intrusions into national economies. Finally, despite the screams of many domestic industries, the UN trade regime includes major steps toward the dismantling of tariff and nontariff barriers.

Third, a notable feature of the regimes concerned with economic openness is that regulations have increasingly moved from controlling activities or practices at borders to regulating domestic economic practices and regulations. Boundaries may be more sanctified and stable, but they are also more permeable to private commercial practices and international economic governance. The regulatory intrusions into national economies are most evident in the regimes for monetary relations, trade, and service or infrastructure industries.

Fourth, global governance has lost out to the increasing influence of market forces in some issue areas, but regimes were disassembled largely when they were seen as unnecessary or even undesirable for international economic stability and openness. The United States was in the vanguard of these disassemblings in areas such as currency exchange rates and the international commercial practices of service industries, but the changes were coming eventually in any case. Another reason global governance is not particularly strong in some international situations is that the relevant international interdependencies are not particularly strong, and the inter-dependencies are being managed adequately by a variety of national and international efforts. This is certainly the case with international health, where the global regime has been weak.

Lastly, there is clearly a trend toward an increasing involvement of non-governmental actors in the negotiations concerning regime creation and reform. At the same time, when crises of openness and stability arise, as has occurred in the balance-of-payments sphere, it is states, through international governmental organizations, that are the ultimate providers of reform and order. Global regimes that promote economic openness may undermine state policy autonomy, but it is remarkable that when serious problems arise it is states (led by the great powers) that must pull the global economy from the fire. The Westphalian international order has definitely been transformed, but at its center is still an order of states based on global interstate institutions affiliated with the UN system.

NOTES

The author would like to thank Hilla Aharon, Will Bain, Kal Holsti, and Raimo Väyr-ynen for comments.

1. The WTO superceded the General Agreement on Tariffs and Trade (GATT) in 1995. Like the GATT, it is not formally a UN specialized agency but belongs to the UN's Administrative Committee on Coordination, along with the UN special-ized agencies. Its future status within the UN system is unclear.

4

Global Governance as a Policy Tool: The Canadian Experience

Denis Stairs

The preoccupation with global phenomena and the problems they generate—all of them real, some of them important, a few of them intractable—is a currently pervasive feature of the thinking of practitioners and observers of government alike. It also permeates the discourse of the vast multitude of transnational interest groups, now routinely described as nongovernmental organizations (NGOs), that are said to represent international "civil society" in the more benign of its manifestations. It is a preoccupation, it hardly needs to be said, that leads easily and naturally to a focus on the need for global solutions. And global solutions, because they seem to require global regulation, global enforcement, and (even more dauntingly) global expenditures, suggest in turn the necessity of global governance.

To describe the phenomenon in this way, however, loads the dice. For the description implies a process of *government* that must somehow apply to the world as a whole.[1] It connotes, in David Easton's (1953) famous phrase, an "authoritative allocation of values." But this is not what the term has always, or even usually, been taken to mean. In practice, its application has been expanded, contracted, and rendered almost infinitely malleable in response to such expository advantage as there may be in making use of it. In the very first issue of the journal for which the phrase itself was selected as the title, James N. Rosenau (1995) conceives global governance "to include systems of rule at all levels of human activity—from the family to the international organization—in which the pursuit of goals through the exercise of control has transnational repercussions" (Rosenau, 1995, p.13). He quotes with approval, therefore, the opinion of the Council of Rome: "Taken broadly, the concept of governance should not be restricted to the national and international systems but should be used in relation to regional, provincial and local governments as well as to other social systems such as education and the military, to private enterprises and even to the microcosm of the family" (Rosenau, 1995, p.14).

To use the term in such a fashion, however, is to use it to apply to almost everything. It therefore applies usefully to almost nothing. In the same journal only two issues later, Lawrence S. Finkelstein (1995) was led, ever so gently, to complain that it was "hard . . . to know what is excluded" by Rosenau's definition "or where to dig into the spaghetti bowl he puts on the table" (Finkelstein, 1995, p.368). Finkelstein himself thinks we should be "concerned with purposive acts, not tacit arrangements" (Finkelstein, 1995, p.369) and therefore suggests an alternative: "Global governance is governing, without sovereign authority, relations that transcend national frontiers. Global governance is doing internationally what governments do at home" (Finkelstein, 1995, p.369). This narrows the focus at least a little, although not by so much as one might think, given that modern governments, as Finkelstein himself is careful to point out, have very broad agendas.

If the contents more generally of the journal in which these observations first appeared are any guide, Finkelstein's understanding of the research agenda matches more closely what scholars in the field are trying in practice to do than does Rosenau's. But in the present context there is little point in pursuing the argument in depth, particularly because it can lead the unwary to rush madly off in different directions (Rosenau and Czempiel 1992; Weiss and Gordenker 1996; Commission on Global Governance 1995). The question currently at hand here is the place of "global governance" in the substance and conduct of *Canadian foreign policy* (and perhaps, by extension, in the foreign policies of certain other powers with similarly limited capacities and comparably vital stakes in the maintenance of a stable international order). This makes it automatically a question of government.

The discussion below is divided into several parts. The first of these considers the character, origins, and practical implications of the central ideas upon which Canada's approach to the construction and maintenance of the world order was founded at the time of "the creation"[2]—that is, in the period immediately preceding the end of the hostilities in 1945—and in the years that followed. These ideas were closely akin to many of the notions that would now be associated with the concept of global governance as understood by practitioners of state (although certainly not by every representative of every NGO).

The second part attempts to identify some of the principal and recurrent characteristics of Canada's behavior in response to the global governance problem. The third focuses on pertinent developments in the rhetoric and substance of Canadian policy more recently and on the domestic political forces (some of them transnationally influenced) to which Canadian decision makers seem to be responding. The latter discussion is accompanied by some brief evaluative comments and some speculations on the extent to which the factors driving Canadian policy may be pertinent to the behavior of certain other states in the international community, as well.

THE CREATION

Like their counterparts abroad, Canadian policy makers approached the construction of the postwar international order under the powerful influence of their most recent experience of world affairs. The failure of the League of Nations—a failure caused by the reluctance of its members (Canada prominently included) to take their collective security obligations seriously—had resulted in a disaster of momentous proportions. Tens of millions of people had died. Notwithstanding the dominant assumption of the policy community in Ottawa during the interwar years, moreover, neither the breadth of the Atlantic and Pacific Oceans nor the initial neutrality of the United States had prevented Canada from being drawn immediately into the hostilities. The latter had come surprisingly close to home. U-boats had devastated shipping along Canada's Atlantic coast; some had even penetrated the Gulf of St. Lawrence. Neither geography nor politics, in short, could be relied upon to sustain an isolationist posture. That being so, a policy of active intervention seemed the better course over the longer run.

The recognition of these realities was compounded by another. During the course of the war itself, the formulation of strategy, the conduct of allied diplomacy, and the management of the hostilities themselves were responsibilities that the great powers (following the Soviet and American entries) had quickly seized for themselves. Ottawa did not seriously object. It was prepared to concede—even though for a time after the fall of France it had been the second largest power on the allied side—that in wartime the big decisions had to be left to the big battalions.[3]

What was acceptable in a time of war, however, was not necessarily acceptable in a time of peace. The great-power allies had run the hostilities as if they were the custodians of a "concert system." There was an obvious danger that they would try to perpetuate this convenient arrangement after the war was over, thereby leaving the lesser powers in a position of diminished influence in the postwar international order. This danger was confirmed by the Dumbarton Oaks draft of the proposed United Nations Charter, wherein the special privileges of great-power status were carefully delineated—permanent membership on the Security Council, along with the veto provision, being only the most prominent among them. To modify the concert premise—to clip the wings of great-power presumption and ambition—thus became an ancillary objective of Canadian policy. This could be accomplished only by active intervention in cooperation with other powers of like mind, and it would require a kind of "multilateral constitutionalism" to make it stick.

There is currently a widespread presumption in Canada, shared by policy makers and attentive publics alike, that Canadian support for the institutionalization of the international environment after 1945 was predicated on an idealist impulse. The fact is, however, that Canadians contributed to the construction of the postwar international order—to the creation, that is, of institutions of global governance—with clearly defined interests in view and on the basis of a "realist" calculus of power from which they derived relatively clear notions of what they could get away with and what they could not. Their primary purpose, it is true, was to ensure that an institutional order would be successfully established. Without that, nothing of substance would have been accomplished. But there was a clear understanding that this objective could not be achieved without the consent of the participating sovereign states. Among these, the consent of some—the United States, the United Kingdom, and the Soviet Union especially—was obviously more crucial than the consent of others. It would not be helpful, therefore, to press Canada's own objectives, or the objectives (as the Canadians thought they ought to be) of any of the other smaller states, either, beyond what the great powers would accept as a maximum degree of constraint upon their own freedom of maneuver. The Canadians thus had no use for the principle of state equality advocated by some of the lesser powers at the San Francisco conference. If such ambitions were pushed too far, they knew very well that the great powers would pick up their marbles and go home. From this, no advantage to Canada, or to the world order itself, could possibly come.

The details of the evolution of the Canadian position on the Charter have been thoroughly explored elsewhere (Eayrs 1972; Holmes 1979; Hilliker 1990; Glazebrook 1947; Reid 1983; Pearson 1972) and need not be recounted here. But the general arguments advanced in defense of Canada's proposals for amending the Dumbarton Oaks draft were a telling reflection of the premises upon which they were operating. In essence, they articulated two fundamental but closely related propositions. The first was that special account needed to be taken in the allocation of decision-making roles within the UN system to powers of the middle rank. The membership of the middle power class was not explicitly defined, although the Canadians were certain that Canada was prominently included. On this score, Canada's war effort and the size of its economy, at a time when the European powers and Japan were in devastated circumstances, left little room for doubt, and they were therefore quick to make practical political use of the temporarily elevated stature that they had so recently acquired.

This did not mean that they wished to challenge the entitlements of the great powers to the privileges—the veto, for example—to which they were most firmly attached. The veto, in any case, was a convenient safety valve, because the effectiveness of the new organization would obviously depend on great-power acquiescence, and because no good could come from a mobilization of the UN as a whole against a great power "aggressor." It did mean, however, that the middle powers ought to have a better chance than the very small powers of being elected, for example, to the Security Council. This was not because power and virtue (or even wisdom) necessarily went together. It was rather because the distribution of the capacity to influence the UN's decisions needed to accord at least roughly with the distribution of capacities for carrying them out. Otherwise, the organization itself would fail for want of legitimacy and efficacy alike.

This view of things was particularly interesting because it was totally in accord with the underlying position of the great powers themselves. The Canadians were not disputing the fact that the UN would be an organization of sovereign states, nor were they challenging the notion that in such an environment the base currency was the currency of power. Their only quarrel was with the categorization of states upon which the Dumbarton Oaks draft had been constructed. The Americans and their colleagues had posited a world of *two* classes: great powers and all the rest. The Canadians and *their* colleagues posited a world of *three* classes: great powers, middle powers, and all the rest. This was a difference over the *implementation* of the principle, not over the principle itself.

To this relatively straightforward expression of Canada's vested "constitutional" interest abroad, there was added another. As these things go, it was fairly ingenious. Given the conditions of the day (it was concocted while World War II was still in progress and while the role of military power in the determination of international politics enjoyed a certain uncontested visibility), it might even be described in retrospect as surprisingly farsighted. Ottawa called it the "functional principle." Given the ideas associated with David Mitrany and the European unity movement that gathered steam in the late 1940s, this seems in retrospect somewhat confusing, but the vocabulary is not essential to the communication of the concept. Reduced to its essentials, the argument was that the real significance of different states in the international community varied not only with their military capabilities (actual and potential) but also with what we would now call issue area. In effect, the world was populated not by *one* hierarchy of power, but by *several*.

It followed that the distribution of roles among participating nation-states might usefully vary from one international organization (UN specialized agency) to another, depending on the organization's mandate. More concretely, states might reasonably expect to be awarded greater prominence in the organizations that dealt with matters in which they had a particular interest and expertise and in relation to which they had an unusual store of assets at their disposal, while having a lesser role to play in agencies that were seized with issues in which they were not directly involved. Canada, for example, might be no more than a middle power in military terms and hence be entitled to no more than a middling and intermittent measure of influence over the triggering of international initiatives in support of collective security. On the other hand, it might be a great power in relation to the production and distribution of food or in the conduct of civil aviation; if that were so, Canada might reasonably lay claim to a significant position of influence in agencies like the Food and Agriculture Organization or the International Civil Aviation Organization (whose headquarters were eventually located in Montreal), and it might have particularly good reason for lending greater weight than the great powers had done to the construction, say, of ECOSOC (UN Economic and Social Council).

It is now, of course, a commonplace to point out that the ingredients of power in an increasingly interdependent world have become more diverse and diffused and that a counting of the battalions can shed light, at most, on only part of the story. But from the Canadian point of view there is nothing new in this argument, even if many Canadians have now forgotten the clarity with which those of their forebears who were present at "the creation"—their minds firmly focused on the Canadian interest—were able to express it.

From the beginning, therefore, Canada was an enthusiastic supporter of both the United Nations and its specialized agencies. Ultimately, this enthusiasm was rooted in the desire to bring as much of the world's affairs under rule-governed environments as possible. The alternative—the perpetuation of a kind of Hobbesian anarchy—carried too high a risk of death and destruction. To tame its abuses required a process of institutionalization. And inside the institutions that resulted, the Canadians (like the Americans, and like everyone else, for that matter) wished to have as much by way of constitutionally legitimated influence as their assets and their arguments in 1945 could give them. Even in the modified form in which it was imbedded in the UN Charter, the "collective security" aspiration might well turn out to exceed the grasp of the UN's members. Some in Ottawa, including the prime minister, came to just that conclusion as early as the fall of 1945, when the defection of a cipher clerk from the Soviet embassy unleashed revelations of a Soviet espionage network in North America. But the process of building an international order had to start somewhere, and the pragmatic exploitation of the opportunity to take some modest steps forward was better than taking no steps at all.

The Canadian interest in multilateral institutionalization extended also, of course, to the construction of the Bretton Woods system (Keating 1993; Plumptre 1977), which was composed of the International Monetary Fund, the International Bank for Reconstruction and Development, and the General Agreement on Tariffs and Trade (the replacement for the ill-fated International Trade Organization). To a large extent, these were the products of tripartite initiatives launched by the British, American, and Canadian authorities.

From the Canadian point of view, the advantages of taking action to secure the stability of the international monetary system and to promote a freer environment for international trade on a multilateral basis were considerable. The Canadian economy was unusually trade dependent; it was later to become more so. This made trade liberalization a relatively easy "sell" at home. At the same time, there were concerns—accelerated by the effect of the war in weakening the economy of Great Britain on the one hand and strengthening that of the United States on the other—that Canada was in danger of becoming overly dependent on a lopsided continental relationship. In economic politics, as in security politics, multilateral arenas seemed to offer at least some relief from having to deal with Washington on a purely bilateral basis. A multilateralist strategy, in short, was a way of modifying the impact on Canada–United States relations of the disparity in the distribution of power between the two players. Here, as elsewhere, Canadians advocated multilateral solutions not simply because they were more "liberal" and more "internationalist" than other mortals—although some of them were certainly that, too—but because such arrangements so clearly suited their geopolitical and geoeconomic interests. Multilateral arrangements were functionally necessary to the continued maintenance and the further development of the international order along many of its varied dimensions, but they also provided opportunities for the formation of coalitions that would have the effect of amplifying Canadian influence *vis-à-vis* the greater powers. This was the counterpart to the American view that multilateral institutions that could be Washington-dominated, if not Washington-controlled, would be immensely useful vehicles for the construction of an international order amenable to the worldview of the United States.

Returning for the moment to the traditional problem of international *security*, the United Nations, as we have already noted, ultimately depended for its effectiveness upon the amity of the permanent members of the Security Council. That condition did not survive the onset of the cold war. In these ominous circumstances, the Canadians were among the first to raise the possibility of establishing a regional collective defense arrangement as a fallback security vehicle for the North Atlantic powers. The creation of the North Atlantic alliance, as viewed from Ottawa, is a well-known tale (Holmes 1982; Eayrs 1980; Reid 1977; Pearson 1973), and it need not be retold here. It is, however, important in the present context to understand the extent to which the Canadians and the Europeans were in agreement on the need for an institutionalized alliance and in their opposition to the initial American preference, which was for a unilateral American guarantee.

From the European point of view, the unilateral American guarantee was a much less dignified—and perhaps also a much less reliable—option. They wanted both the appearance and the reality of a multilateral decision-making framework. So did the Canadians—not so much because they thought the unilateralist option less reliable, as because they thought it "unilateral." They preferred instead that a *table* be created, so that they might have a seat at it. They also gave great emphasis to the concept of an "Atlantic community" within which there would be not merely cooperation in defense but cooperation also in the strengthening and preservation of a liberal political and economic order.[4] This was partly because they interpreted the communist "threat" as a multifaceted political, social, economic, and moral challenge and not merely as a military one. But it was also because, once again, they preferred institutionalized *multilateral* frameworks to noninstitutionalized *unilateral* ones. Like rank-and-file members of a university faculty, they approved of committees and rule-governed environments not just because they were helpful to the efficient performance of specific tasks but because they could be used in addition to keep the powerful under surveillance (even if they could not always be expected to keep them fully in line).

In later years, it became a commonly held assumption that the North Atlantic Treaty Organization (NATO) was the creation of the security policies of the United States. The assumption was not entirely without foundation; in a largely military alliance, after all, military power talks. But the fact remains that the North Atlantic Treaty in its final form represented a considerable victory for Euro-Canadian diplomacy and for a multilateralist institutional principle that the Americans at the beginning would have been just as happy to do without. Its usefulness to the pursuit of what is now commonly described as the American hegemonic interest was a discovery that came somewhat later.

The Canadian preference for multilateral frameworks was also reflected in Ottawa's approach to the Commonwealth of Nations, that peculiar emanation of the British Empire and of its gradual transformation at the hands of an evolutionary process of decolonization. Here, the Canadian role was most obviously discernible in the insistence that the Commonwealth be as broadly inclusive as possible and that adjustments be made so that those states that had decided to pursue a republican option after achieving their independence, rather than maintaining a constitutional linkage to the monarchy, would still be eligible for membership. Because the Commonwealth functioned more by habit and convention than by reference to formal constitutional provisions, and because its purpose was not so much to make "decisions" as to promote a friendly and constructive discourse across the multiplying cleavages of world affairs, Ottawa was not in this case so keen to support the development of an elaborate institutional framework. When a modest secretariat was eventually established in 1965, however, it was willing enough to help with the design and to provide the first secretary-general, Arnold Cantwell Smith, who held the position from 1965 to 1975 (Smith 1981).

To these multilateralist inclinations, one obvious exception was represented by the Organization of American States (OAS). Prior to World War II, the United States had been firmly opposed to Canadian participation in the OAS's predecessor, the Pan-American Union, largely on the assumption that it might open up opportunities for British intrusion into the affairs of the North American republics. After 1945, however, Washington altered its position and began to make the case for Canadian entry, a case that had the support also of the Latin Americans. The Canadians resisted. They had no fundamental interests in Latin America, they pointed out, that they could not pursue by conventional diplomatic means. And their institutional priorities lay first with the United Nations, NATO, and the Commonwealth, which together were challenge enough for their diplomatic and other resources.

But these surface explanations concealed a deeper concern. Ottawa suspected that the United States and the Latin American powers wanted Canada to join the organization for the same reason—that is, because they each assumed that political advantage would accrue to their respective causes from Canadian participation. The Americans would expect Canadian support to lend legitimacy to Washington's position on issues over which they and the Latin Americans disagreed; similarly, the Latin Americans would expect the Canadians to help them with the task of countervailing the influence of American power. Given that Canada had no substantive interest in taking sides and could easily earn disfavor in one quarter or another by doing so, the most prudent response was to avoid the game entirely. It was not until 1989 that Ottawa came finally to the view that circumstances in the hemisphere had sufficiently changed, and Canada's interests in the region had sufficiently expanded, to allow the benefits of membership to outweigh the costs (McKenna 1995).

But the more general pattern of Canadian policy has been clear, and relatively consistent, throughout the postwar period. Ottawa has been an enthusiastic, if pragmatically realistic, supporter of the institutionalization of the international order. Its posture has been a reflection in part of the "lessons" that it acquired from its experience of international violence in the first half of the twentieth century. It has been a reflection also of its desire, as a power of modest means, to multiply its options and maximize its freedom of maneuver by cultivating alternatives to the continental embrace of the United States. And it has been a reflection, finally, of its political, social, and economic interest in the maintenance of an orderly environment for the conduct of international discourse and exchange. At the time of "the creation," Canada was, as it is now, economically prosperous, bountifully endowed with the resources of nature, and geopolitically blessed. Its interest in the development of rule-governed international processes has thus had something in common with the affection of wealthy classes everywhere for the values of law and order.

THE BEHAVIOR

It might now reasonably be asked whether Canada's behavior *in response to specific policy issues* has proved to be consistent with and supportive of its overall strategy. Such a question invites a review of Canadian policies in a wide variety of contexts over a now relatively long period of time. This is not a feasible undertaking in a short space. In the broadest terms, however, there is some truth in the commonly held notion that Canadian diplomats and their political masters have routinely attempted to contribute to the moderation and resolution of international conflicts and, in the process, have strengthened existing international institutions, notably, the United Nations, but sometimes also NATO and (less spectacularly) the Commonwealth. They have also worked actively to promote the UN's specialized agencies, and to cultivate other forms of international "regime," including those bearing on the conduct of international trade. In a few instances— and especially, perhaps, in cases pertinent to the development of the "law of the sea"—their campaigns have begun with unilateral initiatives. These have sometimes been regarded by others as uncharacteristically acquisitive, not to say aggressive. In its own defense, Ottawa has attempted to legitimate its performance on catalytic grounds—that is, as a means of force-feeding the creation of new international law in contexts in which it is badly needed but in which a dramatic stimulus was required to overcome the normal lethargy of the international rule-making process.

On security-related matters, of course, there was never any doubt during the cold war that Canada was a "partisan" on the side of the West, and in East–West confrontations Canadian representatives focused not so much on mediating the issues from "the middle" of the argument as on attempting from time to time to moderate behaviors on the allied side that they thought to be counterproductive because excessively zealous.[5] In many cases, however, they could luxuriate in the knowledge that they had no interest in the substantive outcome of the dispute in question, save that it be peacefully resolved. They could count, too, on this circumstance being well understood by all the other players.[6] Canada's seemingly habitual display of benign detachment in response to other nations' quarrels may have come partly from a liberal political culture accustomed to dealing with internal diversities by pragmatic means. It may have been a function as well of the ease and familiarity with which practiced "old hands" in Canada's professional foreign service could maneuver in international arenas like the UN General Assembly. Certainly it reflected the fortunate array of geopolitical circumstances that Canada happened to enjoy. And it was undoubtedly facilitated by a collection of military and diplomatic assets that were not so great as to seem threatening to others nor so small as to be trivial.

Whatever the forces at work, they ultimately led to a certain Canadian facility with the task of orchestrating multilateral initiatives, and they resulted among other things in a particularly prominent role in the field of international peacekeeping. The latter eventually developed a visibility abroad that was sufficient to lead to Canada's being asked to serve on every peacekeeping mission mounted by the United Nations in the postwar period and a number of other international missions as well (Morrison 1995). In responding so positively, of course, Ottawa was unencumbered by any insistence that Canadian forces never be placed under foreign command—a stipulation that the American armed forces (and the American Congress) have usually not been prepared to relinquish. Rather less helpfully, perhaps, the peacekeeping experience has also generated a vainglorious mythology within Canada itself—a phenomenon that has sometimes worried Canadian politicians, but more often in recent years has presented them with political temptations that they have been unable to resist.[7]

It may here be objected that this account of Canada's encouragement of international institutionalization has stressed the multilateral at too great an expense to the bilateral. There is truth in this. After all, not *everything* can be multilateral. Having said that, however, it is interesting to note that the two most prominent of the bilateral examples (NORAD [North American Aerospace Defense Command] and the Canada–U.S. Free Trade Agreement) are exceptions that sustain the rule. In the case of NORAD (together with a closely related battery of formal and informal continental defense arrangements, some of them bearing on such politically sensitive issues as defense production and procurement), there was initially little choice. The development in the 1950s of a Soviet bomber fleet capable of delivering nuclear weapons on North American targets, when taken together with Canada's physical location between the United States and the USSR, made cooperation in the defense of North America a military necessity. In making their accommodation with circumstance, however, the Canadians insisted—albeit not very persuasively, and often to the bemusement of their allies—that NORAD was not merely a bilateral surveillance, command, and control arrangement but was in effect an extension of the North Atlantic alliance. Canada would be bilateral if necessary, but not necessarily bilateral (Cuthbertson 1977; McLin 1967; Foulkes 1966; Robinson 1989).

Similarly, the negotiation of the Canada–U.S. Free Trade Agreement was initiated by Canada largely in response to the fear of American protectionism, a phenomenon that represented an enormous threat to an economy that even in the 1980s exported more than a third of its GNP, and 80 percent of that to the United States (Doern and Tomlin 1991; Hart 1994; Ritchie 1997). In some quarters, however, the initiative was vigorously opposed precisely because it was a bilateral rather than a multilateral undertaking. The Liberal Party of Canada, then in opposition, at one stage threatened to undo the agreement. This was clearly an unrealistic aspiration. With Mexico now included, and with the Liberals once again in office, there have been attempts instead to multilateralize it even more.[8]

In the meantime, Canada continues to cultivate a presence in such other formally or informally constituted arenas as it thinks show signs of being useful. It cherishes its membership in the G-7. It nurtures its seat in the Asia Pacific Economic Cooperation (APEC). With almost nothing by way of significant security assets to offer, it nonetheless presumed to foster not too long ago a North Pacific cooperative security dialogue. It has withdrawn its standing NATO forces from European soil (although it has made significant contributions to the peace-enforcement effort in the Balkans); nonetheless, it continues to work with the NATO Council and to play an active role in the Organization for Security and Cooperation in Europe (OSCE). It also busies itself with multilateral undertakings in relation to the environment, and it routinely—perhaps *too* routinely—launches what it hopes will be remedial multilateral initiatives in a wide variety of fields, ranging most recently from the sexual exploitation of children to child labor in the sweatshops of Asia and the Pacific and to the control and removal of land mines.

RECENT EVOLUTIONS

This last observation brings us to a consideration of some of the more recent developments that have come to bear on the conduct of Canadian policy. These are as much domestic, perhaps, as international. The traditional patterns of Canadian policy are still clearly present, but the circumstances are not entirely the same. For now, at least, the threat of great-power conflict on the scale of the cold war has been extinguished. At the same time, the ceaseless progress of science and technology has been creating new problems and simultaneously has been drawing our attention more insistently to the serious dimensions of old ones. In the absence of threats to their security of a more immediate and dramatic character, Canadians, like many others, have been able to concentrate increasingly on these somewhat different questions. This adjustment has been taking place, however, in a context in which there is an unsettling uncertainty about the kind of role Canada should now be playing in the world, and why. The cold war was an alarming phenomenon, but at least it provided a set of benchmarks for policy makers. These are now gone, and in consequence the policy community is confronting a freedom of choice from which it can no longer escape, as it previously could do, by making reference to a transparent set of geopolitical or other "national interest" requirements. This existential problem is not so serious, perhaps, in the economic issue area, but in other fields the options now seem to be unusually open ended.

In the floundering that has resulted, there has been evidence of a somewhat desperate clinging to behaviors defined by memories and perceptions (often not very reliable) of past accomplishments. Canada's initial contributions to postwar global governance, as the preceding discussion may have helped to demonstrate, were rooted in real interests and were aimed at facilitating the pragmatic resolution of real problems as they happened to come along.[9] These activities, however, have acquired in more recent times the status of a role, and they have increasingly been associated in the domestic environment with what is mistakenly regarded as a uniquely Canadian conception of how to conduct international affairs and with the expression of a uniquely Canadian set of values. For this Phariseean indulgence, the politicians themselves are at least partly to blame, because they have been understandably prone to glorify foreign policy mythologies for nation-building purposes. The problem has been compounded by a simple ignorance in Canada of the comparable behaviors of governments that are similarly positioned (from geopolitical, economic, military, and other points of view) elsewhere in the international community—the Scandinavian powers and the Low Countries not least among them.

Another contributing factor in this development has been the growing presence in public debates on foreign policy issues of transnationally connected "public service" NGOs. In recent years, these appear to have multiplied in Canada—certainly they have become more visible—in much the same way as they have elsewhere. Their position has been enhanced by the so-called CNN phenomenon. The government has therefore responded to their representations (as well as to some concomitant changes in the Canadian political culture) by encouraging what it describes as the "democratization" of the foreign policy-making process. The details need not be recounted here, but the instruments that it has sought to deploy have included elaborate, and publicly conducted, reviews of both foreign and defense policy, along with a series of annual forums on Canada's international relations (Stairs 1995). To the latter, a wide variety of NGOs have been invited to send representatives, along with journalists, academics, and citizens of other stripes. Communications with the policy community by electronic means have also been encouraged (although the process is still at a relatively primitive stage of development).

The degree to which these and related processes have led to constructive and useful exchanges is a matter that is open to dispute. Thus far, the most visible of the consequences has been to provide the more aggressive NGOs with recurrent (and publicly funded) opportunities for attacking foreign service officers and their political masters for the inadequacy of their response to a long list of alarming international problems. These have ranged from the destruction of the natural environment, the persistence of "basket case" poverty in Africa and elsewhere, the proliferation of stateless refugees, and the uncontrolled dissemination of lethal weapons (great and small) to the violation in many parts of the world of human rights, the resurgence of previously eradicable diseases (and the appearance of some murderous new ones), the exploitation of women and children, and the unsustainable explosion of human populations, to name only an obvious few. In some cases, the criticisms have been particularly interesting because they have been supported by the clear assumption that states, and the state system, although a significant part of the problem, are not a part of the solution. The solution lies instead with "civil society," a society manifested organizationally in the NGOs themselves and morally in the benign and compassionate values of ordinary humankind. The practical implication is that the government of Canada should do what the NGOs tell it to do in environments like the UN General Assembly. More importantly, it should off-load a substantial portion of the public treasure to the NGOs themselves, so that they can get on with the uncorrupted pursuit of transnationally administered remedies to real global problems.

As Kim Nossal has pointed out on more than one occasion (Nossal 1993a; 1995), these consultative processes are far from "democratic," and although the disillusionment of many NGOs with the real workings of international politics is understandable, their indifference to the requirements of constitutionalism is more difficult to fathom. Ultimately, after all, it is only the state that can find, through its power to tax, the resources required for the delivery of public goods. Ultimately, too, it is the state that must assume responsibility for defending the weak against the predations of the strong. Attempting to undermine its legitimacy, particularly in a liberal democratic context, seems to the innocent onlooker a singularly ill-advised endeavor for enterprises that seek above all to serve the interests of the deprived and the dispossessed.

But however that may be, there is no question that the prevailing analytical temper has had an impact on at least the rhetoric of the Canadian foreign policy apparatus. Following to some extent on Boutros Boutros-Ghali's *Agenda for Peace* (1992), this has been represented most noticeably in the adoption of a broader conception of what constitutes security. Although variously described ("common security," "human security," and "shared security" are among the phrases most commonly deployed), in essence it reduces to the notion that serious threats to the human condition are currently posed not by the unleashing of military forces alone but also by authoritarian government, environmental decay, the depletion of resources, economic breakdown, and the other egregious elements in an expanded cavalry of the apocalypse. These are regarded as "security" matters partly because they threaten death and destruction on a scale traditionally associated primarily with war itself and partly because they are assumed to be causes of war in their own right. It follows that the maintenance of international peace and security requires the application not merely of the traditional mechanisms associated with collective security, collective defense, the principle of deterrence, disarmament and arms control, and so on but also the creation and nurture of the underlying conditions of peace. The latter are usually associated with economic prosperity (or at least with a reliable and sustainable pattern of economic growth), the secure conduct of a democratic politics, the maintenance of a healthy and balanced natural environment, and the provision of a suitable level of public services (medical care, education, clean water, and the like), among others.

In the Canadian case, these arguments have been accompanied by proposals for administrative reform that would have the effect of ensuring that initiatives in all such areas would come under an integrated bureaucratic structure, so that trade-offs among them would be explicitly made and explicitly understood (Canada 21 Council 1994). The unstated political purpose, clearly, has been to expose the budget of the traditional defense establishment to a kind of "raiding" in support of alternative approaches to the promotion of a secure world. On "common security" premises, for example, development policy comes to rival defense policy as a vehicle for expressing the fundamental obligation of the state to enhance the security of the environment within which its citizens must prosecute their interests. And if, in the process, the results turn out to be a more agreeable expression of Canadian "values" abroad, so much the better, for Canadians, like Americans, have become increasingly attracted of late to the notion that "soft power" helps, too.[10]

But although the general thrust of these arguments and their accompanying political calculations has been accepted in principle, the practice has been less clear. The problem of assessing the practical results has been complicated by the fact that the government has felt obliged in recent years to mount a major attack on its operating deficit. One of the effects has been a substantial reduction in the funds available for the financing not only of the Canadian armed forces but of development assistance programs, as well. Even the NGOs, many of which are symbiotically dependent on government support, have experienced devastating financial cuts. Canada's ground forces have been stretched to the limit even by the relatively limited deployments entailed in their recurrent peacekeeping and peace-enforcement operations, and increasingly Canada's involvements abroad have taken ancillary form—through the provision, for example, of expert assistance in the running and supervision of elections in countries where democratic practices are still a novelty and of professional training for civilian police forces overseas. These are obviously worthwhile endeavors, and they make an attractive "sell." But in the end the effort they represent must be regarded as relatively modest.

There is a particular irony in this conclusion, given that the expanded conception of security, if taken seriously, connotes an enormously ambitious, time-consuming, and expensive array of enterprises in social engineering. In principle, it should lead to *greater* expenditures, not lesser, and in most cases these would appear to be required over long periods of time, periods more appropriately measured in decades, or even in generations, than in a few months or a few years.

On the other hand, there is always the danger of making the best the enemy of the good. So long as Canadian initiatives are both useful and credible, and so long as there is reasonable evidence of the government assigning at least some of its resources to such tasks as accord with its stated intentions, it can presumably lay fair claim to the proposition that it has given honest encouragement to good works—to works, that is, that mesh with what the tasks of "global governance" might be thought to entail.

CONCLUSION

In the end, it follows from the foregoing that the government of Canada, as it responds to the global challenges posed by global issues, can no more escape the imperatives of its role as the custodian of a sovereign political community than can the government of the United States. The dedicated humanists who do so much in their private and professional lives to advance the manifold objectives of public service NGOs are powerfully—and admirably—drawn to the notion that the welfare of peoples abroad should be as serious a preoccupation of national governments as the welfare of peoples at home. In principle and practice alike, however, the primary obligation of the government of a liberal democratic state is the service of its own. Within the premises of the existing order, this circle can be squared in either of two ways. The first rests on the claim that assigning domestic resources to foreign causes will redound to the interests of one's own in the end. The second depends on there being clear evidence of a domestic political instruction—explicit or implied—that has the effect of authorizing the government, within commonly understood limits, to place the greater needs of "the other" ahead of the lesser needs of its own. The first of these assertions is commonly made. Sometimes, but not always, it is persuasive. The instruction identified by the second is often tacitly assumed. Rarely, however, is it acted upon at so impressive a level as to risk arousing a countervailing domestic response.

For the Western powers, in particular, this problem is ultimately rooted in the contract that is implied by the representative constitutionalism of the liberal democratic state. Until it can be resolved, the question of global governance is likely to remain for Canada, as for other states of like mind, a matter of "making do" and "muddling through." Progress is thus likely to be secured not by the pursuit of a grand design but by the construction of a new institution here, an informal "regime" there, and a great deal of inventive, problem-solving "ad hocery" along the way. From the global problem-solving point of view, most of the creativity in this complex endeavor may have to come from powers, like Canada and the United States, whose fortunate and prosperous circumstances give them a deeply rooted interest in stability and hence in a reformist, rather than a revolutionary, approach to the reengineering of the international environment and the management of transnational problems. As the Canadian case may help to demonstrate, it is the conjunction of the national interest with international order, on the one hand, and with economic capacity (and the other capacities that go with it), on the other, that is the ultimate prerequisite for the will to act.

NOTES

1. The use of the term global, it should be noted, is often as loose as the use of the term governance. Depending on the issue and the context, a lot of the "globe"—even most of it—is commonly left out. The neglect of the omitted may be more implicit than explicit, but it is no less real for being so.

2. The phrase comes, of course, from the title of Dean Acheson's memoirs, *Present at the Creation: My Years in the State Department* (Acheson 1969). The evocation of the Book of Genesis in reference to the statecraft of ordinary mortals was sometimes the cause of wry comment in the Methodist culture that pervaded the Canadian Department of External Affairs. In later years, Acheson himself found the Canadians a trifle precious and, with tongue only half in cheek, described their country as the "stern daughter of the voice of God" (Acheson 1966). It could be argued, however, that the label fits better now than it did then.

3. The most vigorous of prime ministerial lamentations were reserved for cases in which the contributions of Canadian forces seemed to have escaped the notice of those who spoke for the British and American governments and their field commands in describing Allied military exploits. This happened often.

4. The product of Canadian perseverance was the "Canadian article," or Article II. It read as follows: "The Parties will contribute toward the further development of peaceful and friendly international relations by strengthening their free institutions, by bringing about a better understanding of the principles upon which these institutions are founded, and by promoting conditions of stability and well-being. They will seek to eliminate conflict in their international economic policies and will encourage economic collaboration between any or all of them" (Spaak, 1959). Among the skeptics was the United States. Washington eventually decided that it was relatively harmless as the price of Canadian participation, but the initial reservations of the Americans and some of the other players ensured that it would never have much real significance.

5. This could not, of course, be taken too far. The willingness of great powers in general, and of the United States in particular, to put up with the confinements that resulted from operating through multilateral institutions was a function of how much they valued the legitimacy that it gave to their policies and the concrete assistance to which it sometimes led. The Canadians knew very well that the price of a capacity to participate in multilateralist meddling often took the form of a tangible "payment of dues." It also required a finely tuned sense of when to push and when to yield. Such calculations were tuned with particular care during the diplomacy of the Korean War (Stairs 1974; Stueck 1995). Needless to say, there were many occasions on which domestic critics of Canadian policy thought Ottawa was prone to giving in too easily, a phenomenon that became especially evident during the war in Vietnam. Americans who think their statespersons too solicitous of the preoccupations of foreign powers in the United Nations and elsewhere thus have their Canadian counterparts. (The subtleties of the American approach to the intricate balancing exercises that the conduct of an effective multilateral politics requires have been carefully demonstrated by Margaret P. Karns and Karen A. Mingst [1990].)

6. The classic case was probably that of the Suez crisis of 1956. Perhaps because Lester B. Pearson was awarded the Nobel Peace Prize for his role in its resolution, the episode has been greatly overworked and overstudied by Canadian analysts. A helpfully succinct dissection has recently been provided, however, by Pearson's son, Geoffrey A. H. Pearson (1993), who has also had an accomplished career in the Canadian foreign service. The Egyptians were a little uncertain about Canadian loyalties but were persuaded in the end to live with their reservations.

7. This became a particular concern at about the time Pierre Elliot Trudeau succeeded Lester B. Pearson as prime minister, in 1968. Partly because the new government feared it would not be able to respond to a level of public expectation that had become very high, it somewhat denigrated what it described as the "helpful fixer" approach to the conduct of Canadian foreign policy. The first of the six pamphlets that constituted its foreign policy "white paper" noted: "It is a risky business to postulate or predict any specific role for Canada in a rapidly evolving world situation. It is even riskier—certainly misleading—to base foreign policy on an assump-

tion that Canada can be cast as the 'helpful fixer' in international affairs (Foreign Policy for Canadians, 1970, 8). Pearson, then retired, did not approve. But he had no reason to worry. The "helpful fixing" performances have continued, and public expectations today seem, if anything, higher than ever.

8. The principal target of choice has been Chile. The United States having thus far been unable to agree, Canada and Chile have already proceeded on a bilateral basis. The hope is that their agreement will be a "bridge" to Chile's eventual accession to the North American Free Trade Agreement.

9. Even in the 1956 Suez case, for example, the "problem" from the Canadian point of view was a very practical one. The British and French, in particular, had placed themselves in an untenable position. Among the consequences was a breakdown in the normally amicable relations between London and Paris, on the one hand, and Washington, on the other. Leaving aside the cold war saber rattling that had resulted in the Middle East (to say nothing of the deep divisions that had also been triggered in the Commonwealth), this alone was enough to cause nightmares in Ottawa. In these circumstances, Pearson and his colleagues were not trying to follow a recipe. They were simply attempting to facilitate an Anglo-French withdrawal in a way that would restore calm to inconveniently troubled waters.

10. The most influential "position paper" written for the recent foreign policy review made precisely this argument (Saul 1994), and the "projection of Canadian values and culture" is now officially regarded as one of the "three key objectives" of Canadian foreign policy (Canada 1995a). The funding has not yet followed the policy, but that is another matter.

5

Global Governance: The American Perspective

Karen A. Mingst

Globalization, government, globaloney, globalism, global govern-mentality, globality, globaphobia, governance, glocalization, global governance—the academic and policy community, as well as the general public, may be suffering under a glut of *g*-words. Underneath the cacophony of words and concepts are fundamental debates. The first is a debate about how these terms—in whatever form—represent a fundamental departure from conventional international relations theory. The second is a debate within the respective communities utilizing these terms concerning the appropriate terminology, explanations for the trends, and differing evaluations about what these trends mean for policy makers and individuals. This chapter explores both debates, first examining the broader question of how globalization and global governance depart from conventional international relations understandings, then focusing on the way these specific debates are unfolding in the American academic and policy community.

THE CHALLENGE TO CONVENTIONAL UNDERSTANDINGS

Two theories have dominated discussion of international relations historically and in contemporary times: liberalism and realism. Although there are important debates within each of these two traditions, each stands as a separate view of the individual, the state, and the international system.

Liberalism is based on the belief that human nature is basically good and that such goodness makes societal progress possible. Evil or unacceptable human behavior is the product of inadequate or corrupt social institutions and of misunderstandings among leaders. Institutions are the embodiment of liberal thinking: international institutions are designed to facilitate collective action against errant individuals or states seeking to undermine the order implicit in international society. Social change will and ought to occur, but it will occur slowly, affecting all of the various actors because of the interdependence among them. In liberal thinking, the state remains the primary actor, although it operates within an increasingly transnational world of complex interdependence.

In contrast, realism is based on the view of the individual as primarily selfish and power seeking. Individuals are organized into states, each of which acts in a unitary way in pursuit of its own national interest, defined in terms of power. These states exist in an anarchic international system, one characterized by the absence of an authoritative hierarchy. Under this condition of anarchy, states in the international system must rely on themselves. Their most important concern, then, is to manage the insecurity that naturally arises out of the anarchic system. They rely primarily on maintenance of the balance of power and on deterrence to keep the international system intact and as nonthreatening as possible. The primacy of states in the international system is guaranteed by state sovereignty. In such a system, the potential for structural change is low.

Liberalism and realism share a statist view of international politics, particularly dominant in realist thinking. Both tend to see an anarchic international system, although for liberals, complex interdependence may moderate the effects of the basic anarchy. In contrast, globalization and global governance, although emergent from liberal thinking, represent a fundamental departure from the state-centric view of the Westphalian world. They call into question basic understandings of the primacy of the territorial state. They challenge the sovereignty of the state, its ability to exercise autonomy in its daily affairs. They give pride of place to non-state-centered social, economic, and political processes. They expose a view of social change that acknowledges the fundamental and disturbing discontinuities that have "perpetuated poverty, widened material inequalities, increased ecological degradation, sustained militarism, fragmented communities, marginalized subordinated groups, fed intolerance and deepened crises of democracy" (Scholte 1996, 53).

Globalization

Since the end of World War II, academic discourse has acknowledged a certain set of changes occurring in world politics: the increasing scope of actors, interests, and demands in the international system. With the independence of the former colonies in the 1950s and 1960s, the Europeanization of world politics diminished as states in other geographic regions challenged Western hegemony and other international actors emerged. In particular, multinational corporations globalized their operations. Interests of these various actors proliferated, encompassing not only the traditional areas of security and high politics but economic and cultural issues, as well.

In the 1970s, liberal American academics called this process complex interdependence, focusing on how growing interdependence affected world politics by changing the policy alternatives facing individual countries. But interdependence theorists were still ensconced in the state-centric world of international relations theory.

During the 1980s and 1990s, theorists recognized that something deeper was happening, something more fundamental than a mere interconnectedness among states and between states and individuals. Marxists foreshadowed this development, recognizing the increasing power of the internationalist capitalist class, opening up new markets, and forging economic and cultural ties. But even Marxists recognize the continuing persistence of the state.

Globalization challenges that assertion. In its broadest iteration, globalization refers to the "emergence and spread of a supraterritorial dimension of social relations" (Scholte 1996, 46). More specifically,

It denotes a shift in the spatial form of human organization and activity to transcontinental or interregional patterns of activity, interaction, and the exercise of power. It involves a stretching and deepening of social relations and institutions across space and time such that, on the one hand, day-to-day activities are increasingly influenced by events happening on the other side of the globe and, on the other, the practices and decisions of local groups of communities can have significant global reverberations. (Held 1997, 253)

It is a multidimensional condition, involving all spheres of human activity—economic, social, cultural, technological, and political. It is a discontinuous process, in that change is not occurring in a linear direction, and it is not inexorable. What is critical in globalization theory is the recognition that people perceive that this process is actually taking place, although not all are similarly affected.

Globalization poses a number of key challenges. Spurred by technological change and the globalization of economic life, the state is challenged, its sovereignty undermined and constrained, its structures unable to provide the necessary public goods. The state is unable to initiate action but is reduced instead to reacting to globalization. Its sovereignty is compromised and circumscribed. This leads to a disjuncture between the globalized system and people, individuals who continue to be shaped by the framework of the territorial state yet whose confidence in national institutions has been eroded. The disjuncture may result in the resurgence of subnational ties and the reassertion of ethnic and religious identity. No longer does the state-centric world of the realists and traditional liberals exist.

The movement to globalization, to a global economic, social, and cultural scale, is not benign, as some liberals of complex interdependence persuasion suggest. Globalization "divides, fragments, and polarizes" (Cerny 1996, 8). As James Mittelman laments,

> Globalization sets in train conflicts among competing capitalisms, generates deeper or reconfigured intraregional disparities, engenders interregional rivalries among neomercantilist coalitions, and has combined with local forces to consign, at the end of this millennium, 265 million people on one continent to poverty, with little hope for escape in sight. The foremost contradiction of our time is the conflict between the zones of humanity integrated in the global division of labor and those excluded from it. (1996, 18)

American academic literature of globalization focuses on two areas. The first is an evaluation of the agents of globalization—transnational market structures, the competition state intertwined with transgovernmental networks, or institutions like the World Bank or the International Monetary Fund and nongovernmental organizations who are trying to promote a particular mode of government or governance in less developed countries. Such agents serve to integrate all groups into global economic (investment and trade), social, and cultural networks. Through these various agents, individuals are linked to the globalized system: politically, through international political institutions; economically, through the international division of labor; culturally, through global communications; militarily, through nuclear weapons and regional blocs; and through global social movements like feminism, environmentalism, or peace groups (Spybey 1996, 454).

Second, research focuses on the effects of globalization in several different arenas. Several questions are posed. In what ways does globalization result in global economic and political homogenization? The MacDonaldization and Angloification or Hollywoodization of the world are key concerns. How does globalization affect the international hierarchy? To most, there is considerable evidence for a deepening of the North–South divide (e.g., Holm and Sorensen 1995, 14). The more globalization occurs from above, the greater the chasm will become.

What are the effects of globalization on the North? American theorists dwell on this question. Many point to its negative effects on both politics and public policy. For example, Gary Teeple (1995) argues that globalization is responsible for the dismantling of the welfare state and the deepening of the rich–poor divide within the North. The power of trade unions is eroded, and democracy becomes more restrictive. Others are more skeptical about the effects of globalization on the North. They point to evidence that globalization does really not substantially affect wages, employment, and income inequality, particularly in advanced industrialized countries like the United States. As one IMF study asserts,

> the belief that globalization threatens wages and jobs is contradicted by the historical evidence that free trade and the mobility of labor and capital improve global welfare andtend to improve national welfare for all countries involved (Slaughter and Swagel 1997, 11).

Governments and domestic economies are not

> nearly as shackled by economic globalization as is commonly believed. They retain substantial autonomy in regulating their economies, in designing their social policies, and in maintaining institutions that differ from those of their trading partners (Rodrik 1997b, 21).

What are the effects of globalization on individuals? Most find that the destabilization of social cleavages leads to increased individualization (Zürn 1995, 141). Individuals are increasingly alienated as they become further removed from political institutions and their labor increasingly marginalized in the globalization of labor markets. Witness the movement of young women crossing borders to work as laborers, in factories, sweatshops, and the sex trade.

What are the effects of globalization on the state? American political scientists are particularly concerned with the question because state-centered international relations, either in realist or traditional liberal forms, is the dominant paradigm. Globalization theorists attempting to answer the question have found the state increasingly problematic, its autonomy jeopardized and its sovereignty eroded. No longer is the state the center of the international system. It is replaced by uncontrollable global processes, a contestation between the forces of globalization and deconstruction, between globalization and medieval feudalism, between the international and the domestic, between globalized processes and other structures designed to provide collective goods, and between globalization and individuals with competing and sometimes conflicting identities.

Among the minority within the American academy who adopt the globalization framework, most all assess the outcomes of globalization as negative. To those who have adopted the globalization-from-above perspective with its emphasis on detrimental outcomes, global governance is neither possible or desirable. In that sense, the two academic communities— espousing globalization and global governance, respectively—talk past each other, particularly in the United States where the division is most apparent. Only a few explicitly acknowledge that "the extensity, intensity, and impact of issues (economic, political, or environmental) raise questions about where those issues are most appropriately addressed" (Held 1997, 262). These are the questions of global governance.

Similar questions about global governance are raised by another, even smaller, group of academics, those who see globalization emerging from below (Falk 1995). This more idealistic interpretation, closely tied to liberal thinking, posits that globalization has occurred through the web of networks among grassroots groups—social movements and nongovernmental actors all trying to ameliorate harsh conditions imposed from globalization from above (Tuathail, Herod, and Roberts 1997). For that group, global governance designed to manage globalization from below is an attractive possibility.

Global Governance

Academic proponents of global governance, largely an American enterprise, are responding to two troublesome dilemmas. The first is the increasing demand for policy to address global problems versus the recognized weakness of contemporary international organizations and states. That dilemma is universally acknowledged, by liberals and globalization theorists alike. People seek economic and social development, desire a healthy and safe environment, demand transportation networks, and seek help in resolving cultural and religious differences. Yet traditional institutions, according to liberals and globalization theorists, are inadequate to the task. Rather than economic improvement, people see an entrenched underclass and parts of the world in perpetual economic crisis. Rather than functioning international organizations capable of resolving regional and interstate disputes, people see a bungling United Nations, stretched to the limit as far as economic and material resources, lacking leadership and commitment from its state members to engage in effective peacekeeping and peace-building activities in a timely fashion. Confronted with this dilemma, they find another: that many of the demands are being addressed in places and forums other than international organizations and states—the traditional units of analysis. The intent of those who study global governance is to assess both these traditional and nontraditional sources and arenas of governance.

Global governance emerges out of the liberal enterprise of the study of international organizations. Students of international organization largely come from the Grotian view of an international system that emphasizes order among states and normative concerns for cooperation. But that view has increasingly broadened, from a narrow conception of formalized governmental structures like the United Nations to a broader notion of international regimes in the 1980s, wherein states cooperate out of egoistic self-interest, not to achieve any normative outcome, to a yet broader concern with socially constructed international institutions and noninstitutional processes such as those found in nongovernmental actors and social movements. As the institutions subject to analysis broadened, so, too, did the locale of their activity, from the global to the regional, provincial, and local level. As the institutions and locales broadened, so did the issue areas of interest, from economic and political areas to social issues, education, or even the family—issues and transactions that reside largely outside of the control of the state.

As academic inquiry broadened from original liberal concerns, the term in the 1990s attached to these trends became *global governance*. Unfortunately, the choice of terms may be a poor one, because of its close association with the term *government*. And the World Bank's use of the two terms interchangeably and their use of *governance* as "liberal governance" has only added to the confusion in both academic and policy circles.

Global governance is not government. James Rosenau clearly distinguishes between *governance* and *government*:

> Both refer to purposive behavior, to goal-oriented activities, to systems of rule; but government suggests activities that are backed by formal activities, by police powers to insure the implementation of duly constituted policies, whereas governance refers to activities backed by shared goals that may or may not derive from legal and formally prescribed responsibilities and that do not necessarily rely on police powers to overcome defiance and attain compliance. Governance, in other words, is a more encompassing phenomenon than government. It embraces governmental institutions, but it also subsumes informal, non-governmental mechanisms whereby those persons and organizations within its purview move ahead, satisfy their needs, and fulfill their wants. Governance is thus a system of rule that is as dependent on inter-subjective meaning as on formally sanctioned constitutions and charters. (1992, 4)

Thus, global governance is *not* global government; it is not a single world order; it is not a top-down hierarchical process. Rather, *global governance* implies examination of governance activities, from formal to informal, from laws to rules to understandings, at a variety of different locales. Traditional international organizations may be one of the participants in global governance—many of the rules have developed through the institutionalized processes of the United Nations—but they are not the only participants, nor may they be the most critical. The same is true of the state. The state may play critical filtering roles, setting and mediating the rules, but it may play a very insignificant role. That is one of the points of convergence with their globalization sisters, who give even less credence to the state.

Indeed, many of the global governance thinkers look to parts of the world and see no legitimate governing state structures but do see demands being addressed. Nongovernmental, local participatory groups found in Africa, the continent of the "failed state," have implemented economic development. Thus, in these cases, global governance involves a bottom-up activity,

> wherein nascent dynamics of rule making are sponsored by publics or economies that experience a need for repeated interactions that foster habits and attitudes of cooperation, which in turn generate organizational activities that eventually get transformed into institutionalized control mechanisms (Rosenau 1995, 21).

In such cases, there is an understanding that other forms of cooperation have not worked, whether because of a lack of power or legitimacy of the state or because of the imposition of inappropriate policies by external actors unacquainted with local conditions. These new bottom-up arrangements are not only more satisfying to individuals and small groups; they also more effectively meet their needs.

Adherents of global governance generally acknowledge that the need for governance emerges out of the globalization process. The shift in loci of governance may occur because of the tensions between the globalization processes and localization tendencies (Rosenau 1995, 19)—tendencies acknowledged by globalization theorists. The vulnerability invoked by global technological change may "necessitate new forms of global political authority and even governance" (Vogler 1992, 118). This authority would seek to curb the dangers of globalization.

Academic inquiry in the United States—a small minority of scholars—focuses on four areas of inquiry. First, what is global governance? In Ronnie Lipschutz's words, "Who rules? Whose rules? What rules? What kind of rules? At what level? In what form? Who decides? On what basis?" (1997, 83). After two week's discussion of global governance at the annual American Council of United Nations Studies (ACUNS) workshop in the summer of 1996, participants still did not leave with precise definitions and agreed-upon criteria. The contestation over definition, particularly between those of the liberal and globalization camps, continues.

Second, what are the various instruments of global governance, and how representative and effective is each? States still use traditional instruments of governance—diplomacy and international law and organization—as instruments of mutual restraint and as positive instruments to deal with issues of human rights, environmental protection, and development. International organizations and nongovernmental organizations are also active in governance, particularly in the development and implementation of global norms, whether in the form of multilateral treaties or resolutions, all consistent with liberal thinking. Occasionally, these nonstate groups have been charged with the responsibility of implementing decisions of both states and intergovernmental organizations (IGOs).

Research on civil societies and their contribution to global governance, among these instruments of governance, is one of the most dynamic in American academic circles. To more-radical globalization theorists, transnational corporations are increasingly the key actors. How do they use their respective technical expertise, their privileged access to individuals in national and IGO forms, and their coercive economic techniques? What is the role of the major international financial institutions, the World Bank and International Monetary Fund? These institutions are the subject of intense criticism as agents of a destructive globalization that is particularly penetrating.

Third, what empirical evidence do we have of global governance? Case studies of governance on environmental and human rights issues and on women's participation in grassroots development abound, as liberals proudly boast. These are manifestations of globalization from below. But more-radical interpretations of globalization point to evidence in other issue areas—financial intermediation, deficit discourse, global drug culture, or even the global information monopolies—as examples of global governance gone awry (Sinclair 1997). It is in the domain of empirical research that globalization and global governance scholars are likely to have convergent findings. For both, the detrimental affects of globalization and the insufficiency of global governance have become increasingly apparent. Unfortunately, despite the convergent findings, there is little actual dialogue in the American scholarly community between these groups, perhaps because they come from such different theoretical understandings.

Fourth, if there is global governance, that suggests there is a rudimentary global civil society. Several researchers have been examining that concept, including Lipschutz, who argues that an emerging "arrangement of political interaction" runs "parallel" to the conventional state-centered approach,

> one that does not take anarchy or self-help as central organizing principles, but is focused on the self-conscious constructions of networks of knowledge and action, by decentred, local actors, that cross the reified boundaries of space as though they were not there (1992, 390).

Several factors have been responsible for this shift to a global civil society. Sovereignty has shifted away from the state, "both upwards, to supranational institutions, and downwards, to subnational ones"; replaced by the "decreasing ability and willingness of governments to undertake a variety of welfare functions" and "the Gramscian hegemony of the current international system" (399 ff). Yet this strand of research is just gaining scholarly attention. While the community of global governance scholars are pursuing their research agendas, policy circles are baffled.

THE POLICY COMMUNITY

The confusion over globalization and global governance terminology muddies the debates in the policy community. Nevertheless both terms have infused domestic political debates, and there is considerable evidence to suggest that globalization may well be the foreign policy debate in the upcoming years. Recently, *Foreign Affairs* and *Foreign Policy*, two widely read journals in the American policy community, have published articles and whole issues on these debates.

We cannot understand the debate over U.S. ambivalence toward globalization and the anger of a few over the effects of globalization, however, without understanding how the term has entered into the domestic political circles. Nor can we comprehend American ambivalence toward and even disdain for global governance without understanding how those terms have entered the policy debates.

Globalization

Most obververs within the U.S. policy community see globalization as a description of the fundamental trend, the creation of linkages among various parts of the global economy. For many, the trend is descriptively benign, of nominal impact on the U.S. government and thus of minimal concern to the American electorate. To economists like Robert Lawrence, the United States, indeed, is rather isolated from the phenomenon.

> Eighty-two percent of Americans are employed in sectors like government, construction, nonprofit organizations, services, utilities, and wholesale and retail trade, in which international trade is barely a factor. Moreover, America's international interaction with developing countries remains even smaller. In 1994, U.S. non-oil imports from developing countries amounted to just 3 percent of GNP; exports to developing countries were just 2.5 percent. Employment in the foreign affiliates of U.S. multinationals in developing countries is less than 5 percent of overall U.S. manufacturing employment. (Lawrence 1996, 171)

Others are ambivalent about globalization because it seems to have bene-fited them, even perhaps without their direct knowledge. The spread of the capitalist system, particularly with the demise of socialist alternatives, has opened new markets, which the American government has actively courted on behalf of its companies. America can now compete for new resources and markets in Russia, China, and the Vietnams of the newly industrializing countries. Even small-scale producers of rural handicrafts may become more directly linked to handicraft consumers, facilitated by global commu-nication structures (a PEOPLink Web catalogue), and thus will be able to better meet the needs of the consumer markets (Velzeboer 1996).

Whereas Europe, Canada, and the less developed countries may look with alarm at the power of multinational enterprise or with trepidation at the spread of the globalized and homogenized Americanized culture, American policy makers and the public have been largely ignorant of, or ambivalent toward, or occasionally even content with, the "triumph of lib-eral economic ideologies" and have been satisfied with the hegemonic dominance—political, economic, and cultural—that has followed.

That interpretation of a benign or ignorant globalization may be chang-ing. There is a growing vocal antiglobalization movement, increasingly rais-ing its specter on specific issues. Among its spokespersons are Patrick Bu-chanan and Richard Gephardt, who argue that free trade and economic integration, the ingredients of globalization, cause stagnating wages at home and movement of American jobs to the lower-cost producers in the developing world. They are tapping a fundamental and growing concern in the United States—protecting the jobs of American workers. Since the early 1990s, when 66 percent of those polled identified job protection as a very important goal, that number has increased to 83 percent in 1995 (Wittkopf 1996, 100).

The North American Free Trade Agreement (NAFTA) has been the cen-terpiece of the antiglobalization movement and the movement for protec-tion of American jobs (*New York Times*, April 3, 1997, Thomas L. Friedman, "Gephardt vs. Gore"). Congress is the arena in which those special inter-ests seeking to protect affected minorities are most able to make their posi-tion known. In Congress, divisions are not by political party; rather, Bu-chanan Republicans are joined with Gephardt Democrats and then joined with others who represent powerful interests from particularly affected constituencies.

The globalization debate has become a domestic one pitting the groups of "winners" under globalization, who may not actually understand the reason for their "winning" status, against the groups of losers, those who see loss of jobs and stagnating wages and blame the globalized labor market "out there" for their woes. But as everyone acknowledges, NAFTA is not just an economic issue, it is also a foreign policy issue and increasingly a domestic one, as well.

There is evidence that the globalization debate is rippling through to the general population, leading to significant divisions within the U.S. population. In response to a question of whether a global American economy is good or bad, those groups responding that globalization is good are the privileged, particularly college graduates—58 percent of whom responded that globalization is good. Those who see globalization as bad include the marginalized, notably blacks—63 percent of whom saw globalization as bad—and those with high school education or less—59 percent of whom thought globalization was detrimental (*Wall Street Journal,* June 27, 1997, "Opinions Diverge on Globalization"). As these divisions deepen both objectively and perceptually, the debate over globalization is apt to intensify even among the U.S. populace.

GLOBAL GOVERNANCE

Discussions over global governance have not caused the reaction that globalization has wrought. Yet when the policy community and the public equate governance with government, then a spirited discussion is apt to follow. A distinctive component of the American creed, of American political culture, is a popularized belief in individualism *and antistatism.* Surveys of Americans' trust in the United States government show that 55 percent of those polled trust the government "only some of the time," and 21 percent, "almost never" (*Who will Reconnect* 1995).

Global governance is also associated with world government, and world government is too often equated with the United Nations, a place where American money is squandered, where the American vote is demeaned, where inefficiency and bloated bureaucracy is rampant. In more recent times, it is associated with an American military "taking orders" from an incompetent UN command, being dragged through the streets of Mogadishu, or beating a hasty retreat in Bosnia. At best or worst (depending on one's perspective), the current state of global governance "resembles . . . a cross-national policy patchwork, conspicuous for its missing links and unnecessary overlaps" (Reinicke 1997, 136).

There is no better example of how global governance entered into the American domestic debate than the 1996 electoral campaign and the discussion over the World Trade Organization. America has been subject to the GATT's rules and regulations, including its dispute settlement procedures, since its inception in the 1940s. The United States has often initiated those proceedings and been party to its dispute settlement procedures. Yet in the 1996 campaign, coming just when the strengthened World Trade Organization was going into effect, the public debate for the first time centered on the polemic that American trade rules would "never" be subject to review by "foreigners" or, worse yet, to regulation by an international body. In the political rhetoric of the strengthened conservatives, that would be infringement of sovereignty—just like a U.S. soldier wearing a "blue helmet" would make him or her subject to the authority of the international body. Small wonder Buchanan's new book (1998) is subtitled *How American Sovereignty and Social Justice Are Being Sacrificed to the Gods of the Global Economy.*

But in American domestic politics, nothing is that simple. There are no opinion polls that tap the elite's or the public's full range of views about global governance. We have data showing pieces of the global governance puzzle. First, Americans do have a belief in internationalism, but internationalism has both a cooperative and militant face. Eugene Wittkopf's examination of the Chicago Council of Foreign Relations data concludes,

> For good or ill, their foreign policy opinions remain firmly anchored to a structure of largely internationalist beliefs that has proven remarkably resilient (1996, 104).

Even when the public sees a potential economic trade-off between global activism and domestic spending, "large numbers of Americans do not automatically turn inward" (ibid., 103). But the public is still ambivalent; "the recent cacophony of internationalist and isolationist voices" serves as testimony "to the continuing search for structure and purpose in the new world (dis)order" (ibid.).

Second, numerous polls have found general support for multilateralism (Richman 1993, 1996). For example, an overwhelming proportion of those polled (ranging from 69 to 85 percent between 1991 and 1995) feel that when faced with problems involving aggression, the United Nations, not the United States, should take the lead (*Americans Talk Issues* 1995). Americans favor collective, not unilateral, actions.

Third, a majority of Americans support the UN and have since its establishment: they agree that the United States should cooperate with the United Nations (89 percent), that the United States should not pull out (82 percent), and that the United States should increase its participation (53 percent). Kathleen Murray, Louis Klarevas, and Thomas Hartley thus conclude that

> the public, when asked general questions, are highly supportive of multilateralism as opposed to unilateralism. They want the United Nations to take the lead in military actions, they think that the United States should cooperate fully with the international body, that the United States should maintain its membership within it, and a substantial proportion—although not a major-

ity—believe that strengthening it should be a foreign policy priority. (1997, 15)

Of course, this does not equate with support for global governance.

The data does not tap the other dimensions of governance, strengthening localist and subnational civil societies. Nor does the data show, nor can it ever show, whether American leaders will be able to utilize the general supportive trends in favor of internationalism toward support for global governance. But if global governance means relinquishing various degrees of national governmental controls to other groups—formal and informal, domestic and international, social and economic as well as political—if it means a diminution of sovereignty, then the response by American leaders is apt to be a resounding "no."

Supporters of global governance can point to a vibrant civil society nongovernmental sector. Many NGOs emerged from social movements and activities organized around the issues of gender, human rights, and the environment. They work diligently in local-level projects in the United States and in other countries, networking with their counterparts around the world through the global technological revolution (fax, e-mail) and occasionally meeting in international forums in Rio de Janeiro (on the environment), Cairo (on world population), Beijing (on women's issues), and Vienna (on human rights). These are the quiet purveyors of global governance—quiet in that power is diffused away from national governments and capitals to localities and regions. They are part of the building of an embryonic global civil society. And in the United States, as in Canada, this grassroots activism is not hierarchically related to formal government structures and unconnected to formal diplomatic activity. It is building on the growing strength of individuals and organized small groups. And it is this development, along with globalization, that poses the most direct threat to traditional liberalism and realism and their statist approaches.

American civil society has not been able to frame the national public debate and gain the ears of policy makers to the extent that their Canadian and Northern European counterparts have. Yet if global governance is to be strengthened at all levels and in all domains, then the United States–based groups are going to have to seize the initiative vis-à-vis their own government, usurping its power and prestige at critical times.

CONCLUSION

Globalization and global governance debates are destined to be permanent features of both academic and policy discourse in the coming years. If the explosion of interest in the topics during the 1990s is any indication, these debates may well be the single most important debate in the future.

This chapter has addressed two levels of these debates centered in the U.S. academic and policy communities. In the first debate between traditional approaches (liberalism and realism) and globalization theorists, globalization represents a fundamental challenge to the state-centric world of the academicians and the state-privileged world of policy makers. In the second, the debates within the globalization and global governance camps, the major issues and controversies have been exposed. Neither the academic nor the policy communities are monolithic, however. There are significant differences about what these terms mean and who is affected and how. And in the United States there are major differences of opinion over whether these trends are good—leading potentially to a desirable end condition—or bad—leading to an unacceptable and undesirable future. There is undoubtedly more difference of viewpoint among American academicians and policy makers than one can find in other states or regions. Yet neither globalization nor global governance represents mainstream discourse. Traditional liberals and realists share that privileged position.

Why are American theorists and policy makers so wedded to realist and traditional liberal statist discourse long after their counterparts in northern Europe and many less developed parts of the world have increasingly accepted nonstatist globalization and the need for global governance? There are at least three possible explanations for the differences between the United States and much of the rest of the world in the globalization and global governance debate.

First, Europeans and many in the developing world have witnessed the effects of globalization much earlier than those in the United States. The erosion of state sovereignty in the face of the European Union and the predominance of European or other multinational firms has been widely recognized for at least two decades in western Europe. In many less developed countries, state sovereignty has been begrudgingly acknowledged as limited by the onslaught on globalization, multinational enterprises, global markets, and global culture. These trends are only now being recognized in the United States. The tendency is to resist such developments.

Second, losing independence of action and accepting a diminished sovereignty is a particularly unsettling experience for the United States—once the economic hegemon whose multinationals touched every continent and whose own shores remained largely unpenetrated. Changes portending a loss of power and prestige will be fought with gusto.

Third, globalization and global governance challenge the American feeling of invincibility and invulnerability. Such challenges occurred before, notably in Vietnam; but that was a single event from which the United States could escape, leaving others to pick up the pieces. Globalization describes fundamental transnational processes that the United States cannot control. These processes have potentially profound domestic ramifications. If the effects of globalization are detrimental—leading to a demise of state control, to widening divisions between the beneficiaries and the losers—if individuals thereby become increasingly marginalized, then the American myth of continual progress will be exploded. Each generation may not necessarily be better off; people may not just be able to work harder to improve their lot. There may not be any "solution" to the problem. The hegemon is slipping further from its privileged perch. To American theorists and policy makers and to the American public, regardless of political persuasion, these are unnerving possibilities.

NOTE

The author thanks Raimo Väyrynen, Horace Bartilow, and Craign Warkentin for useful comments on an earlier draft.

II

Instruments of Global Governance: Sanctions and Peace Building

6

Sanctions and Incentives as Tools of Economic Statecraft

David Cortright and George A. Lopez

As tools of economic statecraft, economic sanctions and incentives have become commonplace in the 1990s. In recent years sanctions have been imposed for purposes as diverse as containing military aggression (in Iraq and the former Yugoslavia), punishing factional groups that violate ceasefires (UNITA [National Union for the Total Independence of Angola] and the Khmer Rouge), restoring democracy (in Haiti and Burundi), and advancing human rights (in South Africa). Inducement strategies have been employed to curtail nuclear proliferation (in North Korea and the former Soviet Union), to encourage peace processes (in El Salvador and the Middle East), and to facilitate military demobilization (in various African nations). Each approach has direct relevance to a discussion of global governance, as each tool is most effective when employed multilaterally, and each has implications for global norms. Sanctions tend to be imposed in response to acts of aggression or abuse that have already occurred; incentives, on the other hand, are often used to head off a crisis or prevent a recurrence of violence. Much has been written about sanctions and incentives separately, but few attempts have been made to analyze the two approaches together.[1]

Sanctions fall under the rubric of global governance in several respects. If by *governance* we mean the extent to which various international actors, especially nation-states, form highly cooperative linkages in compliance with generally held global norms, sanctions clearly are an important element of post–cold war governance. They fit within the earliest understanding of the global governance concept, when this was discussed in regime terminology (Krasner 1983), and they are part of the 1990s discourse on compliance with norms, as emphasized by the Commission on Global Governance (1995). Within the complex set of rules, mechanisms, cooperative practices, and emerging mores that constitute global governance, sanctions offer opportunities for states to exercise both their international policies and their more narrowly defined foreign policies. Indeed, sanctions are sufficiently complex, if not ambiguous, that they permit both maximum international institutionalization, through the United Nations and regional bodies such as the Organization for Security and Cooperation in Europe (OSCE), and the prospect that powerful single states, such as the United States, may simply commandeer the strategy for their own foreign policy purposes (see Martin 1993; Mansfield 1995).

The use of incentives is equally relevant to the discussion of global governance, although it taps different dimensions of the problem, and can be especially important for creating the long-term foundations of international cooperation. To the extent that global governance means that nation-states now accept certain shared norms in ways that were not previously characteristic of their behavior, incentives may be more important than sanctions to global governance. Indeed the Commission on Global Governance itself recognized the centrality of inducement strategies. Although it acknowledges the place of coercive sanctions in a governance structure, the commission has observed that noncoercive means are the preferred mode of ensuring compliance with international norms (1995, 328).

We believe that both approaches, positive and negative, noncoercive and coercive, must be considered in any analysis of multilateral institutional concerns and enforcement issues relating to global governance. The study of sanctions is most complete when conducted in tandem with its counterpart, incentives. This approach provides a dual focus on the input side, which considers how coercive and noncoercive means reinforce norms, and the output side, which reviews the ways in which leadership preferences in a target-recipient regime are altered through both negative and positive means.

In this chapter we examine the uses of sanctions and incentives and compare their respective costs and benefits. We elucidate the factors that account for success or failure and the conditions under which sanctions and incentives are likely to be most effective. We pay particular attention to the political context of each and their impact on internal dynamics within target-recipient states. We conclude with a discussion of the advantages of incentives over sanctions in building the international cooperation that is at the heart of global governance.

THE ECONOMIC STATECRAFT OF SANCTIONS AND INCENTIVES

Sanctions imposed prior to 1990, when East–West cooperation was rare, were predominantly unilateral, in most cases involving the United States acting alone. Multilateral sanctions were imposed by the United Nations in only two situations: against Southern Rhodesia (in 1965) and South Africa (in 1977). But in the post–cold war era, a new pattern of sanctions use has emerged, with the number of episodes having increased, and nearly all of the major cases having been multilateral, usually under the auspices of the United Nations Security Council. Comprehensive or partial multilateral sanctions have been imposed against Iraq (in 1990), the former Yugoslavia (in 1990), Libya (in 1990), Liberia (in 1990), Somalia (in 1992), Haiti (in 1993), parts of Angola (in 1993), Rwanda (in 1994), and Sierra Leone (in 1997). In July 1996, the nations of East Africa imposed sanctions against the military government of Burundi, with backing from the Organization for African Unity (OAU) and the United Nations. One month later, the Security Council decided in August 1996 (Resolution 1070) to impose limited sanctions against Sudan for that country's alleged support of international terrorism, although actual implementation of the flight ban was delayed to give the government in Khartoum more time to comply with UN demands.

Although not as frequently employed as sanctions, the use of inducement strategies has also become more prevalent. One of the most prominent examples has been the use of incentives to prevent nuclear proliferation in North Korea. In response to Pyongyang's announced intention to withdraw from the Nuclear Non-Proliferation Treaty in March 1993, the United States joined with South Korea and Japan to craft a set of economic and diplomatic incentives that persuaded North Korea to abandon its apparent nuclear ambitions. In the Agreed Framework of October 1994, the United States and its partners offered to provide North Korea with fuel oil, new less proliferation-prone nuclear reactors, and the beginnings of diplomatic recognition. In exchange, North Korea agreed to accept international inspections and controls on its nuclear program. As of this writing, the agreement is holding, and North Korean production reactors and reprocessing facilities remain shut down and under international inspection.

In the former Soviet Union, Ukraine and Kazakhstan were persuaded to give up the nuclear arsenals they inherited at independence in exchange for economic assistance, improved diplomatic relations, and security assurances from Russia and the West. In Bosnia, pledges of economic assistance from bilateral donors and international financial institutions were used to encourage implementation of the Dayton accords. In El Salvador, the United States offered economic incentives both to the Salvadoran government and to the guerrilla forces of the Farabundo Marti National Liberation Front (FMLN) to facilitate peace negotiations and assure implementation of the resulting agreement.

These and other examples demonstrate the relevance and increasing importance of incentives in the prevention of international conflict. They also illustrate some of the complexities and difficulties involved. In the North Korea case, critics charged that the Agreed Framework could be interpreted as a reward for wrongdoing that would encourage other states to engage in similar transgressions in the hopes of obtaining like rewards. Why should Pyongyang be rewarded, skeptics asked, for complying with norms that other states accept without remuneration? Doesn't this undermine the self-enforcing character of norm-based global cooperation?

To some extent, the danger of inducement strategies is that they may inadvertently become a form of appeasement. One way of mitigating this problem is to package incentives in a step-by-step reciprocal process that conditions the delivery of rewards on specific concessions from the recipient. This model is followed in the Agreed Framework accord with North Korea, with each incentive from the United States and its partners tied to clearly delineated, observable steps toward denuclearization by North Korea. This approach can help to overcome the "moral hazard" of incentives and allow for the constructive use of inducement strategies.

CARROTS AND STICKS AS FLIP-SIDE STRATEGIES

Although the economic statecraft literature has tended to treat carrots and sticks separately, in practice they are closely related. Ending a negative sanction may be considered a positive incentive, and removing an incentive can be a sanction. In economic theory, incentives and sanctions are often interchangeable. An incentive is a positive sanction, a sanction a negative incentive. Each is designed to influence the recipient and bring about a desired change of behavior. In diplomatic practice carrots and sticks are usually combined. Incentives may be offered to increase the attractiveness of the preferred course of action; sanctions are threatened if the objectionable behavior is not halted. As Alexander George has emphasized, coercive diplomacy often requires offers in addition to threats to achieve success (George, Hall, and Simons 1971, 25). According to David Baldwin, the intellectual architect of theories of economic statecraft, the use of negative sanctions can lay the groundwork for the subsequent application of positive incentives (1971, 25).

This juxtaposition was played out in a number of prominent sanctions cases during the 1990s. In the former Yugoslavia, the promise to lift sanctions appears to have been an effective incentive in helping to gain the support of the Slobodan Milosevic regime in the Dayton peace process. Battlefield reverses in Bosnia and NATO bombing also played a role in pressuring the Serbs to negotiate. In North Korea, the offer of economic and diplomatic incentives was accompanied by the threat of sanctions and the movement of U.S. military forces in and around the Korean peninsula.

This simultaneous coercive message no doubt enhanced the appeal of the proposed inducements. As George has emphasized, deterrence is most effective, especially for crisis prevention, when it includes inducements for cooperation as well as punishments for resistance (George and Smoke 1974, 608). What the stick cannot achieve by itself, it would seem, may be accomplished by combining it with a carrot (George 1991, 11).

United States policy makers failed to apply these lessons in their response to the nuclear tests of India and Pakistan in 1998. Sanctions were applied against both countries under the provisions of the Proliferation Prevention Act, which requires an automatic cutoff of U.S. aid, trade support, and military assistance to any nonnuclear state that conducts a nuclear test or otherwise engages in an act of overt nuclear proliferation. These congressionally mandated sanctions were all stick and no carrot. They contain no waiver clause and have no provision for the lifting of sanctions. United States diplomats thus lacked the option of offering to lift or waive sanctions as an inducement for nuclear restraint. Later, as U.S. legislators realized that sanctions would impose hardships on American farmers, they voted to exempt the financing of grain exports and called for other exemptions and waivers that weakened the sanctions. Meanwhile, the White House quietly voted to allow World Bank and International Monetary Fund assistance for the two countries on humanitarian grounds, and the force of the sanctions steadily dissipated.

In the weeks after India engaged in testing but before Pakistan followed suit, the Clinton administration made a frantic attempt to offer inducements to dissuade Pakistan from testing. United States diplomats traveled to Islamabad not only to warn of sanctions but also to offer an incentives package that included a lifting of earlier restrictions on military assistance, the delivery of previously embargoed military aircraft, and various forms of financial assistance. The incentives package was too little too late, however. The offers of assistance came late in the process and were insufficient to overcome the enormous domestic political pressures in Pakistan to match India's nuclear tests. Fears of India's military and nuclear capabilities and concerns about the political intentions of New Delhi's Hindu nationalist government were so deeply felt in Pakistan that it would have taken an enormous package of incentives to convince Islamabad not to follow India's example. The assistance Pakistan most desperately wanted, a firm security guarantee against possible Indian aggression, the United States was unwilling and unable to provide. Pakistani leaders also saw that other governments were unwilling to join the United States in sanctioning India and interpreted this as acquiescence to New Delhi's provocative act of testing. Feeling isolated internationally and lacking security assistance, Islamabad felt compelled to proceed with testing and thereby risk U.S. sanctions. This was a case in which the sanctions were ineffectual as a deterrent and the incentives offered for prevention were inadequate. It may also be a case, however, in which the perceived insecurities were so great that no amount of external influence, no matter how heavy the stick or how sweet the carrot, would have been sufficient to prevent the decision to test nuclear weapons.

On the basis of these recent examples, it would seem that four general propositions can be advanced regarding the intermingling of sanctions and incentives. The first generalization posits that *the choice of incentives or sanctions depends on the nature of the problem and the objectives being served.* When the issues involved have a long-term horizon and do not pose an immediate threat to peace, incentive policies are more effective. When there is a more urgent crisis, especially a conflict involving mass suffering or posing a great danger to international security, a more coercive response may be necessary. In a succinct analysis of the Burundi conflict for the Council on Foreign Relations, Michael Lund (1996) advised that a more forceful international involvement at an earlier stage of the crisis might have been more effective than the later attempts at mediation.

When the policy of the targeted regime is perceived as exceptionally heinous (e.g., apartheid in South Africa) or the transgression is a threat to international peace (e.g., Iraq's invasion of Kuwait), incentives must give way to a more coercive strategy. Coercive measures are more appropriate and effective for addressing crises of overt aggression and deadly conflict. Inducement strategies are preferable for creating the long-term foundations for peace and cooperation and ameliorating conflict situations before they reach the crisis stage. One approach addresses the immediate crises of violent conflict, the other creates the long-term conditions for reducing the likelihood of such conflict and establishing the conditions for effective global governance.

A second proposition emerging from scholarly research is *that incentives work best when they are offered from a position of strength rather than weakness.* If conciliatory gestures are made pusillanimously as a substitute for decisive action, the recipient may indeed attempt to exploit the situation and engage in further aggression. According to Martin Patchen (1988, 271), incentives work best when they flow from strength and are accompanied by a latent threat capacity. Russell Leng has similarly observed that offers "are more likely to be effective when the influencer has the requisites for the effective use of negative inducements as well" (1993, 115). When carrots are mixed with sticks, or at least the threat of sticks, the danger of appeasement and encouraging wrongdoing can be diminished.

Third, *the mix of carrots and sticks also depends on the relationship between the parties.* When relations between sender and recipient are distant or highly conflictual, it may be difficult to craft an effective incentives policy. The communication and bargaining aspects of an inducement process are more uncertain when the two sides are hostile and distrustful of one another. At the opposite end of the spectrum, where the relationship is more cordial and offers promise of cooperation, incentives will be easier to initiate and sustain. As Arnold Wolfers (1962, 107–8) has noted, inducements tend to be more effective in cooperative contexts, in which relations between the actors are friendly. In hostile environments, achieving cooperation is by definition more problematic (Patchen 1988, 269).

A corollary to this third proposition may be inferred if we control for the longevity of sanctions. When coercive pressures are maintained for a long period, as in Cuba and Iraq, hostility between sender and target tends to increase. This may set new conditions in which small concessions and incentives can have a major impact on the behavior of the target. We have argued elsewhere that UN sanctions against Iraq were increasingly ineffective, in encouraging Baghdad's cooperation with weapons inspections because the Security Council did not recognize that economic pain may need to be ratcheted down as well as up to achieve political results. The Iraq sanctions have been purely punitive, with no enticements for concessions. We believe that a mixture of sanctions and incentives that rewarded Iraq for partial compliance with UN resolutions would have encouraged further cooperation and achieved greater progress toward the completion of UN-mandated weapons inspections.[2]

A fourth proposition is that *even where there are troubled political relations, incentives can be successful.* Few countries were more hostile and distant from one another than the United States and North Korea prior to 1994, yet the two were able to negotiate a successful compromise to the nuclear crisis with the aid of incentives. The negotiations fared poorly at first, as the two sides traded ultimatums and threats, but a more constructive atmosphere eventually emerged. The bargaining that led to the Agreed Framework was greatly aided by the mission to Pyongyang of Jimmy Carter in June 1994, which helped to break the diplomatic ice between the two countries and opened the door to high-level dialogue.

It may be difficult to commence such a strategy when relations between two countries have been adversarial, but once the process of dialogue begins, mutual accommodation becomes possible. Even in the most contentious circumstances skillful incentives-based diplomacy can bring limited to substantial success.

MAKING SANCTIONS WORK

Although sanctions have become increasingly common, many doubt their effectiveness. Some view sanctions as an ineffective bromide intended to placate public demands for action but incapable of achieving real results

(Hoagland 1993). Eminent scholars share this skepticism. Margaret Doxey, whose work on sanctions has appeared in multiple editions, states that "sanctions will not succeed in drastically altering the foreign and military policy of the target" (1987, 92). If the goal of sanctions is defined in purely instrumental terms, their effectiveness is indeed limited. As Gary Hufbauer and his colleagues at the Institute for International Economics (IIE) have concluded, "sanctions are seldom effective in impairing the military potential of an important power, or in bringing about major changes in the policy of the target country (Hufbauer, Schott, and Elliott 1990). Sanctions serve multiple purposes, however, and these must be assessed as well when calculating impact. As Alan Dowty has argued, "The 'success' of sanctions depends on what goals they are measured against" (1994, 192). Sanctions can serve symbolic or expressive purposes, such as reinforcing international norms. Sanctions can send a message of disapproval to an abusive regime or one of solidarity to its domestic opposition. Sanctions may also serve as a deterrent to prevent future wrongdoing by the target regime or others. These symbolic purposes of sanctions can have an important influence on international affairs, especially in upholding the standards of democracy, human rights, and nonproliferation that have become central to global governance.

Although sanctions traditionally have been considered tools of interstate policy, many of the recent uses of the instrument have involved intrastate disputes. This is most clearly illustrated in South Africa and Haiti, where sanctions were used to advance human rights and democratic rule. The case of South Africa is widely considered a success, whereas sanctions in Haiti proved ineffective and gave way to U.S. military involvement. The case of Bosnia represents more of a hybrid, with sanctions imposed against the truncated state of Yugoslavia as a means of halting its sponsorship of aggression by Serbs within Bosnia. In this case sanctions were considered at least a partial success in moderating the behavior of Serbian authorities in Belgrade. According to a UN report on sanctions in Yugoslavia, based on a 1996 roundtable in Copenhagen sponsored by the OSCE, sanctions were "remarkably effective" in moderating the bellicose posture of the Milosevic regime and were "the single most important reason for the government in Belgrade changing its policies and accepting a negotiated peace agreement" (United Nations 1996; see also Littwak 1995, 117–18).

The most important empirical study of sanctions, conducted by the Institute for International Economics, necessarily focused on officially declared instrumental goals. The IIE study examined 116 sanctions episodes between 1914 and 1990 and found an overall success rate of 34 percent (Hufbauer, Schott, and Elliott 1990, 94). Sanctions made a significant contribution toward achieving the purposes for which they were imposed in one-third of the cases. The IIE study found that sanctions are most effective when economic costs are high for the target but low for the sender, when the sender is much larger than the target, and when the target and sender have extensive trade relations. Sanctions also take time to achieve their political effects—on average, nearly three years (Hufbauer, Schott, and Elliott 1990, 101).

The effectiveness of sanctions depends greatly on swift and comprehensive implementation and rigorous enforcement. Cooperation among the states capable of trading with the target is essential. In many cases, however, sanctions have been either poorly implemented or ineffectively enforced. In Haiti, sanctions suffered from inconsistency (the initial Organization of American States embargo left gaping loopholes) and flawed implementation (the Governors Island Agreement lifted sanctions before the actual return of exiled president Jean-Bertrand Aristide). Many nations lack the legal, administrative, and institutional capacity for implementing and enforcing multilateral sanctions. In the case of the former Yugoslavia, implementation steadily improved during the course of the sanctions regime as regional European institutions made important and innovative contributions to enforcement. The European Union and the OSCE established Sanctions Assistance Missions to monitor commercial traffic, and NATO and the Western European Union created a Sharp Guard naval interdiction force in the Adriatic Sea. These innovations made the sanctions against the former Yugoslavia the most effective in history, according to the UN report (United Nations 1996). The Yugoslav example suggests that the active participation of regional security institutions may be crucial to enhancing sanctions effectiveness.

The case of Nigeria under the Sani Abacha regime illustrates the problems that result from a lack of consensus among international actors. Partial sanctions were imposed against Nigeria following the 1993 annulment of election results and the November 1995 execution of Ogoni activists, but regional states and the major powers were unwilling to support stronger measures. The OAU was reluctant to condemn its largest and most influential member. As Peter Lewis (1998) has noted, Nigeria's leading creditors and trading partners in Western Europe sought to preserve ongoing commercial interests and parried proposals to impose tougher sanctions. An oil embargo against Nigeria could have been enforced readily and would have had a major impact on the regime in Abuja, but the lack of international consensus precluded the effective use of sanctions. Whether the Nigeria sanctions debate will be rekindled in the future depends on the willingness of Abacha's successors to fulfill their pledges to restore democracy and respect human rights.

One of the most important empirical findings from the IIE study is that financial sanctions have a higher success rate (41 percent) than do the more widely imposed general trade sanctions (25 percent) (Hufbauer,

Schott, and Elliott 1990, 63 ff). This finding is ambiguous, because financial sanctions seldom appear alone; but the implication is that financial pressures may be more effective than trade sanctions. Financial sanctions include such measures as the freezing of foreign assets, the cancellation of financial assistance and debt rescheduling, the withholding of credits and loans, and restrictions on travel, commerce, and communications. These forms of financial pressure are often found in combination with trade sanctions and add powerful leverage against a target regime. Assets freezes allow coercive pressures to be targeted against the economic and political elites responsible for wrongdoing. Financial sanctions also tend to have a multiplier effect within the target country. When external governments or multilateral institutions freeze assets or ban lending and investment activities, financial institutions abroad and at home may be prompted to reconsider their commitments as well. Banks are acutely sensitive to uncertainty and the perception of risk, and they may be reluctant to make commitments in nations facing financial sanctions. Because financial sanctions are more focused and exert pressure primarily on elites, their humanitarian consequences for vulnerable populations are less severe than broader trade sanctions. This has important significance for the moral legitimacy and political effectiveness of sanctions and can help to ensure that economic coercive measures achieve greater political gain and less civilian pain.

The conventional theory about how sanctions are supposed to work assumes that political change is directly proportional to economic hardship. The greater the economic pain caused by sanctions, the higher the probability of political compliance. Johan Galtung has termed this the "naïve theory" of sanctions, because it fails to account for the efforts of the target state to adjust to or counteract the impact of sanctions (1983, 26–27). It is assumed that the population in the target state will redirect the pain of sanctions onto political leaders and force a change in policy. As David Baldwin has observed, however, "the economic effects of sanctions do not necessarily translate into political impact" (1985, 63). There is no direct transmission mechanism by which social suffering is translated into political change. This is the case even in the most democratic of countries and is especially so in the authoritarian or dictatorial regimes that are the usual targets of sanctions.

Economic sanctions may actually strengthen a target regime and generate a rally-round-the-flag effect. A regime may adopt defensive measures that enable it to withstand the pressures of economic coercion or that redirect the hardships onto isolated or repressed social groups while insulating power elites. The latter form of adaptation is especially evident in Iraq's response to UN sanctions. Rather than causing political disintegration, sanctions may evoke nationalist sentiments and generate autarky in the target country. In some cases sanctions may enrich and enhance the power of elites who organize and profit from smuggling and illicit trade activities. In Haiti, military and business elites close to the regime of Raoul Cedras controlled the black-market trading of oil and other vital commodities. In the former Yugoslavia, hard-line militia groups used their control of checkpoints and transportation routes to enrich themselves and consolidate political power. Some amount of leakage is inevitable in a sanctions regime, as shortages and rising prices create opportunities for profiteers, but when these operations become large-scale and fall under the domination of the political elites who are the target of sanctions, policy objectives are often undermined.

Although sanctions sometimes cause a rally-round-the-flag effect, they can also generate an internal-opposition effect. Sanctions may empower internal political forces and render more effective their opposition to a regime's objectionable policies (Eland 1995, 32–33). As a report of the United States General Accounting Office has observed, "if the targeted country has a domestic opposition to the policies of the government in power, sanctions can strengthen this opposition and improve the likelihood of a positive political response to the sanctions" (United States 1994, 12). In the case of South Africa, the opposition African National Congress actively encouraged stronger international sanctions and gained moral and political support from the solidarity thus expressed by the international community. Sanctions did not have a huge economic impact in South Africa, but the combination of external sanctions and the civil resistance campaign of the United Democratic Front helped to bring about a sweeping political transformation (see Davis, 1995). In Nigeria the lack of a strong, coherent domestic opposition was a major constraint on the potential effectiveness of sanctions. As Lewis (1998) notes, opposition efforts within Nigeria have suffered from division, demoralization, and opportunism. The absence of a powerful and united democratic movement clouded the prospects for effective sanctions against the Abacha regime.

The prospects for an internal-opposition effect depend substantially on the degree of support for sanctions within the target nation. When credible civil organizations and human rights movements within the target country support international sanctions, the moral legitimacy and likely political effectiveness of those measures is enhanced. In its 1993 study, *Dollars or Bombs*, the American Friends Service Committee argued that sanctions are morally justified when there is "significant support for sanctions within the target country among people with a record of support for human rights and democracy, or by the victims of injustice" (1993, 9). In her review of the ethics of sanctions, Lori Fisler Damrosch emphasizes the importance of internal opposition in both the South African and Rhodesian cases: "I attach great significance to the fact that the authentic leadership of the majority populations called for the imposition, strengthening, and perpetuation of sanctions" (1993b, 302).

A greater use of targeted financial sanctions may be a way of reinforcing internal opposition effects while minimizing the prospect of a rally-round-the-flag effect. By avoiding harmful impacts on vulnerable populations, targeted measures deny political elites the opportunity to rally broad political support. Instead of punishing the general population, assets freezes and similar measures apply pressure primarily on the political and military elites responsible for wrongdoing. There are limits to how much sanctions can be fine-tuned, but attempts to focus coercive pressures on elites can yield positive dividends. Targeting economic pressures against decision makers is the strategy that is most likely to produce the desired political changes within target nations. Combining this approach with support for democratic opposition movements offers the greatest opportunity to achieve the desired policy change within the target nation while minimizing adverse humanitarian consequences.

MAKING INCENTIVES WORK

Incentives can be either conditional or nonconditional. Cooperation theorists have emphasized what might be termed the power of positive reciprocity, the ability of cooperative gestures to induce similar behavior in others. Robert Axelrod (1994) and others have found that the simple tit-for-tat process, in which one party responds in kind to the gestures of the other, is a highly stable form of cooperation. Incentive policies go beyond the concept of narrow reciprocity, however. Inducements are sometimes offered as part of a long-term process in which no immediate response is requested or expected. This is the so-called pure form of incentives in which there is little or no explicit conditionality (George and Smoke 1974, 608–9). The purpose of incentives in such instances may be to establish the basis for cooperative relations in the future or to help rebuild a society ravaged by war in the hope that this will prevent a renewal of bloodshed.

There are many particular forms of incentives, but the most powerful inducement for peaceful relations in the world today is access to the emerging system of political cooperation and economic development among the major states. A zone of relatively prosperous democratic peace now stretches from Japan and Australia to North America and through much of Europe. The states in this zone are characterized by economic cooperation and development, democratic governance, and peaceful relations. One can be critical of the inconsistencies and inequalities within and among these nations and their exploitation of others; but the fact remains that access to this system of peaceful cooperation is an attractive inducement for many countries. The promise of improved political and economic relations with the major powers, especially the United States, has often served as an inducement for cooperation. For the countries of central and eastern Europe, the lure of integration with the European Union and NATO is a powerful incentive. Conditioning access to the system of peaceful cooperative development on the observance of civilized rules of behavior can be an effective inducement for the prevention of conflict. Paul Schroeder has described this process as "association–exclusion," contrasting it with traditional "compellence–deterrence" (1994, 35). The greatest hope for a more cooperative future lies not in the power to punish, according to Schroeder, but in the creative use of association to reward those who abide by civilized standards of behavior while excluding those who do not. This approach is in keeping with the Commission on Global Governance's preference for noncoercive strategies of norm enforcement.

The history of the cold war illustrates the benefit of incentives in generating a positive response. Lloyd Jensen (1984) finds in his review of American–Soviet arms negotiations that concessions by one side tended to be reciprocated by the other. William Gamson and Andre Modigliani (1971) examine eight episodes in which the West made conciliatory gestures toward the Soviet Union from 1946 to 1963. In seven of the eight cases, the Soviet Union reciprocated with cooperative behavior. By contrast, when faced with hostile actions, each side tended to respond with "refractory" actions and increased belligerence. Perhaps the most dramatic recent case of positive reciprocity occurred in September 1991, when President George Bush announced the unilateral demobilization of U.S. tactical nuclear weapons from ships and submarines and the removal and dismantlement of nuclear artillery and short-range missiles in Europe ("An Assault on Nuclear Arms" 1991, 24–28). This bold initiative was promptly reciprocated by Soviet president Mikhail Gorbachev, who announced a similar and even more sweeping withdrawal and dismantlement of tactical nuclear weapons from Soviet land forces and naval vessels ("Nuclear Weapons: Going, Going" 1991, 54). The Bush initiative was prompted by a desire to reign in the far-flung Soviet nuclear arsenal at a time of rapidly disintegrating Soviet authority and thereby limit the danger of de facto nuclear proliferation. The reductions were highly effective in diminishing the nuclear danger and constituted the largest single act of denuclearization in history.

The Bush–Gorbachev nuclear reductions and other mutual concessions at the end of the cold war were a partial reflection of Charles Osgood's important concept of graduated and reciprocated initiatives in tension-reduction (GRIT) (1962). The GRIT strategy goes beyond simple reciprocity and proposes a sophisticated series of conciliatory measures designed to reduce tensions and distrust (see George, Farley, and Dahlin 1988, 705–7). The initiating side announces a series of accommodating steps and continues these actions even in the absence of a reciprocal response. If the other side exploits the situation or acts in a hostile manner, the initiating side responds in kind, although only to the limited extent necessary to restore the status quo. If the other side reciprocates positively, the pace of conciliatory action is accelerated. The point of the strategy is to foster a sense of common identification and mutual interest in further cooperation and to reduce distrust and animosity.

The nature of the objectives sought is one of the most important variables affecting the potential effectiveness of incentives. Just as sanctions are more successful in achieving modest or limited policy changes, incentives are more likely to achieve small-scale change than sweeping political transformation. Arnold Wolfers has argued that incentives are most likely to be effective in the area of "low politics," in which national sovereignty and territorial integrity are not at stake (1962, 107–8). It is extremely difficult to persuade a state to trade territory or national security for economic benefits. On the other hand, if security assurances and the rewards of political association are included in the inducements package, even far-reaching political change may be achievable. Denuclearization successes in Ukraine and Kazakhstan were facilitated not only by economic inducements but also by broader security and political assurances. The pursuit of major political objectives may be possible, but in such cases larger and more comprehensive inducements will be necessary. There may be some circumstances, however, such as attempting to prevent Pakistan's nuclear tests, in which the scale of necessary assistance is beyond the capacity and will of even the most powerful states.

The experience of attempting to use incentives for intrastate conflicts has been uneven. In El Salvador, the promise of U.S. aid and recognition was used effectively to induce both the government and the FMLN to implement the 1992 peace accords. Each side found greater benefit in accepting the benefits offered by the United States than in continuing the armed conflict. As Raimo Väyrynen notes, the use of inducement strategies in Bosnia has been less successful (1997a). Despite major commitments of financial assistance from the European Union, the World Bank, and other international actors, Croats and Muslims have refused to cooperate in Mostar, Serbs and Bosnian government representatives have made little progress in creating a genuine federal structure. Because of the deeply rooted nature of the conflict in Bosnia, even large-scale inducement efforts have been unable to overcome local hostilities.

The most successful incentives strategies are those that are focused on a single objective and consistently sustained over time. When there are multiple or conflicting objectives, the inducement process is likely to be confused and ineffective. Competing interests and agendas are a particular problem in the application of aid conditionality by international financial institutions (see Nelson and Eglinton 1993). The World Bank has emphasized "structural adjustment" policies, which often require reductions in public sector spending, but the bank has also made commitments to alleviating poverty, which may necessitate major public investments in infrastructure, job creation, and social welfare. Structural adjustment policies may also conflict with military demobilization programs, such as those in Mozambique and Uganda. The joblessness and economic hardship caused by adjustment policies can make employment more difficult to find for demobilized combatants.

The perception of value is one of the most important variables in the success of incentives. In economic theory, an incentive is calibrated to increase the value of the option preferred by the sender over what the recipient would otherwise choose. An incentive seeks to raise the opportunity cost of continuing on the previous course of action by changing the calculation of cost and benefit. The scale of the incentive depends on the magnitude of the desired change in behavior. The greater the change, the larger the required inducements. In the area of nonproliferation policy, Virginia Foran and Leonard Spector have developed the concept of a "reservation price," which they define as the lowest price a potential proliferator will accept for giving up its nuclear program (1997). The reservation price includes the sunk costs already invested in the nuclear program. For countries such as India and Pakistan, which have invested a vast quantity of scarce economic resources and a huge amount of political capital in their nuclear programs over decades, the reservation price is likely to be spectacularly high. In the case of North Korea, on the other hand, in which the nuclear program was only partially completed when the crisis broke in 1993, the sunk costs were much lower and could be matched by the United States and its South Korean and Japanese partners. According to Spector and Foran, the magnitude of an incentives package must be commensurate with the proliferator's sunk costs.

Access to advanced technology is a highly valuable incentive. This is especially true in developing countries but applies in industrialized nations as well. William Long has found that access to technology raises the perceived value and utility of an incentives offer and is highly effective in encouraging bilateral cooperation (1996a). Because technology is so crucial to both economic development and military capability, it has value to the most fundamental objectives of government. The lure of military technology is especially great, although an overemphasis on weapons transfers can have counterproductive economic and political consequences. The World Bank and other international financial institutions now recognize excessive expenditures on weapons as an impediment to sustainable development. Arms sales and an emphasis on military inducements may also reinforce a bias toward the use of military force to solve complex political problems and devalue the search for more nonviolent, civilian-oriented approaches to conflict prevention. Offering access to civilian technology carries none of these risks and is the preferable means of offering technology inducements.

The effectiveness of incentives also depends on credibility, which requires that the sender have a reputation for fulfilling pledges and a demonstrated ability to deliver the promised reward (Fisher 1969, 119–23). Promptness in delivering a promised reward is especially important. The swift fulfillment of a pledge increases the influence of the promised reward, and raises the likelihood of positive reciprocation (ibid., 124). Delays in the implementation of an incentive may impede cooperation. In Gaza and the West Bank, the failure of international lenders to deliver on the financial pledges made at the time of the 1993 Israeli–Palestinian accords has contributed to political problems and delays in the implementation of the peace process. Promises whose fulfillment rests far into the future are less effective in encouraging compliance. Cooperation theory emphasizes the importance of a quick response to conciliatory gestures as a way of assuring additional cooperation. According to Axelrod, the shorter the response time, the more stable the relationship and the more enduring the cooperation (1994, 185).

Incentives can be offered either by a single state such as the United States or a multilateral institution such as the World Bank or the Council of Europe. Each approach has advantages and disadvantages. A single nation usually can decide upon and implement an incentives strategy more effectively than a coalition. A single actor may also be better able to deliver on a promised reward and communicate a coherent objective. On the other hand, coalitions or multilateral institutions have more market power and a greater potential for offering security assurances. Transnational participation is crucial to the process of global governance and more readily strengthens the legitimacy of international norms. Multilateral involvement is especially important in peace implementation and post-conflict reconstruction. The enormous costs associated with rebuilding countries such as Bosnia or Angola make it impossible for any single country to shoulder the burden alone. A disadvantage of multilateral actors is that sustaining a coherent policy commitment over time is more complex, especially if the inducement strategy involves security commitments and the provision of financial assistance. Differences among the senders may also send confused or contradictory messages to the recipient.

Economic power is important to the effectiveness of inducement strategies. The larger the market power of the sender or senders, the greater the potential for offering economic incentives. This helps to explain the leadership role of the United States and other major industrial nations. These considerations of power are important; they are not, however, sufficient. Reliability, political will, and the soundness of the underlying policy are more important to success than raw capabilities. The United States plays a leading role as both an individual sender and a major player in multilateral coalitions and institutions. Most of the major cases of incentives policy involve the United States acting either alone or in partnership with others. Whether in fashioning the incentives package for resolving the nuclear crisis in North Korea, initiating and sustaining the Dayton peace process for Bosnia, or attempting to keep a lid on simmering disputes in Macedonia and Kosovo, American leadership has been decisive. Although Washington has been at times inconsistent in its commitments to global governance and has used international coalitions to advance its own foreign policy interests, the importance of the United States to the prospects of international cooperation is indisputable.

As with sanctions, the effectiveness of inducement strategies depends on how they affect internal political dynamics within the recipient nation. External attempts to change policy must be able to influence the political preferences of important actors within the recipient country. In his analysis of trade policy, Long (1996b) demonstrates how commercial preferences and technology transfers appeal to particular groups and constituencies within the recipient nation who are willing and able to mobilize on behalf of the reforms sought by senders. By targeting benefits to stakeholders and potential allies within the recipient country, senders are able to use incentives with maximum political effectiveness. Etel Solingen has observed a linkage within some developing countries between support for trade liberalization and acceptance of cooperative security and nuclear nonproliferation goals. The political constituencies committed to economic globalization, according to Solingen, are less inclined to favor overt nuclearization and assertive nationalism (1995, 214). Solingen recommends using trade preferences to encourage these political dynamics: "Coalitions favoring steps toward denuclearization could be rewarded with a variety of trade benefits, investments, selective removal from export control list, debt relief, and the like" (ibid., 218).

Attempting to achieve targeted influence in this way is a delicate matter. It is always better to frame incentives as assistance rather than compellence. Overt attempts to influence can backfire if they are perceived as interference or manipulation. Offering incentives that influence domestic politics requires finesse and aplomb and a keen sensitivity to the traditions and culture of the recipient nation. Just as sanctions can generate a rally-round-the-flag backlash, inducement efforts may spark nationalist resentment and denunciations of attempts to "bribe" the recipient nation. Seemingly irrational concerns about national pride can override utilitarian calculations of cost and benefit. As with sanctions, incentive policies must consider the possibilities of unpredictable responses within the recipient nation.

Ultimately the success of an inducement strategy depends on subjective factors. As Denis Goulet observes, "an incentive system can only sway a subject who is disposed to respond" (1989, 11). Moral and cultural considerations can be as important to the success of an incentives offer as purely material factors. Baldwin makes the same point in noting that the value of an incentive depends on a recipient's perceptions of the situation and the baseline of previous expectations (1971, 23). The intended beneficiaries of an incentive offer will always be the final judge of its effectiveness, which makes the assessment of a recipient's subjective feelings crucial to the prospects of success. Incentive policies can have unanticipated negative consequences if senders are insensitive to internal political dynamics. Incentives delivered to military elites or to corrupt political leaders can weaken the standing of constituencies seeking democratic reform and undermine the long-term prospects for cooperative behavior (Morgenthau 1962, 308). Understanding the likely internal consequences of inducements and targeting benefits to empower the supporters rather than the opponents of reform are key elements in the strategic design of incentives policy.

Goulet has proposed an approach to incentives policy that encourages popular participation as the key to mobilizing political support within the recipient nation (1989, 145, 159–61). This approach differs from strategies that target rewards to elites. The distinction lies in the nature of the recipient's internal political dynamics. If there is popular concern about selling out to foreign influence, or if there is a recalcitrant leadership that refuses to reform, a nonelite strategy may be preferable. Making an offer that is appealing to popular forces can help to minimize concerns about external interference (Forsberg 1996, 10). Crafting proposals that benefit popular movements rather than narrow elites may empower such constituencies to overcome obdurate leaders. By enhancing the involvement of nonelite groups and empowering them to acquire political and economic rights, this approach targets assistance to those who often need it most while providing concrete inducements for domestic constituencies to mobilize on behalf of reform and cooperation.

COMPARING SANCTIONS AND INCENTIVES AS TOOLS OF GLOBAL GOVERNANCE

We conclude our essay with a comparison of sanctions and incentives as useful instruments for norm enhancement and sustenance in a political environment in which governance is increasingly global. One important difference between sanctions and incentives is in their cost to the senders. In narrow accounting terms, a sanction is not a cost. When countries impose an embargo on an offending state, this does not show up as a line item in the national budget. As a result, some policy makers naïvely consider economic sanctions a kind of "foreign policy on the cheap" (Elliott 1993). In reality sanctions impose significant costs on private companies and local communities, but because these losses do not appear as specific government expenditures, they are easy for political leaders to overlook or ignore. By contrast, foreign assistance, loan guarantees, and other forms of financial aid are listed as specific budgetary allocations, which can make them easy targets for budget cutters, especially in an era of fiscal austerity. On the other hand, trade preferences and technology incentives appear to be relatively cost free to governments and have become a favorite tool of economic statecraft.

Although trade incentives do not require budget allocations, they have financial implications. United States budget legislation mandates that reductions in revenue from any source, including the lowering of tariffs, must be offset by tax increases or compensating budget reductions. Because trade incentives increase the overall level of commerce, however, they usually result in greater government revenues. Trade incentives also open up new opportunities for commerce that can benefit domestic constituencies (Long 1996a, 19–33). Whereas sanctions impose costs on particular industries and communities, trade incentives can bring benefits to these groups. As a result, domestic constituencies in the sender state may gain a stake in maintaining trade preferences and provide political support for sustaining the incentives policy. As noted earlier, incentives can create similar dynamics within the recipient country. In contrast with sanctions, which cause hardships for both sender and recipient, trade incentives bring benefits to both. They are a classic win-win proposition.

A related advantage of incentives is that benefits can be designed and targeted to ameliorate the root causes of conflict. Väyrynen (1997a) emphasizes the importance of structuring incentives packages so that they overcome resource imbalances and other underlying sources of violence. Whether the primary needs are economic, political, or security related, inducement strategies can be packaged and delivered to meet those needs and lessen the likelihood of conflict. In the case of Ukraine, security assurances were added to the package of economic benefits offered to Kiev as a way of addressing concerns about Ukrainian vulnerability vis-à-vis Russia. This targeting of resources to meet specific political objectives is an important way in which incentives differ from sanctions. Whereas sanctions take away resources or deny benefits to contending parties, incentives add resources. When these rewards are targeted strategically to address the sources of conflict, the effectiveness of incentives is enhanced.

Incentives also differ from sanctions in their relation to market forces. When incentives are offered, there is no natural tendency, as with sanctions, for black marketeers or third-party actors to step in and circumvent trade restrictions. As Eileen Crumm observes, "Where market forces work against negative sanctions, they can reinforce positive ones" (1995, 326). Many scholars have noted that economic sanctions generate countervailing pressures that can undermine the effectiveness of such measures. A tightly enforced embargo will raise the price of imports in the target country and in the process create powerful motivations for cheating (see Kaempfer and Lowenberg 1995, 61–72). By contrast, an offer of incentives such as foreign assistance or concessionary loans will not create market pressures for another party to do likewise. Competing offers of assistance may result from political motives, but they are not generated by market forces. During the cold war the United States and the Soviet Union vied to provide incentive offers, but such competition is less likely now. Positive incentives work in harmony with the natural forces of the market and thus have a significant economic advantage over negative sanctions.

Sanctions and incentives also have differing impacts on international trade and the prospects for economic cooperation. One of the most significant, some would say most hopeful, characteristics of the post–cold war world has been the widespread expansion of free markets and the substantial increase in international commerce. Richard Rosecrance has spoken of "the trading state" phenomenon as a powerful antidote to war and armed conflict (1987). Expanding trade and economic interdependence can establish a long-term foundation for peace and enhanced international cooperation. The use of economic sanctions runs counter to this trend. Peter van Bergeijk argues that the greater use of negative sanctions may threaten the expansion of trade, thereby weakening the incentive for political cooperation that comes with increasing economic interdependence (1994, 12). By contrast, positive measures encourage trade and international cooperation and thereby contribute to the long-term prospects for peace. Incentive policies provide a basis for long-term cooperation and understanding and create the foundations for international stability.

Perhaps the greatest difference between sanctions and incentives lies in their impact on human behavior. Drawing on the insights of behavioral psychology, Baldwin identifies key distinctions between the two approaches. Incentives foster cooperation and goodwill, whereas sanctions create hostility and separation. Threats tend to generate reactions of fear, anxiety, and resistance, whereas the normal responses to a promise or reward are hope, reassurance, and attraction. Threats send a message of "indifference or active hostility," according to Baldwin, whereas promises "convey an impression of sympathy and concern" (1971, 32). Incentives tend to enhance the recipient's willingness to cooperate with the sender, whereas negative measures may impede such cooperation. Roger Fisher argues that "imposing pain may not be a good way to produce a desired decision" or to influence another's actions (1969, 28). Whereas threats and punishment generate resistance, promises and rewards tend to foster cooperation (ibid., 35).

These differences have important implications for the conduct of political communications. One of the drawbacks of sanctions is that they close off channels of commerce and interaction, which can intensify misunderstanding and distrust. Inducement strategies do not carry this burden. Because incentives create less resentment and obstinacy in the recipient, communication is clearer and more precise, and negotiations are more likely to succeed. Punitive measures may be effective in sending a message of disapproval, but they are not conducive to constructive dialogue. Whereas sanctions may generate communications gridlock, incentives open the door to greater interaction and understanding (Long 1996a).

Our conclusion from the foregoing analysis is obvious. We agree with the Commission on Global Governance that incentives are preferable to sanctions as a means of reinforcing norms of global governance. We second Roger Fisher's conclusion that "the process of exerting influence through offers is more conducive to international peace than the process of exerting influence through threats" (1969, 106). Although inducement strategies are not appropriate in every setting, and may be counterproductive if employed in the face of overt military aggression and gross violations of human rights, they have many advantages over punitive approaches. Incentives have the ability to generate positive reciprocity and can establish the basis for enhanced cooperation and trust. A diplomacy that employs carrots more often than sticks offers hope for transforming the international system and creating a more cooperative and peaceful world order. Because of their unique ability to add resources in situations of need and to create a climate of reassurance and cooperation between previously distrustful parties, inducement strategies offer greater promise for addressing both the long-term sources of conflict and the requirements of global governance. Sanctions will continue to be necessary as an immediate response to violent and abusive behavior; but incentives can build the long-term foundations for greater peace and understanding.

NOTES

1. Examples of such disparate treatments include Cortright and Lopez (1995) and Cortright (1997). A recent attempt to analyze the two strategies together can be found in Cortright and Lopez (1998, 113–34). This chapter is a major revision and updating of this earlier argument.

2. For a full examination of this argument, see Lopez and Cortright (1998).

7

Liberal Democratic Regimes, International Sanctions, and Global Governance

Kim Richard Nossal

As the reactions of the international community to the Indian nuclear tests on May 11 and 13, 1998, demonstrate, it is common for many foreign policy makers to reach almost reflexively for sanctions when they engage in the processes of global governance. At the same time, however, these same policy makers must deal with a thorny paradox: the tool of statecraft to which they are so attracted has a notoriously poor record of success. Policy makers—and students of sanctions—have devoted considerable energy to exploring how sanctions work and how they could be made more effective, either as a tool for individual states in their foreign policy (United States 1992; Canada 1994) or as instruments of global governance (Commission on Global Governance 1995, 2; Stremlau 1996; Minear et al. 1998; for a critique, see Nossal 1999).

However, although policy makers and scholars have looked far and wide for the determinants of sanctions success, they have tended to overlook one important variable: the impact that regime type has on the success or failure of international sanctions as an instrument of global governance. This chapter seeks to examine the variable of regime type, particularly to look at the record of sanctions as a means of securing political change. It begins from the observation that of the more than one hundred sanctions episodes over the course of the twentieth century, there have been relatively few cases in which one can conclude unequivocally that sanctions were "successful"—where a successful result is defined as one in which the sanctioner (or "sender") secures the desired political change in the sanctioned state (or "target"), and the use of sanctions alone (rather than other tools of statecraft) can be deemed responsible for that change of policy.

Indeed, it can be argued that there have been only fourteen such cases of sanctions success since 1945. This number is derived from the comprehensive survey by Gary Clyde Hufbauer, Jeffrey J. Schott, and Kimberley Ann Elliott in which each sanctions episode was scored on a scale of one to four according to whether a target country's government changed its behavior; another scale measured whether sanctions were deemed to be the significant cause of that change (Hufbauer, Scott, and Elliott 1985). Sanctions were deemed to have worked when the episode scored a four on both scales. Although their scaling exercise has been widely criticized for being both crude and highly subjective, on the whole it can be argued that the results reached by Hufbauer and colleagues do not violate commonsense observation.[1] To the Hufbauer cases I added recent episodes in which sanctions alone have achieved the political change desired by the sanctioner. A summary of the cases is shown in table 7.1.

One intriguing observation about this list is that in twelve of the fourteen cases, the sanctioned country had a functioning multiparty electoral system at the time of the sanctions episode. This begs an obvious question: Is there a relationship, previously overlooked by students of sanctions, between sanctions effectiveness and regime type? This chapter explores whether such a relationship does exist and whether sanctions of states with multiparty electoral systems are more successful than sanctions of countries without this political feature. I conclude, however, that although there appears to be a coincidence between regime type and sanctions success, explanations of the effectiveness of sanctions in these cases must include other factors. But there can be little doubt that regime type plays an important part in the synergies necessary for the effective use of sanctions, a conclusion that has considerable implications for the use of sanctions as instruments of global governance.

SANCTIONS: ASSUMPTIONS AND PARADOXES

One of the most persistent questions facing those who use—and those who study—international sanctions is whether and how this instrument of statecraft works. This is an issue that has dominated the discussion about sanctions at least as far back as the aftermath of World War I when the question was whether sanctions, employed by members of the League of Nations, could be effectively used to deter governments from using force and aggression in their foreign policy. The sanctions enthusiasts of that era believed that they had found a peaceful alternative to war, one that would produce the desired political effect (avoidance of the resort to the use of

Table 7.1   Sanctions "Successes"

Sanctioned State	Sanctioning State or Coalition	Year	Issue
Netherlands	United States	1948-49	Dutch policies in Indonesia
Britain	United States	1956	Suez crisis
Israel	United States	1957	Israeli occupation of Sinai
Finland	Soviet Union	1958-59	Putative "tilt" toward West
Sri Lanka	United States	1963-65	Expropriation of oil companies
India	United States	1965-66	Agricultural policy
South Korea	United States, Canada	1975	Nuclear reprocessing
Taiwan	United States	1976	Nuclear reprocessing
Canada	Arab states, Arab League	1979	Moving Canadian embassy to Jerusalem
New Zealand	France	1985-86	Release of French agents convicted of *Rainbow Warrior* bombing
Lesotho	South Africa	1986	Harboring ANC militants
South Africa	Numerous states	1940s-90s	Dismantling apartheid
Kenya	Western states	1991	Adopting multiparty system
France	Australia	1995	Resumption of nuclear testing

force by states) without the huge costs of going to war against an aggressive state. Woodrow Wilson, the president of the United States, outlined the thinking in what has become the classic statement of sanctions theory: "A nation that is boycotted is a nation that is in sight of surrender. Apply this economic, peaceful, silent, deadly remedy, and there will be no need for force. It is a terrible remedy. It does not cost a life outside the nation boycotted, but it brings a pressure upon the nation which, in my judgement, no modern nation could resist" (quoted in Hufbauer, Schott, and Elliott 1985, 8).

Implicit in Wilson's assertion is the theory that has informed the use of sanctions throughout the twentieth century, from the measures institutionalized by the Covenant of the League of Nations to the present. In a nutshell, sanctions theory is driven by assumptions of rationality in decision making, overlaid with what in essence is a liberal democratic assumption about the relationship between the governed and those who govern. The theory suggests that international sanctions work in the following way: sanctions interrupt normal economic intercourse, and in so doing, they deprive political communities of the good things necessary to sustain life and community; faced with such disruptions in the supply of good things, rational governors of a sanctioned community will do whatever is necessary to continue to have access to those good things and will alter their behavior in such a way as to stop the sanctions.

But this model of the rational, pain-avoiding political leadership has a liberal democratic corollary: if the governors of a sanctioned state are not rational enough to make such a calculation, then they will incur the anger of the country's citizens, whose interests will be most affected by a disruption in economic intercourse. The internal quarrels produced by this anger will result in the governors removal from power, either in constitutional ways, such as through elections or a parliamentary caucus coup, or in unconstitutional ways, such as a real *coup d'état* by the military or a palace coup. However the removal is achieved, the net effect will be that governors whose policies attract international sanctions will be swept from power by the governed and a new set of governors who will make the right rational choice will be put in their place. This is what Johan Galtung, writing about Rhodesia in the 1960s, terms the "naïve theory" of sanctions (Galtung 1967); it is also commonly called the subversive purpose of sanctions (see, e.g., Lindsay 1986).

In the eighty years since the creation of the League of Nations and its system of sanctions to be imposed against those governments that violated the covenant, sanctions have been advocated—and imposed—for a range of reasons and with a range of intended effects. But always the sanctions debate has been dominated by one seemingly small question: Do sanctions work as Wilson suggested they would? In other words, when a "sending state" imposes sanctions against a "target state," does this tool of statecraft produce the desired political change?

Attempting to answer this question has spawned a large literature debating the effects—and the effectiveness—of international sanctions (for an excellent survey, see Doxey 1996). The effort to answer this question has also produced an odd policy paradox. On the one hand, there is widespread agreement among those who study economic sanctions that this tool of statecraft does not work well. It is true that, as David A. Baldwin (1985) reminds us, such an analytical conclusion very much depends on how one defines "work". But the vast majority of students of sanctions appear to agree that if the goal of sanctions is defined as producing immediate political change in the behavior of the government of the target state, then sanctions are generally an ineffective tool. Indeed, the list of scholarly studies testifying to the general ineffectiveness of sanctions as a means of prevailing in conflicts of interest between governments is long and stretches over at least the past three decades; one could usefully begin with Galtung (1967) and end with such recent studies as those of Robert Pape (1997) and Clifton Morgan and Valerie Schwebach (1997).

On the other hand there is an increasing body of evidence that demonstrates unequivocally that sanctions "work" only too well at producing negative effects on others besides the government of the target state. Sanctions hurt the civilian population of the target state, the countries that border the target state and are thus sideswiped by international sanctions, and even domestic groups within the sending state—all without necessarily causing the governors of the target state to change the behavior that prompted the sanctions in the first place. Some studies focus on what is called "civilian pain"—the impact of sanctions on the governed of a target state (Damrosch 1993b; Weiss et al. 1997). Others focus on the often unintended consequences of international sanctions. For example, a number of studies have explored the impact of sanctions on children (Harvard Center for Population and Development Studies 1993; Harvard Center for Public Health 1991). In a similar vein, Lori Buck, Nicole Gallant, and I have examined the tendency of sanctions to have highly gendered effects (Buck, Gallant, and Nossal 1998).

The policy paradox is that despite the overwhelming evidence that sanctions simply do not work as their enthusiasts claim, they nonetheless continue to be a favored instrument for global governance, in response to behavior deemed wrongful in international politics. Confronted with an action they deem to be unjust or wrong—the execution of a political prisoner, the rigging of an election, the harboring of a suspected terrorist, the widespread violation of human rights, the testing of a nuclear weapon—many political leaders continue to reach almost reflexively for the sanctions option. Moreover, these leaders commonly shrug off the observation that the instrument they are reaching for will have little impact. Instead, they assert that this time it will be different; this time the sanctions will indeed work. And government leaders are not alone in their optimistic enthusiasm for sanctions. Members of nongovernmental organizations (NGOs) also see sanctions as a favored policy instrument. As a result, throughout the 1990s the idea that sanctions are a sound instrument of policy remains alive and well, not only at the level of individual states, but also at the multilateral level. Since the end of the cold war, the United Nations has imposed multilateral sanctions against the former Yugoslavia (including Serbia and Montenegro), Somalia, Libya, Liberia, Haiti, Rwanda, and Sudan; in addition, an arms embargo was imposed against UNITA, one of the sides in the civil war in Angola (Doxey 1997; Conlon 1995).

One of the reasons sanctions continue to be so popular in the 1990s—despite the considerable evidence that they produce great civilian suffering but little political change—lies in the fact that sanctions remain an excellent policy option for foreign policy decision makers who wish to demonstrate that they are *doing* something in response to behavior by others in the international community deemed to be wrongful. In this view, it does not matter that study after study serves up the conclusion that sanctions don't work; it does not matter that study after study shows that sanctions have a negative impact on the poor and the marginalized in the target state. Rather, the policy maker can brush aside these academic quibbles and argue that doing something is not only better than doing nothing but is also better than using other compulsive tools of statecraft such as force, assassination, or subversion. As I have argued elsewhere (Nossal 1989), international sanctions continue to be attractive to policy makers (and to their publics) in large part because of their punitive capacity. They might not produce political change; they might produce all manner of negative effects on the civilian population; but sanctions remain an excellent tool for punishing behavior deemed to be wrongful.

But it can be argued that there is another and more particular reason sanctions remain an attractive option in the 1990s. This is the case of South Africa and the role that sanctions are widely believed to have played in the collapse of apartheid in the early 1990s. Thus, when confronted with some case of international wrong needing to be righted, the tendency of policy makers, those in the NGO community, and many others, is to point to the role of the sanctions imposed by the international community against South Africa in the 1980s in the collapse of the apartheid regime and to argue that the South African case provides solid evidence that sanctions do indeed work.

One can hardly quarrel with the general conclusion that the sanctions imposed by the international community against South Africa in the late

1980s played an important part in prompting the National Party in South Africa, in Audie Klotz's phrase, to negotiate itself out of power (Klotz 1995a, 159). Indeed, the collection of studies on the impact of sanctions on South Africa edited by Klotz and Neta C. Crawford makes quite clear that the wide range of international sanctions played a crucial role in creating a political–economic environment that was antipathetic to apartheid (Crawford and Klotz, 1999). To be sure, Crawford and Klotz conclude that these sanctions *contributed* to rather than caused the collapse of apartheid. In other words, as Crawford notes, sanctions "were only one of several forces at work" in securing change in the behavior of the South African government (Crawford 1997, 58). Other factors cited by Crawford included the role of armed struggle, both inside South Africa and in the southern African region, and structural changes in the South African economy. Similarly, one could point to the important role that capital flight played, as individual investors and bankers in the United States decided that the civil unrest in South Africa was raising the risk to unacceptable levels. We also must include the impact of changing norms, in other words, the impact on white South Africans of the longer-term change in thinking about the rightness of racial discrimination that was occurring in other countries and that had led to a massive increase in opposition to the idea of apartheid.

REGIME TYPE AND INTERNATIONAL SANCTIONS

But there is one possible explanation of sanctions success in the South African case that has not been explored in any great detail in the sanctions literature. To what extent can the success of international sanctions in this case be attributed to the nature of South Africa's domestic political system? In other words, can we discover a linkage between regime type and the success of the sanctions in this case?

Although sanctions theory is largely built on the assumption that there is a deep and intimate relationship between government behavior and the preferences of individuals in civil society, there has not been a great deal of research into the relationship between political form and the success of sanctions. The comprehensive survey of more than one hundred sanctions episodes by Hufbauer, Schott, and Elliott is indicative. Hufbauer and colleagues examine numerous "political" variables in their efforts to determine the causality of sanctions success or failure, but they do not include regime type among these variables (Hufbauer, Schott, and Elliott 1985, 41–55).

To be sure, there have been generalized observations about the ability of certain types of regimes to resist the impact of sanctions. I have suggested elsewhere (Nossal 1993b) that the record of sanctions failures shows clearly that military dictatorships, oligarchies, human-rights-abusing governments, and indeed all regimes with illiberal forms generally find it easy to resist the punitive impact of sanctions. Such regimes simply pass on the costs imposed by international sanctions to the governed, relying either on a degree of public support for the regime or on the superordinate power of the armed forces and security apparatus to deter (or repress) political opponents—or, more commonly, on a mixture of both these factors. The longstanding sanctions against North Korea and Cuba—in place for well over three decades—demonstrate the ability of illiberal regimes to withstand even the most crushing and comprehensive sanctions. The international sanctions against Iraq, Libya, Myanmar, and Nigeria have been of somewhat shorter duration, but these illiberal and nondemocratic regimes have also been unmoved by the punishments.

The quintessential case of the willingness (and ability) of the governors of illiberal regimes to pass on the costs of international sanctions to their populations is Iraq. The government of Saddam Hussein has remained indifferent to the humanitarian impact of the international sanctions regime that has been in place since 1990 and which has been continued primarily at the insistence of the governments of the United States and Britain. The regime in Baghdad has actively avoided any policy change that would bring relief to the Iraqi civilian population; on the contrary, it continued to acquire weapons of mass destruction, as Iraqi defectors and UNSCOM (United Nations Special Commission on Iraq) inspectors made quite clear, thus ensuring that the sanctions would continue to be imposed. Indeed, the regime often spent conspicuously on projects, such as lavish presidential palaces, that made it easy for American and British officials to counter pleas from other governments to ease the sanctions regime against Iraq (Cordesman and Hashim 1997; Dowty 1994; Alnasrawi 1993; Center for Economic and Social Rights 1996; Hoskins 1997).

A more detailed exploration of the relationship between sanctions failure and the political attributes of the target of sanctions has been undertaken by Dina Al-Sowayel and Sean Bolks. They conclude that regime type invariably affects the duration of sanctions episodes (Al-Sowayel and Bolks 1998). For his part, Robert A. Hart Jr. has tested the "democratic peace proposition"—the idea that democracies do not go to war with one another (Morgan 1993; Russett 1993; Ray 1995)—in the case of international sanctions (Hart 1996). Hart hypothesizes that the democratic nature of a regime will also have an impact on the use of economic sanctions. Examining eighty-one sanctions episodes, he demonstrates that sanctions imposed by democracies are more "successful" than those imposed by nondemocratic regimes (a conclusion, it might be noted, that could also be a function of the fact that democracies tend to be richer and thus have more economic clout to make sanctions "successful").

Hart focuses on democratic *senders*; but what about democratic *targets*? Do sanctions imposed on regimes that have liberal democratic forms—or polities that have some liberal democratic features—have a higher chance of succeeding in altering behavior? Here we encounter another paradox: the sanctions literature seems to have been so transfixed by sanctions *failures* that students of sanctions have tended not to focus on the unequivocal sanctions successes—in other words, when sanctions, or the threat of sanctions, "worked" exactly as sanctions theory predicts—and explored possible reasons for that success.

SANCTIONS SUCCESSES

Among the many sanctions episodes since 1945, only fourteen stand out as unequivocally successful, in the sense that the target state was prompted to alter its behavior by the use of sanctions. These cases are outlined in table 7.1. A brief thumbnail sketch of these sanctions episodes demonstrates the dynamics of success in each case.

Netherlands, 1948–49. In the latter half of 1948, the police action taken by the Dutch government against the new Indonesian republic caused a deterioration in relations between the Netherlands and other Western countries, particularly the United States. Although the administration of Harry S. Truman suspended Marshall Plan aid to the Netherlands Indies in December 1948 in response to a new wave of arrests of Indonesian leaders by Dutch authorities, it was not until February and March 1949 that overt threats of economic sanctions were made by the United States to pressure the Dutch government into granting Indonesia sovereignty. After the Dutch government stalled for time by proposing a compromise that would have excluded Indonesian leaders such as Sukarno, the United States increased its threats against The Hague. On March 31, 1949, the U.S. secretary of state, Dean Acheson, went so far as to openly threaten the Dutch foreign minister, Dirk Stikker, with a termination of aid under the European Recovery Program (ERP, or Marshall Plan) if the Netherlands did not bend. Marshall Plan aid was crucial to postwar Dutch recovery. Stikker later recalled that "it was absolutely a must—you couldn't do without it" (cited in Hufbauer, Schott, and Elliott 1985, 192). Within three weeks, the Dutch government had abandoned its intransigence, leading to the granting of full independence to Indonesia in August 1950.

Britain, 1956. Following the attack on Egypt by Britain, France, and Israel, a plan was proposed by the Canadian government to have the United Nations introduce a peacekeeping force to settle the dispute. As part of its effort to secure British acceptance of the UN plan, the U.S. administration of Dwight D. Eisenhower blocked British access to its International Monetary Fund reserves to pay for oil supplies in the Western Hemisphere and refused to provide support to the Bank of England's efforts to maintain the value of the pound. The United States sanctions, together with widespread condemnation of the attack on Egypt from other Commonwealth countries, prompted the British government to back down.

Israel, 1957.   In the aftermath of the 1956 Suez crisis, the Sinai Peninsula remained occupied by Israeli forces, with the prime minister of Israel, David Ben-Gurion, asserting that the Sinai was henceforth part of Israel. The Israelis eventually agreed to withdraw from most of the Sinai, but Ben-Gurion insisted that Israel would continue to occupy Gaza and Sharm el-Shaikh. To exert pressure on the Israeli government, president Dwight D. Eisenhower privately threatened to suspend American economic aid to Israel and, more importantly, to amend the U.S. Income Tax Act, which makes contributions to the state of Israel a tax-deductible expense for American taxpayers. On March 16, 1957, Ben-Gurion yielded to the American threat and ordered the withdrawal of all Israeli forces from the Sinai (Hufbauer, Schott, and Elliott 1985, 262).

Finland, 1958–59.   The general elections of July 1958 brought a Social Democratic government under Karl August Fagerholm to office, creating a fear in the Soviet Union that Finland would abandon the careful course steered by J. K. Paasikivi and Urho K. Kekkonen since the late 1940s, a course that sought to ensure that Finland would do nothing that conflicted with the interests of the USSR. Part of the Paasikivi–Kekkonen line involved tying the Finnish economy closely to the Soviet Union; thus, for example, Finland never accepted Marshall Plan aid. However, Finnish membership in the Nordic Council in 1955 and a progressive increase in trade with the West was seen in Moscow as a harbinger of the "loss" of Finland to the West, particularly under a politician like Fagerholm. As a consequence, over the autumn of 1958, the Soviet government pursued an escalating policy of economic and other sanctions against the Fagerholm government, canceling discussions on a range of economic issues, discontinuing trade, and trying to leave little doubt in the minds of Finns that having Fagerholm as prime minister would be exceedingly costly. The pressure worked: on December 4, 1958, Fagerholm resigned. In January 1959, after Kekkonen had traveled to Leningrad to personally assure Nikita S. Khrushchev that Finland would be a "good neighbor" of the USSR, all economic intercourse resumed (Väyrynen 1969).

Sri Lanka, 1963–65. The Sri Lankan Freedom Party (SLFP) government of Sirimavo Bandaranaike was both one of the inspirations for and one of the first targets of the Hickenlooper amendment, an initiative by Senator Bourke B. Hickenlooper, Republican of Iowa, to deny U.S. development assistance to governments that expropriated or nationalized U.S. property without appropriate compensation. In 1962 the Bandaranaike government nationalized a number of American and British oil companies operating in Sri Lanka and refused to move quickly to compensate the companies. The U.S. government responded in February 1963 by halting aid. Negotiations over compensation lingered through 1963, prompting the companies affected to halt shipments of oil to Sri Lanka in January 1964. In general elections held on March 22, 1965, the United National Party under Dudley Senanyake, which had promised to settle with the oil companies and have U.S. aid restored, defeated the SLFP; within five days a preliminary compensation agreement had been reached (Hufbauer, Schott, and Elliott 1985, 324–28).

India, 1965–66. In June 1965, the United States administration of Lyndon B. Johnson terminated both long-term and short-term food aid under Public Law 480 as a means of pressuring the Indian government to place greater priority on domestic agricultural production and reduce India's dependence on external sources of food; added to the list of American demands was that the Indian government devalue the rupee and institute a more aggressive family-planning program. The Johnson administration called this keeping India on a "short tether." The short-tether exercise worked: between December 1965 and March 1966, the Indian government responded by altering its policies in all areas desired by the administration in Washington (Hufbauer, Schott, and Elliott 1985, 405–8).

South Korea, 1975. In June 1975, the South Korean government publicly announced that it would purchase a nuclear reprocessing plant from France. This was seen by the U.S. administration of Gerald Ford as part of a wider program by the government in Seoul to establish a nuclear weapons program. Washington responded by threatening to disrupt the civilian nuclear power program also being pursued by the South Korean government. Not only did the U.S. government threaten to veto financing for the purchase of reactors for civilian power generation; it also persuaded the Canadian government to tighten the terms of financing for nuclear sales to South Korea. On January 29, 1976, it was confirmed that South Korea had abandoned its plan to purchase the French reprocessing plant (Hufbauer, Schott, and Elliott 1985, 505–7).

Taiwan, 1976. The Ford administration pursued a similar strategy toward the Republic of China on Taiwan in 1976. Reports by the Central Intelligence Agency revealed that Taiwan was secretly reprocessing spent fuel, either from Canadian reactors that had not been closely safeguarded since the Canadian government's derecognition of the Republic of China on Taiwan, in October 1970, or from South Africa. In January 1976, the U.S. government imposed sanctions on nuclear transactions with Taiwan, holding up licensing applications for two power reactors and also a shipment of fuel. The sanctions were made public in August 1976, and in September the government in Taipei responded by promising not to acquire nuclear reprocessing capabilities; in early 1977, it closed the Institute for Nuclear Energy Research, where the secret reprocessing was alleged to have taken place (Hufbauer, Schott, and Elliott 1985, 540–43).

Canada, 1979. During the campaign that preceded the May 1979 elections, the Progressive Conservative leader, Joe Clark, sought to woo the Jewish vote in Toronto and Montreal by promising to move the Canadian embassy in Israel to Jerusalem. Clark also promised that a Progressive Conservative government would keep its election promises (unlike the Liberal government, which had promised in the previous election not to impose wage and price controls and once in office had reneged on that promise). When the Conservatives were elected, Clark reiterated his promise. Because it was likely that a move to Jerusalem by Canada might trigger moves by other countries, a number of Arab states imposed sanctions against Canada and threatened Canadian businesses with links to the Middle East with boycotts and disruptions. After heavy lobbying by Canadian corporations and media stories with headlines like "Arabs' Reply Could Cost 55,700 Jobs," Clark shelved the plan (Takach 1990).

New Zealand, 1985. On July 10, 1985, agents of the French secret service—the *Direction Générale de la Sécurité Extérieure*—blew up the Greenpeace ship *Rainbow Warrior* in Auckland harbor, killing a photographer on board. Subsequently, two of the agents involved—Dominique Prieur and Alain Mafart—were arrested by New Zealand authorities and put on trial for murder. They pled guilty to manslaughter and on November 22, 1985 were sentenced to ten years in prison. However, the French government (and French public opinion) took the view that Prieur and Mafart were army officers acting under orders, not criminals, and therefore should be returned to France. The New Zealand government of David Lange not only rejected outright French requests that the agents be returned to France but also insisted that France issue an apology for the incident and pay reparations.

The French government responded by imposing a series of administrative blockades on the importation of agricultural products from New Zealand and threatened to block New Zealand butter from the entire European market, a sanction that would have cost some NZ$300 million a year. But because 20 percent of New Zealand overseas trade was with Europe, the Lange government soon capitulated and accepted a suggestion made by the Dutch prime minister that the matter be referred to third-party arbitration. The arbiter, Javier Pérez de Cuéllar, the secretary-general of the United Nations, recommended that the agents be released to France to spend three years on Hao, a French-owned island in the South Pacific. In return, France would issue an apology, pay New Zealand $7 million in reparations, and promise not to block access to New Zealand products. Although Lange had vowed publicly on numerous occasions that he would never authorize the release of the agents, his government agreed to the terms. The agents were transferred to Hao, where they were widely and publicly praised by the French government—and eventually transferred to other duties well before the end of the three-year period specified in the arbitration (Thakur 1986).

Lesotho, 1986. Although Chief Leabua Jonathan, prime minister of Lesotho, generally pursued a policy of maintaining good relations with South Africa, frictions developed after the South African government established the Transkei *bantustan* in 1976. In particular, South Africa objected to the fact that Lesotho harbored more than ten thousand South African refugees, among them members of the military wing of the African National Congress (ANC). When Jonathan refused to expel the ANC members, South Africa imposed an economic blockade against Lesotho on January 1, 1986. Completely surrounded by South African territory and highly dependent on the movement of goods, services, and remittances from Lesotho nationals working in South Africa, the South African sanctions provide the one clear case where sanctions had precisely the effect claimed for them by the "naïve theory": within three weeks of the imposition of the sanctions, Jonathan was ousted in a relatively bloodless coup by the defense forces. The new military government expelled sixty ANC members; shortly thereafter, South Africa agreed to a $2 billion water project in Lesotho that had been under consideration for two decades and which, when completed, would involve substantial royalties paid to Lesotho.

South Africa, late 1980s. Although a variety of sanctions had been imposed against South Africa in response to apartheid in that country in the years after the formal embrace of apartheid in 1948, it was not until the outbreak of sustained civil unrest in the townships in 1984 that the sanctions movement gathered force. Gradually, more and more comprehensive measures were enacted with the intention of prompting South African whites to abandon apartheid and introduce a multiracial system. By the late 1980s, a range of comprehensive sanctions, imposed by a range of actors, both governmental and nongovernmental, were in place. Table 7.2, adapted from Neta C. Crawford's survey of sanctions against South Africa, shows the range of measures imposed against the apartheid regime.

Although apartheid was brought to an end over a period of years, one could date the beginning of the end from January 18, 1989, when P. W. Botha suffered a stroke and was replaced as president later in 1989 by F. W. de Klerk. The key initiatives taken by de Klerk included the unbanning of the ANC and other antiapartheid groups (February 2, 1990), the release of Nelson Mandela (February 11, 1990), rescinding the legislation of "petty apartheid" (June 1, 1990), and the abolition of the legislative bases of "grand apartheid" (June 5, 1991). Although there is considerable evidence that de Klerk's initiatives were accompanied by the waging of a violent rear-

Table 7.2 Sanctions against South Africa

Type of Sanction	Primary Senders	Year Initiated
Diplomatic	Individual countries, International organizations	From 1950s From 1960s
Arms	UN voluntary measures UN mandatory measures	1963 1977
Oil	OPEC Commonwealth and EU United States	1973 1985 1986
Sport	Olympics Commonwealth	1964 1977
Culture	Various	1970s
Finance	Individual banks Netherlands Commonwealth	1970s 1977 1985
Divestment trade	Private actors India Jamaica Denmark, France and United States coalition	1970s 1946 1959 1985

Source: Adapted from Neta C. Crawford, "Humanitarian Consequences of Sanctioning South Africa," in Weiss et al. 1997, table 3.1, p. 64.

guard action by the South African security forces, the ANC reciprocated, formally suspending its armed struggle and agreeing to participate in the negotiation of a new constitution for a multiracial state. The first multiracial balloting was held on April 26–29, 1994, and Mandela was installed as president on May 10, 1994.

Kenya, 1991. The government of Daniel T. arap Moi had for many years been brushing aside Western criticism of Kenya's official one-party policy and the repression of efforts to organize constitutional opposition to KANU (Kenya African National Union), including the assassination and imprisonment of anti-KANU activists and numerous killings by security forces. Despite the regime's repression, in August 1991 a new opposition movement, the Forum for Restoration of Democracy (FORD) was formed. Called a "discussion group" to circumvent the law proscribing parties other than KANU, FORD pressed for the establishment of a multiparty system. In November 1991, the regime arrested many of FORD's leaders; at the same time, an investigation revealed that one of Moi's closest allies, Nicholas Kiprono Biwott, had been implicated in the February 1990 assassination of Robert Ouko, the foreign minister who was emerging as a challenge to Moi. The response of Western governments and international financial institutions was to impose a suspension on economic assistance. Faced with a cutoff of international financing, Moi capitulated immediately: in December, the constitution was revised to legalize political parties.

France, 1995. The case of the Australian sanctions against France in 1995 is somewhat of an anomaly, because the sanctions imposed against France in response to the decision by the government of Jacques Chirac to resume nuclear testing in the South Pacific were taken by nonstate actors rather than by the Australian government (Nossal and Vivian 1997). But there can be little doubt that the range of often highly inventive and imaginative sanctions imposed against things French by hundreds of thousands of Australians over the southern winter of 1995 should be considered a sanctions episode, even though the sanctions invoked by the government of Australia were limited to relatively restrained diplomatic measures. Ordinary Australians, by contrast, showed little such restraint. Anti-French sanctions of all sorts were eagerly embraced by state governments, municipalities, political parties, nongovernmental organizations, entertainers, radio and television hosts, unions, neighborhood associations, schools, and a huge array of individuals. French diplomatic missions were often paralyzed by the refusal of unions to service them; their phone and fax lines were jammed by crank callers, often urged on by radio talk-show hosts. There were widespread boycotts of French products and services, which caused a temporary collapse in trade. Indeed, the widespread antipathy toward the French government easily spilled over to antipathy toward anything simply sounding

French—with attacks against French restaurants and patisseries and even people with French names.

The widespread anger—and the sanctions that came with that anger— appears to have taken the government in Paris by surprise. Watching as the French relationship with Australia deeply deteriorated between May, when the resumption of the tests was announced, and September 1995, when the first test was held, the French government relented—somewhat. It cut short the planned series, stopping the testing program after six, rather than eight, tests. Paris also announced that it was closing its South Pacific testing sites for good and would be signing the Comprehensive Test Ban Treaty.

DISCUSSION AND ANALYSIS

It should be noted that in all but two of the cases outlined above, lines of causality between the imposition (or threat) of sanctions and the change in the target's behavior is relatively straightforward. Had "senders" not threatened or imposed sanctions against the Netherlands, Israel, Finland, Sri Lanka, India, South Korea, Taiwan, Canada, New Zealand, Lesotho, Kenya, or France, it can be argued that there would have been little or no change in the behavior of these governments. Moreover, in each of these cases, sanctions were the predominant instrument of statecraft used. In that sense, one would be justified in concluding that sanctions worked in these cases.

By contrast, causality in the British and South African cases is less easy to trace. It can be argued, for example, that the British capitulation in November 1956 was prompted not so much by the American sanctions as by the expectation that unless the face-saving compromise proposed by the Canadian foreign minister, Lester B. Pearson, was accepted, the British government would be condemned outright by the United Nations. But there can be little doubt that the economic measures used by the Eisenhower administration concentrated minds in London. Indeed, in this case, it would be prudent to conclude that a mixture of factors were at work.

The South African case is even murkier. Indeed, students of South African politics (as opposed to students of sanctions) tend to argue that numerous factors brought white South Africans to a realization that the kind of South Africa that had existed in the halcyon days of apartheid in the 1950s and 1960s was no longer sustainable (Price 1991; Klotz 1995a; Crawford and Klotz, 1999). Sanctions invoked by governments to pressure the South African state into change is generally seen to be only one of these factors. As Crawford and Klotz note, unraveling the causality in the South African case will be difficult; the role of sanctions in that process is likely to remain essentially contested.

Even noting the more contested causality in the British and South African cases, however, there remains the intriguing commonality among all but two of the successful cases of international sanctions: all but Lesotho and Kenya had functioning multiparty electoral systems at the time that the sanctions episode occurred. Could it be argued that there might be a relationship between the effectiveness of sanctions in these cases and the fact that, with the exception of Lesotho and Kenya, those on whose shoulders the burdens of sanctions normally fall most heavily—the governed—had an opportunity, even if only eventual and in some cases highly manipulated by dominant parties, to engage in electoral punishment of the governors whose policies attracted the international sanctions in the first place? In short, is it significant that, with the exception of Lesotho and Kenya, the only clear cases of sanctions success involve political regimes that had electoral systems?

Three important caveats must immediately be entered. First, I am not suggesting that all of these systems were liberal democracies. Clearly there were important differences among these countries. On the one hand, Britain, Canada, Finland, France, Israel, the Netherlands, and New Zealand were (and are) liberal democracies, all featuring relatively universal suffrage; relatively fraud-free elections; relatively unrestrained political competition among political parties; a relatively firm commitment of all the players in the political game to the rule of law, constitutionalism, and the idea of the necessity of the consent of the governed; and a generally firm commitment of the governors to tolerate a "loyal" opposition. At the time of the sanctions episodes surveyed here, India and Sri Lanka were functioning democracies, even if the commitment of Indians and Sri Lankans to liberal principles might be open to question.

By contrast, one could not describe South Korea and Taiwan in the mid-1970s or South Africa in the late 1980s and the 1990s as liberal democracies. In both these cases, one or more of the important elements of liberal democratic governance was missing from the political structures or practices of each of these countries. Yet each of these countries at the time of the sanctions episode had either a functioning multiparty system or an electoral procedure that permitted the expression of political dissent (or both). To be sure, the electoral system may have been deeply rigged, and the opportunities for the expression of political opposition might have been overtly constrained (as in Taiwan, for example, where opposition candidates were constrained to run as independents); or the commitment to actually holding elections might have been less than firm (as in South Korea, where the functioning of the electoral system was punctuated periodically by declarations of emergency rule and martial law). But in both of these political systems there was an active political opposition and opportunities for that opposition to be expressed. Although these countries cannot reasonably be considered liberal democracies in the mid-1970s, they do not fit easily into other political pigeonholes.

Characterizing the South African political system under apartheid is even more difficult. Certainly the apartheid system, with its deeply rooted discriminatory and exploitative practices and its foundational assumptions about the necessary inequality of human beings based on skin color, was manifestly neither democratic nor liberal. Moreover, the apartheid regime actively denied to the majority of citizens the key elements of liberal democratic governance—the vote—and thus the means by which the hypothetical notion of the consent of the governed can be operationalized. Similarly, the apartheid regime could and would brook no political opposition other than that which confined itself to a narrow space and was fundamentally accepting of apartheid. Other expressions of political opposition to the governors, even when expressed nonviolently, were inexorably met with a range of coercive and often lethal practices, ranging from attacking protesting crowds with dogs, whips, and bullets to widespread extrajudicial executions. However, although the apartheid regime was deeply illiberal and as deeply undemocratic, it also had some undeniably liberal democratic elements. In particular, South Africa had a functioning electoral system, even if the participation in that system was limited to those with a certain skin pigmentation and to those who were prepared not to fundamentally challenge the regime.

Second, I am not suggesting that fear of electoral punishment was a factor in any of the sanctions cases explored here. In one instance, Sri Lanka, the capitulation to foreign pressure came in the form of the electoral defeat of the government whose policies had attracted the sanctions in the first place. But in the other cases, the direct shadow of upcoming elections played no part in the dynamic. The fairly rapid capitulations of the Dutch, British, Israeli, Finnish, Indian, South Korean, Taiwanese, Canadian, or New Zealand governments when confronted with the imposition or threat of sanctions did not seem to be motivated by upcoming elections. Elections had just been held in France, and so Jacques Chirac was unlikely to have been moved by electoral considerations in his decision to cut short the program of nuclear tests. In South Africa, legislative elections were held in September 1989, some seven months after de Klerk replaced B. W. Botha as leader of the National Party, but it is not clear that there was a relationship between those elections, in which the vote for the National Party actually fell, and the introduction of de Klerk's reform package. Rather, as I argue below, it would appear that a functioning electoral system interacts with another key variable to produce sanctions success.

Finally, it is also important to note that I am also not suggesting that when a regime has a functioning electoral system it will readily succumb to sanctions. On the contrary: there are times when a target with a functioning electoral system will resist international efforts to sanction it quite successfully. Indeed, Hufbauer and colleagues report at least twelve cases where sanctions against liberal democracies failed, almost as many as are surveyed in this chapter. The case of the sanctions imposed against India in response to its nuclear tests provides a useful example of the capacity of democratic regimes to resist sanctioning. The Bharatiya Janata Party government of Atal Behari Vajpayee successfully resisted international sanctions, buoyed by widespread support among ordinary Indians for the policy of going nuclear.[2] One could readily imagine some other liberal democratic states, such as the United States, Britain, or Japan, refusing to bend to sanctions imposed by others in the international community.

However, there are three other important commonalities among the cases surveyed in this chapter. The first is that in most cases, the target had a high degree of dependence on the sender and a high degree of vulnerability. In nine of the fourteen cases, the governments that gave in most readily to sanctions pressure—the Netherlands, Israel, Finland, Sri Lanka, New Zealand, South Korea, Taiwan, Lesotho, and Kenya—were all weak and highly dependent on the sender for the good or service being withheld. In the cases of the Netherlands, Israel, South Korea, Taiwan, and New Zealand, the governments bent only because they felt they had no choice; in the case of Finland, the "offending" government was forced to resign; in the case of Sri Lanka, the government was voted out of office; in the case of Lesotho, Chief Jonathan's choices were made for him by Lesotho's defense forces.

By contrast, one could not make the same argument about dependence and weakness in the British, Indian, Canadian, South African, and French cases. However, one could argue that in each of these cases the governments involved decided to cut their losses rather than try to create a sustainable position. Thus, the British government might well have weathered the storm of international criticism; it might even have managed its dependence on the United States for financial support. However, the loss of both concrete and symbolic support from its friends and allies would have made it hugely costly to try to sustain the Suez adventure. The Indian government could have resisted the Johnson administration's pressures, but it is clear that the government in New Delhi calculated that it would be better off with American Public Law 480 aid than without it. In 1979, the Canadian government was in no way dependent on business with Arab states and could have resisted the pressures generated by the sanctions had they not been amplified by the corporate community within Canada and had the Progressive Conservatives not been in a minority situation in the House of Commons. For its part, France was not at all dependent on Australia or on economic intercourse with Australians, but there can be little doubt that the rage that swept the Asia Pacific in the middle of 1995 severely weakened French standing in the region; Chirac's *volte face* in September 1995 makes most sense if it is seen as an attempt by Paris to stanch the progressive deterioration in French relations throughout the Asia Pacific rather than as a result of weakness stemming from dependence.

The South African case is more contested, for there is disagreement on how dependent South Africa actually was on those who were imposing sanctions in the late 1980s. Clearly the dynamic of deprivation, as it evolved in the South African case, did not work as cleanly or as unambiguously as it did, for example, in the Lesotho case. Nonetheless, it could be argued that the progressive squeezing of white South Africans in the late 1980s—economically, through divestment and other economic sanctions; psychologically, through such measures as cultural and sports sanctions; militarily, through combat losses in regional wars; and politically, through the increasing ungovernability of the black areas of the country—revealed to white South Africans the degree to which their attachment to apartheid had made them pariahs and had made South Africa both weak and vulnerable (even if that weakness and vulnerability did not spring directly from dependence on those who were administering the sanctions).

The second commonality is that in most of the cases explored in this chapter, the threat or imposition of sanctions was accompanied by often considerable domestic political opposition, with the government being pressed, either publicly or privately, to bend to the demands of the foreign sanctioner. The existence of vulnerability, dependence, or weakness plays an important role in giving rise to this opposition, it often being argued that the national interest would be better served by pursuing what is invariably called a "more cooperative" policy. However, the existence of such opposition, it can be argued, is a crucial prerequisite for the capitulation that is so necessary for sanctions to work. For *domestic* opposition has the effect of legitimating *foreign* opposition to the target government's position and thus legitimating capitulation to those foreign demands.

The third commonality is that in seven of the twelve cases where the government being sanctioned chose to change its behavior (rather than being forced from office)—that is, the cases involving the Netherlands, Britain, Israel, India, Canada, New Zealand, and France—governments were headed by individuals operating in a political culture deeply suffused with democratic ideas and the practices that flow from them, notably the idea that community decisions are best made following full and open discussion and debate; the idea that opposition to the governors in power and the advocacy of alternative policies are both legitimate forms of political expression; and the idea that it is possible for one set of governors to be replaced with another by peaceful means. It can be argued that from an attachment to these ideas also flows a receptivity to backing down in the face of compelling argument from critics.

It is only when one puts together all of these common elements—the existence of vulnerability or weakness; the existence of domestic opposition; the existence of a forum or set of practices that allows that opposition to be expressed, channeled, and perhaps directed against the governors; and the receptivity of governors to having their minds changed—that one can see how regime type can have an impact on sanctions success. Remove one or more of those elements, and the likelihood is that sanctions will be less than effective as a means of compelling the political change desired by the sanctioner. Remove vulnerability or dependence, and the pressure for capitulation diminishes (as the case of India and the May 1998 nuclear explosions reminds us). Remove pressure for capitulation, and it is likely that domestic opposition diminishes. Similarly, if there is high domestic support for the course of action being sanctioned, capitulation is unlikely (again the Indian case is instructive). Remove the channels, structures, and processes for the expression of opposition to the government line that is deemed legitimate, and it is likely that the degree of vulnerability, the degree of weakness or dependence, or the level of domestic opposition to the policies that are attracting the sanctions will be unimportant to the outcome. Finally, remove the receptivity to argument and debate that is so deeply embedded in liberal democratic practice, and it is likely that the resistance of individual leaders to foreign pressure will increase, no matter what the cost to the community as a whole.

CONCLUSION

The argument in this chapter is not that liberal democratic governments necessarily make better targets for sanctions. Rather, I have tried to account for the observation that the overwhelming majority (twelve of fourteen) of sanctions successes occurred in cases where the target political systems were liberal democracies (the Netherlands, Britain, Israel, Finland, Canada, New Zealand, France), had democratic if not fully liberal forms and practices (India, Sri Lanka), or had a functioning multiparty electoral system (South Korea, South Africa), or an electoral system that permitted formal opposition (Taiwan). And it might be noted that even the two outliers (Lesotho and Kenya) had begun life as sovereign postcolonial states with democratic forms even if at the time of the sanctions those forms had been distorted and manipulated.

However, although the coincidence between sanctions success and political form can be observed, it is no means clear or self-evident how or why sanctions seem to work so well in countries that are either liberal democracies or have some of the structures, forms, and practices we associate with liberal democratic politics. Certainly we cannot conclude that there was a direct electoral connection (except in the case of Sri Lanka, where the government was voted out of office and replaced by a party that had promised, inter alia, to abandon the policies that were attracting international sanctions). Only one of the changes in political behavior (that in South Africa) occurred in the shadow of an election.

Rather, I have hypothesized that the existence of a democratic (or pseudodemocratic or protodemocratic) polity does not in itself explain sanctions success; for example, one would have a hard time conjuring a scenario in which the United States, the world's quintessential liberal democracy, was successfully sanctioned by other states. Instead, I have hypothesized that sanctions success comes from the interaction of the weakness and dependence of the target on the sender, the existence of a domestic opposition that is able to be expressed legitimately and noncoercively, and a political culture that is receptive to policy change.

The dynamic identified in this chapter suggests a number of implications about the effectiveness of sanctions as an instrument of global governance. First, and most narrowly, it suggests that we should draw lessons about the role of sanctions in bringing apartheid in South Africa to an end with some care. I have argued that although South Africa can be considered a case of sanctions success, it could be hypothesized that among the factors that led to that success was the South African political system and the dynamics of opposition we saw in the other cases of success. Needless to say, more detailed research will have to be done before we can establish an unambiguous connection between South Africa's unique political form in the 1980s and the impact of sanctions, but the preliminary evidence offered in this chapter suggests that the nature of the South African political system may well have contributed to the success of sanctions in that case.

A second, broader, implication of the analysis in this chapter is that we should continue to view with some skepticism the enthusiasm for the use of sanctions as a tool of global governance. The cases surveyed in this chapter suggest that the assurances of foreign policy makers that their sanctions policies will be effective tools for bringing pressure on recalcitrant states to conform with global norms should be questioned—unless the state they are talking about targeting not only has a democratic form of government but also is weak, vulnerable, and dependent.

NOTES

1. I (subjectively) made three modifications to the Hufbauer results. I removed two cases to which Hofbauer and colleagues had assigned a 4/4 score: the United

States versus the Dominican Republic (Case 60–1) and the United States versus the United Arab Republic (Case 63–1)—on the grounds that they overweighted the impact of sanctions in the Dominican Republic case and overweighted the success of U.S. sanctions against the UAR. I added two cases that Hufbauer and colleagues had scored as 4/3: the American sanctions against Britain after the Suez crisis of 1956 and the Arab sanctions against Canada in 1979 over the Jerusalem embassy issue. It can be argued that in both these cases, the outcomes would have been different without the existence of the threat or imposition of economic sanctions.

2. For example, a poll conducted by the *Times of India* immediately after the tests showed that support for the tests among Indian public opinion stood at 91 percent. *Toronto Globe and Mail*, May 14, 1998.

8

New Norms in the Field of Peacemaking: The Challenge of Implementation

Albert Legault

The great theoretical debates on peacekeeping touch upon numerous issues, from the process of conflict resolution to the difficult political and economic reconstruction of collapsed or failed states. This chapter sheds new light on these problems and better integrates the internal and external conditions necessary to establish a peace process into a framework that will help determine when intervention by the international community is appropriate.

PEACEKEEPING OPERATIONS AND THE PHASES OF CONFLICTS

Since the 1960s, the majority of studies on conflicts have identified three major phases within a conflict: the preconflict phase; the conflict itself, distinguishable by the outbreak of armed violence; and the postconflict phase characterized by the elaboration of the terms of the peace settlement (Bloomfield and Leiss 1969; Barringer 1972). This chapter uses these three phases to throw new light on peacemaking and peacekeeping operations.

Peacekeeping operations refers to the complete range of operations, from preventive diplomacy to peace consolidation operations including peace enforcement, traditional peacekeeping, and nontraditional (second-generation) operations. The absence of the term *peacekeeping* in the UN Charter indicates that these operations have evolved through time and practice. Today, the words *peacekeeping* and *United Nations* are intimately connected, and very few question the significance of the operations undertaken by the blue helmets.

151

Figure 8.1 presents a summary of the main elements of peacekeeping.

The absence of proper definitions within the Charter increases the difficulty of defining the terms used in the figure. *Peacemaking* is the most difficult term to define, as it applies during all three phases of a conflict and during all types of peacekeeping operation. Nevertheless, *peacemaking* as a generic term reflects an orientation or a political process that is established in tandem with missions or operations deployed by the UN to maintain peace and international security. This parallel process has always existed in peacekeeping operations. The secretary-general or his representative negotiates a political resolution to the conflict while peacekeeping operations unfold simultaneously. This has long been the source of criticism that UN peacekeeping operations have preserved the *status quo* rather than actively assisting in the resolution of a conflict (Diehl 1993, 105).

The use of phases to demonstrate the differences between traditional and nontraditional peacekeeping reflects the scope and the complexity of the problems to be resolved. In the first case, with the exception perhaps of the Congo, all traditional peacekeeping operations took place in the postconflict phase, after hostilities had ceased or the belligerents had agreed on the terms of an armistice or a cease-fire. Traditional peacekeeping was a quick fix, a dressing one would put on a wound so as to stop the "bleeding." Often with some luck, peacemaking or diplomatic efforts did the rest, resulting in a peaceful conflict resolution.

In second-generation operations, in which the intervention of the UN takes place during the conflict itself, the tasks of the peacekeepers are infinitely more complex and diversified, and the missions often require more than ten thousand personnel. Furthermore, the mandates are often ambiguous, impractical, or overly ambitious. They may include, for example, the separation of the belligerents and the demobilization of the armed parties, the reestablishment of a legitimate government, social and economic reconstruction, and the holding of national elections supervised by third parties while at the same time providing help, food, protection, and shelter to millions of refugees. Finally, most of these interventions take place during an internal conflict, making it extremely difficult for the UN to preserve its impartiality or to act without appearing to favor one of the parties. This raises the question of whether the UN can intervene in internal conflicts without taking sides, in accordance with its mandate to be impartial, universal, and cooperative.

UNITED NATIONS PEACEKEEPING AND
CONFLICT RESOLUTION THEORY

Why do operations undertaken by the UN sometimes fail and sometimes succeed? To answer this question it is important to bring in the contribu-

Figure 8.1   Peacekeeping Operations and Phases of Conflicts

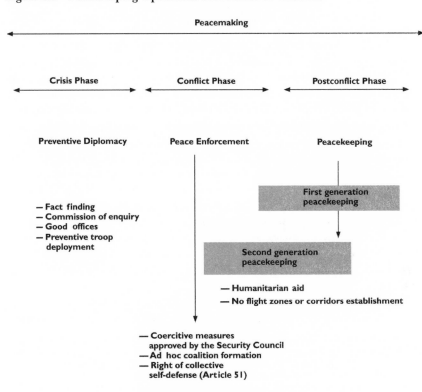

tion of conflict theory. Among the most important questions raised in the literature on conflicts, three key questions are relevant for this study. What systemic or external conditions are necessary for conflict resolution? What internal conditions are likely to lead to conflict resolution? And finally, what are the main transformations required to ensure that these two levels can be integrated?

External or Systemic Conditions Necessary for Conflict Resolution

According to Robert Jervis, four conditions are required for peaceful resolution of a conflict: (1) the great powers have to agree on a common strategy; (2) all parties must abandon expansionist ambitions; (3) peace must be preferred to war; and, finally, (4) agreements have to lead to a shared perception of strengthened mutual security (quoted in Tow 1993, 95). As early as the 1960s, Lincoln P. Bloomfield questioned whether a regional or local conflict could be resolved by superpower intervention (Bloomfield and Leiss 1969). Fen Osler Hampson reminds us that the end of the cold war has had a considerable impact on the resolution of regional conflicts. He emphasizes that several scholars have observed a direct link between the improvement of East–West relations since the end of the cold war and settlements negotiated in Angola, Namibia, El Salvador, and Cambodia. Hampson further notes that the failure or success of a peacekeeping operation depends essentially on the role of third parties, because their presence is crucial to ensure a permanent support and assistance structure throughout the duration of the operation (Hampson 1996, 12–13).

In reality, these conditions rely upon two determining factors: first, the presence of a neutral third party that attempts to resolve the conflict; and second, the existence of conditions that make belligerents opt for peace rather than war or, at least, a negotiated settlement rather than continued hostilities. These elements are supported by a double structure: a cooperative structure composed of third parties and a conflictual structure composed of adversaries. Thus, a conflict transforms itself, with the intervening third parties, from a dyadic structure into a triadic structure. The way these structures unfold constitutes the heart of conflict resolution.

The cooperative structure is normally put into place before the establishment of an operation, as it is normally composed of the negotiating parties that are trying to impose a political settlement on the conflict. Great powers, regional powers, and participating states may be part of this political arrangement, as well as personnel from the organization in charge of the operation, be it the UN, NATO, or any other regional body that tries to settle the conflict. There may be some or much divergence of views between the members composing the cooperative structure, but this structure is generally more cooperative than conflictual. If the divergence of views is too great, no operation is likely to be undertaken.

On the other hand, the conflictual structure is generally composed of the belligerents whom the cooperative structure is trying to separate or to reconcile. The structural characteristics of the conflictual structure vary ad infinitum—some parties are externally supported, and the polarization may be complex—but in general, the polarization of the conflict is based on a dyadic opposition.

It is through the junction of these two structures (cooperative and conflictual) that the conflict henceforth basically dyadic is transformed into a triadic structure, the cooperative structure being essentially the third parties that try to contain, settle, or negotiate the conflict. The presence of a double structure is undoubtedly what best characterizes second-generation operations. As a whole, there is no ideal situation. There is always conflict within cooperation and cooperation within conflict, but cooperative structures present more opportunities for cooperation than for conflict, and conflictual structures more opportunities for conflict than for cooperation.

The cooperative structure can be erected during the preestablishment phase or during the formal start-up phase of an operation. In the first case, a "contact group" will be established, composed of the intervening parties to the crisis, and in the second case, an "enlarged contact group" will be created, composed of representatives whose states are supplying troops for the operation, especially within the command and control element.

The existence of a cooperative structure does not necessarily mean that the conflict will be resolved. Many reasons militate against third-party interventions. Great powers do not want to become an international police force; regional powers, as a rule, do not possess sufficient equipment or logistics to enforce peace in a local conflict or do not have the political will to act. Robert O. Matthews also emphasizes the importance of the transnational system in the resolution of conflicts (1989, 3). Fen Hampson concludes rightly that intervening parties require the support of other third parties, and he notes that a "multilateral negotiation system" with a double structure is required for the working of a regional or local peace process (1996, 12–13, 233). Other conditions necessary for conflict resolution will be examined later. For the moment, the internal conditions necessary for the working of such a process must be reviewed.

Internal Conditions Necessary for Conflict Resolution

The works of William Zartman and Maureen Berman and of Raimo Väyrynen dealing with internal conflict analysis are most useful for this study (Zartman and Berman 1982; Zartman 1985; Zartman 1986; Väyrynen 1991). Zartman concludes that four conditions are necessary for the realization of an internal peace process, although these conditions do not need to be present in the same way or at the same time. These conditions include a "hurting stalemate" between the two parties, a "looming catastrophe," the existence of a "way out," and the presence of "legitimate representatives." A stalemate implies either the exhaustion of the parties or the fact that neither of them is able to win the war. The "looming catastrophe" is the escalation or expansion of the conflict to unacceptable levels, and a "way out" presents itself when the parties find an acceptable political resolution to the conflict that allows them to "save face." The presence of "legitimate representatives" implies the likelihood that agreements will be respected in the future because they have been negotiated by known representatives and supported by the population. If these conditions exist, then a conflict has reached its "ripe moment."

The difficulty with the notion of a "ripe moment" in a conflict is that it is a variable that will regress indefinitely in time, because it is always after the fact that one knows that the point chosen was the right one and not a temporary step in the deescalation or escalation of the conflict. We are all prisoners of history, and uncertainty is common to all social sciences. Counterfactual analysis (what would have happened if different conditions had existed?) is no more reassuring, as it is a research method based on pure speculation. However, these reservations aside, most will agree that conditions for conflict resolution are present when the belligerents cease preferring war over peace or, more positively, when they prefer peace to war. At such times there occurs "a shared perception of the desirability of an accord" (Haass 1990, 27).

Beyond these considerations, several problems exist, especially in the case of collapsed states. Their reconstruction is no small task, and the experience of the UN in Somalia was revealing in this regard. It is often necessary to rebuild these states from the bottom up and to legitimate the whole process of building a civil society. As Zartman states:

> Either the rebellion leaders and local warlords can be brought together, under the theory that the source of the problem must be the source of the solution . . . and leaders with the will and means to *break* security must be given the legitimacy to *make* security; or new elites must be helped to emerge from the closet, representing the leaders of a civil society (teachers, labor leaders, elders, religious figures, and civil servents), the best of the ruled being called on to replace the worst of the rulers. (Zartman 1995, 269)

This aspect of the problem must be underlined because it is linked to one of the previously mentioned conditions, namely the presence of "legitimate representatives." The UN is at times put in the position of having to legitimate leaders who were recently considered war criminals. Nevertheless, in several situations, the most radical elements of a society are eliminated, brought before international tribunals, or simply ostracized from the new society.

The Dynamic Transformations Necessary for Linking Conflictual and Cooperative Structures

Many scholars have studied the processes of dynamic transformations within a conflict, but the elements of proposed answers have not been sufficiently precise to translate into prescriptive rules of conflict resolution. Nevertheless, the hypotheses put forward by Väyrynen remain attractive. He suggests that four potentially dynamic transformations during a conflict should be studied in depth: (1) the transformation of actors; (2) the transformation of issues; (3) the transformation of rules; and (4) structural transformation, that is, changes in the distribution of power or qualitative changes in the relations between actors (Väyrynen 1991, 4–6).

These variables are widely used by experts who deal with the role of third parties in conflict resolution. For instance, both Robert Jervis (1989) and Richard Haass (1990) see the necessity of a shared sentiment of strengthened mutual security, one that addresses both the transformation of issues and the potential transformation of the rules, through confidence-building measures for example, as a means to strengthen security within a region. Kalevi Holsti enumerates conditions for a just and equitable peace that deal with the structural transformation of the conflict (1991, 337–39). The multiplicity of actors, in particular, in the case of ethnic conflicts, points to the constant transformation of power relations between actors (Fournier 1995; Markakis and Fukui 1994).

Although there is no magical solution to a conflict, structural transformations are most likely to allow for a smooth integration of the cooperative and conflictual structures. In general, these structural transformations result either from victory and the imposition of a new order, as was the case in Europe in 1815 with the Congress of Vienna or in 1945 with Yalta; or from the existence of efficient international organizations able to impose a negotiated settlement, as was partly the case during the Gulf war; or from intermediate structures created to promote peace in a region or a conflict.

All dynamic changes in a conflict imply either a change in the environment or changed perceptions by adversaries as to their goals (Legault et al. 1979). It does not seem possible to operationalize these variables without using dichotomous categories. With regard to the conflictual structure, the elements that appear to be the most important are those that affect the overcoming of a temporary cease-fire or the regression from such a cease-fire into further hostilities. These characteristics, shown in table 8.1, indicate the possible transformations.

Table 8.1   **Characteristics of the Transformation of a Conflictual Structure**

Regression of the Status Quo	Maintaining the Status Quo	Overcoming the Status Quo
Adversaries prefer war to peace	Acceptance of a ceasefire	Adversaries prefer peace to war
Existence of war strategies (looking for a military victory)	No comprehensive settlement	Comprehensive settlement
Hate propaganda and indoctrination	Mission of interposition humanitarian aid or assistance	Establishment of cooperative strategies between the different branches of power
Development of authoritarian military or civilian structures	Agreement between the host nation and the UN for deployment of troops	Building and legitimization of new institutions
No or limited freedom of the press	Appointment of a representative of the Secretary General to ensure the coordination between the UN and the deployed force	Democratization, respect for human rights, and reinforced security and cooperation

The determining element remains that parties prefer peace to war, and only this criterion allows the conflictual structure to evolve and overcome the status quo. The converse is also possible: a regression of such a status quo can occur if the belligerents prefer to renew hostilities and return to war strategies to realize their political objectives. Maintaining the *status quo* is the intermediate position between the two. The most difficult choices are made in this phase, when third parties, by making the necessary effort, may lead the conflictual structure to overcome the status quo.

Regarding the cooperative structure, the dichotomy is the presence or absence of intervention. An intervention can be carried out by a military or civil force for the purpose of peace enforcement, traditional or nontraditional peacekeeping, or peace building. Conversely, the cooperative structure can abstain from intervening if it is judged that the costs or risks are too high or that the international situation does not justify it. These characteristics are shown in table 8.2.

To sum up, certain external conditions are necessary for the establish-

Table 8.2   Characteristics of the Transformation of a Cooperative Structure

Regression of the Status Quo	Maintaining the Status Quo	Overcoming the Status Quo
Absence of immediate interest in the international community	Search for solutions through arbitration, mediation, and conciliation	Negotiation of a comprehensive settlement
Half-measures or absence of resolutions on the part of the Security Council	Elaboration of a consensus in the Security Council	Implementation of a peace process according to fair and equitable terms
Deterioration and disintegration of local or regional structures	Setting up, if necessary, of a contact group	Negotiation of agreements to ensure peace, social reconstruction, and security
History follows its course despite the pressure to resolve conflict	Coordination between the group and the Security Council	Reintegration of opposition forces in the political scene
	Setting up, if necessary, of a peacekeeping operation	Respect for democracy and human rights

ment of a peace process, particularly the presence of a double-structured multilateral negotiation system that transforms a polarized or multipolarized conflict into a three-party structure. The necessary internal conditions for the implementation of an equitable peace process are the existence of a cease-fire or the cessation of hostilities, followed or accompanied by comprehensive or partial settlements of the conflict. This process can start only if the parties to the conflict prefer peace to war, regardless of their motives. Finally, these two structures can only function efficiently if they are linked by a structure of negotiation.

Structures of Negotiation

The international community can choose to remain indifferent to wars between its members when it is not directly concerned about the outcome of a conflict. In regard to the international system as a whole, this is nevertheless a stable situation, because this scenario deals with the converse of intervention. In figure 8.2, the theoretical line of stability runs diagonally from the lower left quadrant to the upper right quadrant. The system is particularly stable when the two structures (conflictual and cooperative) meet in the construction of peace. The two right quadrants depict the situation with or without intervention. In the upper right quadrant, the two structures (conflictual and cooperative) meet in the construction of peace, and stability is the product of the positive interplay between the cooperative and the conflictual structures. In the lower right quadrant, stability is produced through the transformation of the internal structure, without external intervention, and by accommodation to peace.

The two left quadrants depict the same situation, with or without intervention, but in unstable conditions. In the upper left quadrant, the cooperative structure enforces peace. The instability of the situation is externally imposed, but in a positive way, at least from the viewpoint of the cooperative structure. Negotiations give way to the will of the international community to redress the situation, as in the Gulf war in 1990–1991 or in Korea in the early 1950s. In the lower left quadrant, no intervention occurs and instability is the product of the evolution within the conflictual structure alone. The conflictual and cooperative structures do not meet; events are left to themselves and history follows its course.

To conceive of a peace process as a system of multilateral negotiation with a double structure has both advantages and disadvantages. The main advantage is that it presents an accurate depiction of reality. The main disadvantage is the difficulty in knowing how these two structures can be linked together into a coherent goal-oriented process; any peace process implies costs and risks for both the cooperative and conflictual structures. As David Carment (1994) notes, it is uncommon that the objectives pursued by intervening states do not meet their interests (instrumental motivations) or are not underlain by affective considerations. In addition, the evaluation criteria are not inevitably the same for all actors, and what originally should have produced positive results can very well produce dysfunctional results within the conflictual structure when implemented (Diehl 1993, 92–106).

The need for a consensus within the Security Council can involve give-and-take negotiations as well as issue linkages, and the risk of intervention can be greater for some powers than for others, depending on the type of operations envisaged. Conversely, the risks incurred inside the conflictual structure by parties that accept or refuse peace proposals or plans are not the same. Participants within the conflictual structure often risk losing all their power or being compelled to share it. As Brian Job states, the establishment of a durable peace process often depends on the perceptions of internal threat shared by the regime in power (1992, 17). Under these con-

Figure 8.2   Stability of the System under Various Conditions of International Response

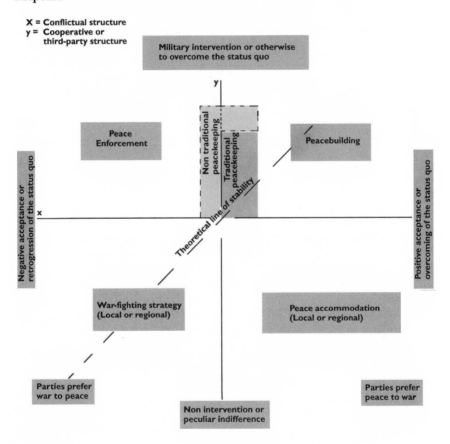

ditions, Hampson concludes, the goal of actors is "to survive" and not to "share power" with "those that seek to overthrow them" (1996, 5). Or, again, as David Carment reminds us, the "elites may be uncommitted to the negotiation process because of gains to be had by prolonging the conflict" (1994, 576).

From the previous discussion it is evident that one cannot present in an integrated framework of analysis a series of adjustable criteria that would work in both directions and in the same manner for the two structures. All that one can put forward is a series of required criteria to link the conflict to the cooperative structure, and a different series of criteria to allow transformations inside the conflictual structure, which will in turn allow bridges to be established between the two structures. In the case of the cooperative structure, we do not retain the number, size, or costs of operations as criteria, because they are not necessarily valid criteria to determine the efficiency of a peace process. For instance, the United Nations Protection Force (UNPROFOR) cost billions of dollars and involved the deployment of tens of thousands of personnel without real results. In addition, political costs, which are difficult to measure—such as the support (or lack thereof) of great powers for their local allies (e.g., Russia and the Serbs, China and the Khmer Rouge)—represent important political risks for the participants.

The risk criteria have to be considered in a broad sense. Studies of peacekeeping operations tend to present the risks as a function of the probable degree of hostility in a given environment, which in turn is defined by the type of mission considered. John Hillen presents the spectrum of UN peacekeeping operations in a diagram with the level of belligerency in the operational environment on the y-axis and the level of force required to implement the mandate on the x-axis. Thus one progresses from classical peacekeeping observation missions to second-generation peacekeeping operations and finally to peace enforcement operations (Hillen 1994, 56). Mats R. Berdal, after making a meticulous examination of second-generation operations, distinguishes three fundamental types of operations: those marked by a comprehensive political settlement, those in which governments have come out victorious from a civil war and remain responsible for demobilization and demilitarization (e.g., Uganda, Ethiopia in 1993, Eritrea), and finally, those that constitute coercive disarmament interventions in collapsed states (Berdal 1996, 18–20). Although they are not mutually exclusive, these categories have relevance in that they take into account the risks associated with different types of peace processes. To characterize the political aspects of the cooperative structure, these three criteria, slightly modified, are used to determine three different peace processes: a process based on comprehensive political settlements, a process of relegitimation of the government in place through the implementation of partial agreements, and a process of coercive intervention, in the case of collapsed states (see table 8.3).

In addition, several strategic elements have to be kept in mind in the assessment of the conditions of efficiency in the cooperative structure. These elements have already been mentioned in the course of the analysis and do not constitute a surprise. On the other hand, it is necessary to add tactical elements, as previous studies, notably that of Paul Diehl, demonstrate clearly that even the most promising peace plans often meet with failure if one is not able to separate the belligerents (Diehl 1993, 62–91). The more completely the belligerents are separated, the more efficient the mission will be. Similarly, results will often be mixed if the geographical situation does not allow for the clear separation of the groups in conflict, and risks will be even higher if a mission has to face troops or guerrilla forces on the ground.

In the conflictual structure, elements of transformation also appear to be important. These concern not the profile of efficiency but rather the potential of transformation, whose most important elements, without mentioning them all, include criteria listed in table 8.4.

In all cases, just as in the cooperative structure, pure situations do not exist. A specific operation can present characteristics that tally with several cells in table 8.4 or can shift from one stage to another as the operation unfolds. Strategic elements have a structural nature, whereas tactical elements are mostly determined by a decisive factor in the conflictual structure: the attitudes of the host state or parties to the conflict. According to Diehl, this variable is a determining factor in the evolution of an operation, and it constitutes, according to Hampson, one of the two criteria (the other being the end of violence) that determine the lasting character or success of an operation (Diehl 1993, 169–71; Hampson 1996, 207).

Table 8.3   The Profile of Efficiency in the Cooperative Structure

Context	Type of Intervention	Strategic Elements	Tactical Elements
Favorable	Legitimization of the political structure on the basis of comprehensive political settlements	Security Council consensus; creation of a contact group; support of regional powers; cooperation of states providing troops	Implementation of an effective ceasefire; clear separation of belligerent parties; cooperation of civil and military parties
Mixed	Relegitimization of the authorities	Mixed consensus in the Security Council; absence of leadership by a state; *ad hoc* or partial settlements	Scattered geographic layout of the belligerents; weak control over arms transfers into the region
Unfavorable	Coercive disarmament in collapsed states	Absence of settlements; repetitive exhortations by the Security Council	Presence of guerrilla or well-armed groups; absence of control over elements that are detrimental to law and order

Table 8.4   The Potential of Transformation of the Conflictual Structure

Context	Type of Intervention	Strategic Elements	Tactical Elements
Favorable	Legitimation of the political structure on the basis of comprehensive political settlements	Presence of legitimate representatives; a "way out" for all the parties; elaboration of democratic consociational mechanisms I	Demobilization and demilitarization of the parties in conflict; reconstruction of civil and military powers; linkage of economic and security problems
Mixed	Relegitimation of the authorities	Sanctions and rewards linked to progress on the ground; emergence of a central authority or a temporary leader	Partial or asymmetric demobilization in favor of the new authorities; holding of free elections, if possible
Unfavorable	Coercive disarmament in collapsed states	Marginalization of the most radical elements; persistence of factionalism and rivalries between clans	Widespread violence and absence of civil or military administrative structures

Any peacemaking process implies substantial structural transformations that are dependent on what happens in both the conflictual and cooperative structures. Bridges of negotiation are established through third parties that can modify the rules of the game by favoring equitable and balanced peace settlements, and through the judicious use of both the "stick" and the "carrot" to bring both sides to a lasting peace settlement (Hampson 1996, 11–12). It is only when these two structures converge that one can speak of a peace process that is oriented, directed, and controlled.

In second-generation operations the question of knowing whether to intervene has been most acutely raised. The structural transformations that have just been discussed are only one aspect of the transformation of a conflict. They specify only favorable, mixed, or unfavorable conditions for an intervention. Other sources of transformation are as important, notably the evolution and practices of the UN on the subject. It is therefore useful to look at the global context wherein new norms have appeared in the areas of human rights, civil reconstruction, and stabilization of the political structure of states. All these aspects have been partly discussed in the preceding pages, but it is important to understand how these processes tend to become legitimated through the operations of the UN.

THE NEW NORMS OF INTERVENTION

The UN can intervene to reestablish peace and security by virtue of Chapter VII of the UN Charter, whose wording clearly addresses actions to take in case of threats to the peace or breaches of the peace. In its history the

UN has attempted only twice to reestablish the peace: in Korea in 1950 and in Kuwait during the Gulf war in 1990–91. In the first case, most jurists agree on the juridical basis for the action of the UN. It related to Article 51 of the Charter, which enshrines the right of individual or collective self-defense. Other procedures could not be considered, because they required the unanimous vote of the five permanent members of the Security Council, and the USSR was, at the time, out of the Security Council. As a last resort, the resolution, "Uniting for Peace," was introduced to force the General Assembly to discuss the issue, but this did not correct the procedural flaw attached to the operations of the United Nations in Korea. With regard to the Gulf war, the judicial dispositions of the Charter were respected, although some experts questioned the decision of the Security Council because a breach of the peace had not been determined (in accordance with Article 39) before Resolution 688 went into effect, and the UN mandate was given to an *ad hoc* coalition instead of an international army raised in accordance with Articles 43 to 47 of the Charter.

Does the recent evolution of the UN confirm that its charter is a "living constitution"? Or, on the contrary, does it weaken the "constitutional integrity" of the organization?[1] There are some significant implications here: how can, or should, the Security Council exercise its quasi-legislative function? In addition, new norms are emerging in the case of internal-conflict resolution involving the UN: political settlements based on power-sharing agreements and the relegitimation of political authorities through the holding of free elections.

The Quasi-Legislative Authority of the Security Council

Since the creation of the UN, the Security Council has always had quasi-legislative power concerning threats to the peace or breaches of the peace, because it is the only organ able to act on the subject.[2] Whether one speaks of "legislative" or "quasi-legislative" power is not of great importance here, as this often depends on the definition that one wants to use.[3] Frederic Kirgis defines the three characteristics of the legislative power of the UN as follows: "[The decisions] are unilateral in form, they create or modify some element of a legal norm, and the legal norm in question is general in nature, that is, directed to indeterminate addressees and capable of repeated application in time" (1995, 520). The list of recent decisions of the Security Council taken in accordance with Chapter VII of the UN Charter is long (Roberts 1996, 47–48). Among them, one can mention the decision to impose an arms embargo on Somalia in January 1992 (Resolution 733), the authorization of the first military–humanitarian operation of the UN in Somalia in December 1992 (Resolution 794), the economic sanctions against Haiti in June 1993 (Resolution 841), and the authorization, in July

1994, of the resort "to all means necessary" to facilitate the return of President Jean-Bertrand Aristide in this same country (Resolution 940).

In all these cases, the decisions of the Security Council have been made without particular justifications being provided by members of the council as to the elements that threatened peace, international stability, or regional security. One must admit that the Security Council has a rather elastic notion of what constitutes a threat to peace and international security. More recently, the Security Council has decided to include the violation of human rights in the category of threats against peace. This decision, according to some analysts, constitutes a self-interpretation of the Charter that allows no possibility of judicial review (Malone and Cockell 1996, 13). For other analysts, it even constitutes a threat to multilateralism, in that it amounts to some form of unilateral privatization of Security Council enforcement action (Quigley 1996).

The decision to create courts for crimes committed against humanity in the former Yugoslavia (May 1993) and in Rwanda (November 1994) also has immediate consequences for members of the UN.[4] The statutes of these courts make provision for their precedence over national courts, and directives to this effect have been brought to the attention of the member states of the UN. In addition, Article 4 of the statutes of the court, established to judge crimes in Rwanda, grants to the court the power to prosecute in accordance with Article 3 of the Geneva Conventions and the additional Second Protocol. This article and protocol apply to internal armed conflicts. Kirgis notes, "It is absolutely impossible to believe that such a decision could be true to international criminal law" (1995, 524). In short, some of the recent decisions of the Security Council lend credence to the arguments of jurists worried by the tendency of the council to make unilateral decisions, without possibility of appeal, about what can be demanded of members of the international community.

United Nations interventions for humanitarian assistance purposes are also a potential source of controversy. Most humanitarian assistance operations have taken place with the consent of the host state, but sometimes, when confronted with the absence of a rightfully constituted authority, as in Somalia, they have undertaken the operation without consent. The recourse to Chapter VII to set up these operations constitutes a practice that the crafters of the Charter had not foreseen. Despite this, there has not been significant opposition to these operations within the international community. As Kirgis underlines, the tendency has been to evaluate these operations according to their cost and efficiency or on the basis of their success or failure rather than in terms of the validity of the legal innovation made by the Security Council (1995, 535).

On the whole, it is not exaggerated to speak of a UN constitutional crisis; and yet it would be wrong to ask that the organization hold to the strict principles of the Charter as the only foundation for its decisions. The UN has evolved, and so have the practices of the international community. However, as the report of David Malone and John Cockell indicates, much prudence is required in this evolutionary process:

> The Security Council must seriously consider whether it is to be only a political body, or also a law-making one. If it is to be solely political, then it should make only political decisions for specific cases and not engage in judicial functions. If the Council does wish to exercise judicial functions, then these must be applied with more care and according to principles and precedent. To date, law-making by the Security Council has been carried out in a clearly political fashion, and it will not likely be allowed to continue to do so indefinitely by the international community. (Malone and Cockell 1996, 13)

This separation of the political and judicial functions of the Security Council is not really relevant to a study of the UN's adaptation problems or to an explaination of the dichotomy between "judicial determinism" and "adaptable creativity."[5] To say that the UN must demonstrate much circumspection in justifying its quasi-legislative decisions seems obvious. If one can sometimes speak of "abuses of power" by the Security Council, one cannot indeed reproach it for having abdicated its responsibilities. This is all the more true since the organization has imposed new norms for the implementation of peace processes in internal conflicts. The judicial argument concerning the lack of constitutionality of certain Security Council decisions remains nevertheless persuasive.

Power Sharing and the Search for Democratic Values

Malone and Cockell make a distinction between the UN approach to internal conflicts that focus on "ideology or on control of state resources" and those that focus on "ethnic identity and group autonomy." In the first category, one includes such cases as the civil wars in Cambodia, El Salvador, Mozambique, and Nicaragua. In the second category, the situation is more complex, and one has to envisage some form of "power sharing" between rival ethnic groups "through such devices as regional autonomy, minority vetoes over government policy, and seat reservations for minorities in offices at the national level" (Malone and Cockell 1996, 14–15). In practice, it is not clear that these categories are as exclusive as one may think. All internal conflicts focus on control over power structures and the allocation of resources. However, in terms of policy advice, the authors of the report are correct: "Settlements based on majoritarian politics are easier to achieve and more likely to endure than interethnic power sharing" (ibid., 15).

In both types of conflicts, the Security Council intervenes in the internal affairs of a state. The practice is therefore innovative if one holds to a restrictive interpretation of the Charter. This transgression of Article 2(7) of the Charter must be interpreted as a temporary suspension of the prerogative of the state until the return of a politically stable or effective government. From a legal point of view, the UN attempts in all cases to reach an agreement with the host state so that all parties concur in the intervention. From a normative point of view, however, the procedures reveal a far more noble and complex purpose: the implementation of a peace process that rejects the resort to force as a way to resolve conflicts. From a political standpoint, it is probable that conflicts of the first category are better characterized by the search for a peace process in which democratic values (free elections, respect for democratic principles and human rights) take priority, whereas in conflicts of the second category, settlements based on some form of consociational arrangements are more likely.

The case of El Salvador clearly constitutes a "negotiated revolution" (Brody 1995; Karl 1992). Although it is true that much remains to be done, El Salvador is, nevertheless, now a pluralistic democracy with an independent supreme court, new security forces, and an improved human rights record. The San José Agreement, concluded in Costa Rica (July 26, 1990) was the first comprehensive agreement on human rights to be negotiated by the UN in the framework of a peace process. The New York Agreement (December 31, 1991), followed by the creation of ONUSAL (Observer Mission in El Salvador), the UN mission in charge of supervising the peace process (replaced by MINUSAL [Mission of the United Nations in El Salvador] in May 1995) and the Mexico Agreement (January 16, 1992) allowed the UN to demobilize and to demilitarize the belligerents, to build from scratch a new civilian police force, to reform the country's judicial system, and to supervise the presidential and legislative elections in March and April 1994. The operation itself had three divisions: a human rights division that came under the secretary general of the UN, a military division, and a police division. An electoral division was added later to ONUSAL as well as a unit, created in 1994, to deal with the delicate problem of land redistribution.

Successful conflict resolution in El Salvador began in 1987 with what became known as the Esquipulas II agreements, which were a driving force that allowed for the creation of a third-party negotiation structure whose main role was assumed by the UN. The case of El Salvador underlines a point made earlier: the implementation of a peace process depends also on basic conditions within the conflictual structure. In others words, the dynamics of international law and the actions of third parties are determining factors, but it is also necessary that favorable political conditions exist in the conflictual structure for the two structures to lead to a comprehensive peace settlement process.

Instances of peace processes based on power-sharing agreements are also instructive. The case of Cyprus, in particular, is a classic case of failure, in which third-party intervention occurred in a conflict that had not yet reached its "ripe moment," leading to a deadlock rather than a resolution to the conflict. Cambodia, on the other hand, is an example of the relative success of a peace process based on a power-sharing agreement, to the extent that free elections, under international supervision, have taken place in Cambodia. In contrast with Cyprus, where all political actors continue to assume their role, the Cambodian Khmer Rouge have practically been eliminated from the political scene by their refusal to participate in the peace process. In addition, many defections have taken place within their ranks, and the government in place appeared to control the situation, at least until the summer of 1997. If one adds the crisis in the former Yugoslavia to our assessment, it is probable that IFOR/SFOR (Implementation Force/Stabilization Force) plays a role in this similarly significant transformative process, in which again, a third-party intervention leads to the elimination or marginalization of the most radical elements in a conflict.

The UN has thus taken the lead in many important transformations within internal conflicts. Peace plans put forward by third parties have had two important normative effects: a process of democratization was initiated, and in some cases a process that might lead to a consociational arrangement has taken place. These developments are of great importance for the future of the UN and the international community. They are a vibrant testimony to the evolution of the UN and its capacity to adapt to situations that are not only difficult but were considered inextricable not long ago.

CONCLUSION

There is no magic recipe that provides a solution to the current UN crisis or a resolution to the recurrent internal conflicts that draw the attention of the international community. Our review of theoretical debates demonstrates the complexity of problems and the difficulty in discerning necessary conditions for the transformation of the conflictual and cooperative structures into an efficient and durable peace process.

The international system is undergoing a metamorphosis, and the Security Council, obsolete as it is, has not yet abdicated its responsibilities. There is evidence of a strong link between the way parties behave in ethnic conflicts and the way the international community responds to these challenges. An absence of reaction strengthens elites in their perceptions that their acts of violence will go unpunished and that they can maintain specialized institutions in the exercise of violence (Carment 1994, 574). Conversely, frequent negotiations aimed at transforming collapsed states can encourage the development of democratic institutions respectful of human rights and democratic freedoms (ibid., 1994, 574).

A firm answer to the question of when to intervene and when to abstain from intervention remains elusive. However, some elements of the answer are clear. First, the peace process has to be supported by the regional powers, great powers, and third parties. Second, comprehensive peace settlements create more favorable expectations for the resolution of a conflict than partial agreements. Third, tactical elements such as the separation of belligerents and the existence of well-conceived demilitarization and demobilization plans must also be taken into consideration. From a normative perspective, it appears that the international community is willing to intervene in internal conflicts, but it is necessary to recognize at the same time that the UN is exhausted, that its resources are limited, and that several states resent being told how to behave by the international community.

Three points must be made here. First, as long as the Security Council remains fundamentally status-quo oriented while continuing to put forward global-conflict settlement proposals based on the dynamics of international law and of peace processes, the international community will only be the better for it. After all, if the "end of history" conveys effectively the Hegelian notion that history has reached its term through the triumph of democracy, then it is also reasonable to think that democracies should promote democracy and help countries to become democratic. Second, peace processes, as the title of the work of Fen Osler Hampson (1996) indicates, have to be nurtured. In this regard, international organizations are indispensable, because they have a universal character and can create a sense of a common goal. Finally, despite the conservative attitudes of some international jurists, only new ideas can effectively serve as legitimate standards to establish norms. These ideas should be introduced gradually and must be based on the rejection of violence as an instrument of conflict resolution. Here, the danger comes not so much from institutional weaknesses or judicial negligence by the Security Council as from the fact that in some circumstances, the strongest and the most powerful states do not relinquish the resort to force and thus legitimate the principle of double standards or the rule that might is right.

The main difficulty in the establishment of a peace process is the linkage between the conflictual and cooperative structures so that both are peace-oriented. Negotiations are possible only if the two structures are held in balance. In reality, what is being asked of the international community is that the international system be ordered according to principles of equal and just peace and based on a real liberalism and an international community bound by solidarity—what Barry Buzan calls a "gemeinschaft" (1993, 333).

NOTES

Funding from the Social Sciences and Humanities Research Council of Canada made this work possible. The author wishes to thank his research assistant, Dr. Thierry Gongora, for the editing of this article in English.

1. For a positive interpretation of the evolution of the UN, see Kirgis (1995). Joaquin Tacsan, former legal counsel for Costa-Rican president Oscar Arias Sanchez, recipient of the Nobel Peace Prize for his role in the peace process in Central America, argues that the terms of the debate are situated somewhere between the neopositive legal school and the sociological jurisprudence school of public policy, of which the leading figure was Myres S. McDougal. According to Tascan, it is necessary to establish links between the two schools in order to correctly asses "both the influence of decision making on international law and the impact of legal norms on the process by which actors attempt to resolve their conflicts" (1992, 14).

2. According to Chapter VI, which deals with the pacific settlement of disputes, the Security Council uses quasi-judicial powers in accordance with Article 37(2) of the Charter, in particular if it reaches a decision on the merit of a conflict and if the Security Council's conclusions contain normative statements or recommendations that could have normative consequences (Kirgis 1995, 527).

3. The phrase *legislative power* is judged to be improper by some analysts, because the Security Council is not a body elected by a majority, it is not representative of the international community, and the right of veto is not in accordance with democratic values. The responsibility of the Security Council to act in the name of all members of the UN imposes a crucial and solemn obligation: to act in accordance with the Charter and the provisions of other international legal agreements. In this regard, it is difficult to believe that the International Court of Justice has the necessary legitimacy to carry out legal examination of the decisions of the Security Council in matters of peace enforcement. The Security Council remains, therefore, the sole master of the legal examination of its decisions (Reisman 1993).

4. These courts were created in accordance with Chapter VII of the Charter, although they are considered subsidiary organs of the Security Council in accordance with Article 29 of the Charter. Serbia and Montenegro have stated their opposition to such a practice unforeseen in the Charter, on grounds that the Security Council assumed responsibilities beyond the scope of its "implicit powers." Kirgis nevertheless considers this decision to be constitutionally defensible, because the Security Council availed itself of Article 39, the decisions of the court remain free from political control, and the procedure followed for the establishment of the courts is essentially valid (1995, 523).

5. Kirgis takes a more ambiguous position than Malone and Cockell. He writes:

> At the same time, if the Council is to be effective in the long run, it needs to demonstrate that it is using the powers judiciously. In this context, it needs to make, and to demonstrate that it is making, a genuine effort to determine what the threat to international peace actually is, and how serious it is. It may be that such late-twentieth-century phenomena as the mobility of masses of people across international borders, the communications explosion and the attendant heightened concern for the suffering of people at the hands of their own

governments, the diminishing significance of traditional international boundaries with the rise of nonstate nations and their claims for recognition, and the widespread availability of highly destructive weapons to nongovernmental actors, as well as to governments, lead unavoidably and quite properly to a much expanded definition of "threat to international peace" than could have been intended fifty years ago. (Kirgis 1995, 516–17)

9

Enforcement without Military Combat: Toward an International Civilian Police

Robert C. Johansen

THE CONTRIBUTIONS OF ENFORCEMENT TO HUMANE GLOBAL GOVERNANCE

Readily available technologies of destruction, peoples' capacity for collective violence, and environmental fragilities make all contemporary societies, even the militarily most powerful, highly vulnerable. Because people have no choice but to live within territorial boundaries that have become highly permeable, peace and human security can no longer be achieved without ensuring that all people everywhere obey at least a few fundamental rules that prohibit genocide and severely threatening actions, whether of a military, migratory, or environmental nature. Indeed, global governance that provides an overarching set of enforceable norms seems the only way of overcoming the self-defeating behavior summed up in both the security dilemma and the tragedy of the commons, each encompassing a series of approaching calamities that threaten the human species because of possibilities for economic and environmental disruption and collective violence. Difficult though it may be to accomplish, peace and security can be substantially enhanced only by taking further steps to domesticate the international system (Johansen 1996).

Experience with the enforcement of law in domestic, democratic societies demonstrates that people comply with basic legal norms out of habit, convenience, conviction, or some combination of these but not primarily because they cower before heavily armed law enforcers. They feel a sense of commitment to the legal order and live amid a pervasive culture of com-

173

pliance. Moreover, when explicit enforcement mechanisms *do* determine behavior, for most people the enforcement consequences they seek to avoid are embarrassment, social opprobrium, and monetary fines. Only those we label as socially deviant seek to escape legal norms through drastic means that invite the risk of arrest at gunpoint and prolonged imprisonment.

Although within democratic societies most people willingly comply with most laws most of the time, some instruments for even coercive enforcement *are* necessary to ensure respect for human rights and a minimal level of social and economic predictability, cooperation, and personal security. In international relations, enforcement is particularly difficult because of the weakness of social bonds, ethical constraints, and legal and political institutions across ethnic, religious, and state boundaries. As a result, since ancient times many people—although not all—have considered wars to be legitimate instruments for settling intersocietal disputes, because governing functions *between* societies have been nonexistent or extremely unreliable. Even the human species' best effort at prohibiting aggressive war and instituting community-wide enforcement, the United Nations Charter, "governs" international conflicts primarily by asking the great powers, through the Security Council's collective security mechanism, to employ military force if all else fails to maintain the peace. The failures of collective security are legion, and even when faced with the most obvious of needs, such as addressing unconscionable deeds of genocide in Bosnia or Rwanda, the international community has not cooperated well to halt vast human suffering.

Until very recently, governments have not sought to establish a rule of law in world affairs in which *individuals*, rather than entire societies, would be held accountable to fundamental norms of peace and human rights. A permanent international criminal court legally competent to try individuals has not even existed, although the international community is now poised to make significant breakthroughs in this regard.

Few people disagree with the idea that the existing prohibitions against genocide and war, established in the Nuremberg and Tokyo war crimes tribunals after World War II, ought to be enforced. Yet most governments and individuals have never committed themselves to international measures that could enforce fundamental norms of peace and human rights at reasonable cost. If we want to counter the mental and moral inertia sustaining today's war-prone, inequitable international system, we need to question the widespread assumption that it will be impossible to hold individuals accountable to international law until we can hold states accountable to law through collective security mechanisms. In this chapter, I reject the notion that the international community's inability to hold national governments strictly accountable to fundamental legal norms is sufficient reason to abandon the search for more imaginative means by which to hold individuals, including officials, accountable to international law. Even imperfect initiatives to hold *individuals* accountable are normatively preferable to a focus on military instruments designed to hold *states* accountable, because the former emphasize personal responsibility to honor specific norms in a way that wars of enforcement against entire societies never can. The initiatives emphasizing individual accountability also contribute more directly to political precedents essential for constructing a more peaceful world community in the long run. More successful forms of UN *police* enforcement might be able to contribute as much to the enforcement needed in global governance as efforts to achieve UN enforcement through military combat.

This chapter demonstrates that desirable, practical steps to enforce law on individuals and to deter mass killing can be taken without jeopardizing any country's legitimate security interests if more governments and citizens commit themselves to these goals: (1) to hold individuals accountable, insofar as possible, to fundamental international norms of peace and human rights, including the prohibition of genocide and other crimes against humanity, crimes against the peace (aggressive war), and other war crimes; and (2) to aim at strengthening UN capabilities for employing civilian police and legal enforcement more extensively and for providing war-torn societies with a flexible justice package, including highly trained UN police, conflict experts, and internationally sponsored judicial proceedings where needed. This strategy would encourage or require individuals, regardless of rank or position in society, to honor widely agreed upon international norms of peace and human rights. For the international community to pursue this direction, would mean, at the top of the political hierarchy, taking war crimes investigations, indictments, and extraditions far more seriously. At the bottom of the political hierarchy, it would mean international or regional agencies attending sensitively enough to local people's interests and needs in war-torn societies or failed states to encourage local consent to and participation in the administration of a UN justice package with the goal of transforming conflicts from lethal to nonlethal modes of containment or resolution.

This analysis proceeds, first of all, by explaining what is meant by enforcement and by defining several other concepts for this analysis. After briefly noting some contributions of UN military operations, economic sanctions, and peacekeeping to the enforcement of compliance with the norms of peace, the main part of the analysis focuses on past and potential contributions that UN civilian police and related judicial proceedings can make to peace and security.

Norms of Peace

The "norms of peace" refer collectively to prohibitions of crimes against the peace (aggressive war), war crimes (e.g., mistreatment of civilians or prisoners of war), crimes against humanity (e.g., genocide or other mass killing), and gross violations of human rights that constitute a threat to the peace or cause numerous civilian deaths (e.g., "ethnic cleansing" in Bosnia–Herzegovina or the obstruction of efforts by relief agencies to avert mass starvation in Somalia in 1993). Although these international norms protect human rights as much as they govern matters of war and peace, I refer to them as the norms of peace to simplify the narrative and reflect the Security Council's preference to rationalize its interventionary actions by relating them to its primary responsibility for maintaining peace.

Enforcement

Enforcement is used here to mean UN actions, ranging from positive inducements to military coercion taken under Chapter VII of the UN Charter, to ensure that states comply with the well-established norms of peace and new Security Council decisions that may be made to maintain peace and security. The term frequently refers to economic sanctions or military action against a country, but it can also include war crimes tribunals and the use of domestic courts to enforce international law on individuals. An action to deprive a UN member of its vote, in accord with Article 19, because it is delinquent in paying its dues is also a form of enforcement. The distinguishing feature of UN enforcement is that, unlike peacekeeping, it does not wait for the consent of a lawbreaking state or other party to take action against those committing misdeeds.

Despite the tendency to associate coercive and punitive actions with enforcement, a more complete and profound understanding of enforcement recognizes that in a general sense enforcement is "merely" a form of authoritative influence on a potential or actual lawbreaker to deter or prevent normatively unacceptable behavior. In this more general sense, enforcement at some points overlaps with compliance based on consent. Thus what I have described as the distinguishing feature of enforcement, namely, its coercive element, may not always be heavy handed or even highly visible. In fact enforcement at its best achieves compliance without employing guns or using violence. A potential outlaw, after assessing costs and benefits, may consent to obey the law after all.

To be sure, enforcement denotes an element of finality: illegal actions must cease. Yet in some instances finality is not immediate and may be achieved without military force. For example, a domestic law requiring a person to provide an accurate accounting of income for the purpose of taxation is usually enforced through a system of interest penalties for failure to pay the proper amount of income tax at the prescribed time. Similarly, UN economic sanctions against South Africa, designed to end *apartheid*, were enforcement actions. Yet this enforcement instrument did not produce immediate results, nor was the outcome of sanctions, once they had been initiated, at all certain. Even if they had not succeeded in ending apartheid, they would still be considered enforcement actions. In short, actions need not be military or always effective to be considered enforcement.

Cultures of Compliance and of Military Enforcement

Successful enforcement in the global arena, as in the local community, often is nested within what might be called a culture of compliance—beliefs, values, norms, symbols, institutions, and sanctions—rather than relying entirely or even primarily on sheer physical force. Although important, cultural factors are not frequently emphasized in domestic law enforcement; similarly, they are almost never addressed in discussions about how to innovate in the field of UN enforcement. However, unless they are given serious attention, the inertia of the quite different, existing culture of military enforcement, or more simply, the "culture of combat," rooted as it is in political realist thinking about the importance of preparation for military combat and the requirements of a militarily competitive balance of power system, will overshadow even modest suggestions to implement a new multilateral strategy of enforcement, as the lack of serious response to Boutros Boutros-Ghali's *Agenda for Peace* (1995) has made clear.

The point is not that military thinking is unimportant but rather that it is only one part, and often a distracting part, of a broad spectrum of enforcement instruments within a culture of compliance. This culture includes elements of positive inducement (e.g., development assistance to a state conditioned upon policies aimed at social integration and respect for human rights), mutual obligation (e.g., reciprocal respect and cooperation in agreeing to submit any disputes over allegedly genocidal treatment of minorities to an international tribunal), and enforcement (e.g., arrests of indicted persons who leave shielding sanctuaries, UN-directed freezing of assets of elites violating the norms of peace, preventive deployments of UN forces to deter military aggression, or more traditional military action in the interests of collective security and in response to threats to the peace).

A culture of compliance is manifested when a constabulary or police agency representing the community is authorized by the community to enforce norms established by the community on members within the community, and to conduct such enforcement within prescribed procedures guaranteeing a maximum of fairness and a minimum of violence. In contrast, a culture of military enforcement is encouraged when, in normal international relations, one country threatens or uses force to enforce norms that it interprets in a manner it unilaterally deems appropriate to advance its interests against another party. A culture of compliance can easily degenerate into a culture of combat if an enforcing agent does not represent the community, if the norms to be enforced have not been established by the community, if disputes over the meaning of the norms are not settled impartially, if the enforcement mechanism itself denies equal respect for human lives, or if a pattern of enforcement develops in which the norms are applied to some but not to all members of the community. Conversely, a culture of combat can evolve into a culture of compliance if the conditions noted previously are increasingly met.

United Nations enforcement has functioned at the interface of these two cultures, endorsing collective violence in some cases but attempting to do so only after international norms have been impartially applied to a government's conduct and the use of force has been authorized by Security Council decision. Whereas police enforcement and a culture of compliance are usually mutually reinforcing, military enforcement and a culture of combat sustain each other. Existing support for military instruments greatly impedes the domestication of international conduct that is essential if the international community seeks to make enforcement more reliable at a reasonable cost. When it is either impossible or undesirable to develop a globally centralized UN military capability, then innovations in nonmilitary areas take on added importance. Although conventional usage of the term *enforcement* includes strategies ranging from mild inducements to major military activity under Chapter VII of the Charter, enforcement is ethically more desirable and politically more feasible when it achieves compliance by relying on police and legal instruments rather than military means. Although a strictly nonviolent strategy is not a defining element of enforcement, such a strategy is an aspiration toward which short- and long-term goals should aim. Although even a well-developed culture of compliance will not be able to eliminate all illegal acts, in many cases a potential outlaw, after assessing costs and benefits, will ultimately decide to obey the law after all.

Impartiality

Confusion arises if and when observers of UN operations believe that the desire for impartiality necessarily means doing nothing to halt illegal behavior. To avoid terminological confusion, I use the term neutrality to refer to the stance of UN peacekeepers who passively do nothing in the face of clear violations of fundamental norms, to avoid taking a stand for or against a particular adversary. I use *impartiality* to refer to UN actions that attempt to uphold, even forcefully, fundamental norms by holding all actors equally accountable to the norm, without regard for the nationality of wrongdoers. A neutral observer is passive and refuses to alienate either of the sides in a dispute; an impartial official is active and adheres impartially to established rules, even if so doing alienates one or more violators of the rules. Both terms can be distinguished from *partiality*, which is exhibited when UN personnel (inappropriately) impose rules on one nationality but not on its adversary. In my parlance, *peacekeepers* may often remain *neutral* because they seek to perform valuable buffering functions while operating within a state-centric frame of reference, aiming to maintain good diplomatic relations with all concerned, even offenders. Civilian *police* normally apply law *impartially* on individuals, regardless of nationality and without expecting the alleged offender to be pleased about arrest. Although police may be unarmed or less heavily armed than peacekeepers, the former may be less neutral and more impartial. In this usage, *neutrality* and *impartiality* may sharply diverge. For example, if almost all illegal acts in a two-sided conflict are committed by one party, a neutral observer who does nothing to stop illegalities fails to uphold the law with impartiality.

Peacekeeping

For the purposes of this analysis *peacekeeping* includes (1) traditional monitoring and buffering activities of UN forces and (2) expanded activities of election monitoring, demobilizing belligerents, and administrative functions to facilitate transition from war to peace. These activities are carried out by contingents of armed forces or civilian police contributed by member nations for special UN duty to patrol borders or cease-fire lines in order to defuse misunderstandings and to prevent incidents between adversaries from escalating. The classic examples are the two United Nations Emergency Forces (UNEF I and UNEF II) that served as buffers between Egyptian and Israeli forces. Whether operating in limited monitoring roles or more expanded administrative tasks, UN peacekeeping forces are deployed with the consent of the adversaries, carry only light arms, fire their weapons only as a last resort in self-defense, usually maintain a neutral posture between two or more adversaries, and do not perform generally coercive functions.

Compliance and Enforcement

A culture of compliance contributes to enforcement in diverse ways. If a culture of compliance, which includes norms and values as well as UN police and internationally assisted judicial processes, eventually results in obedience by most parties to a major international norm such as the prohibition of genocide, for example, it *is* enforcement. In general usage, *to enforce* means "to urge," as well as "to bring about through coercion." Article 41 of Chapter VII clearly anticipates several nonmilitary enforcement measures. Whereas peacekeeping traditionally was authorized under Chapter VI of the Charter, which deals with pacific settlement, enforcement has been authorized under Chapter VII. More recently, enforcement mechanisms under Chapter VII have been invoked for a variety of military and nonmilitary UN enforcement operations in Iraq, Rwanda, Haiti, Somalia, and the former Yugoslavia. The Security Council established the war crimes tribunals for the former Yugoslavia and Rwanda with a Chapter VII decision, marking the first time that a UN enforcement mechanism took this judicial form and reminding us of the flexibility that may be employed in considering enforcement instruments. Of the many instruments that comprise enforcement, each contributes differently to enforcement, to a culture of compliance, and thereby to humane global governance.

THE CONTRIBUTIONS OF UNITED NATIONS MILITARY ENFORCEMENT, ECONOMIC SANCTIONS, AND PEACEKEEPING TO A CULTURE OF COMPLIANCE

Both positive and negative UN experiences with military combat, economic sanctions, and peacekeeping demonstrate the need for and promise in expanded police enforcement. Although space does not allow treatment of these alternative instrumentalities here, the humanitarian crises in Somalia, Sudan, the former Yugoslavia, Rwanda, Zaire, and elsewhere in the 1990s have demonstrated the international community's lack of enthusiasm for undertaking military combat to enforce the norms of peace. Even the apparently successful use of military force against Iraq's annexation of Kuwait constitutes a rare exception, and the subsequent erosion of support for the military option illustrates the limits of even overwhelming military power in a clear-cut case of aggression.

Regardless of where one stands on the spectrum of opinion regarding the advisability of the UN's acquisition of military force, it seems unlikely that the UN will establish its own military capability in the foreseeable future. Realism requires us to acknowledge that military combat frequently exacts unbearable political, military, and moral costs. Indeed, that is precisely why stronger UN action was rejected in many recent conflicts. Because UN members are reluctant to support military enforcement in most cases, whether for good or for dubious reasons, we might make a virtue of necessity and explore whether more creative space lies outside the realm of both traditional peacekeeping and the resort to large-scale military force. The claim is not that this space can provide a panacea. It is the more modest claim that the international community has undervalued an approach to enforcement that could be potentially useful in some cases, if only because all other avenues, including the feeble enforcement and follow-up made familiar in Rwanda and Bosnia, are unpromising in comparison.

The amazing growth in the number of instances in which economic sanctions have been considered or employed in recent years attests to the difficulties of employing military force for enforcement and the lack of imagination in developing other Article 41 enforcement instruments. Economic sanctions have several merits: They exert coercive power, so when coercion is needed they offer the world community leverage to encourage a noncomplying country to change its behavior. Because they are usually less costly than war in human and financial terms, political support for them can more readily be generated than for military enforcement. They are morally preferable to military enforcement because they almost always result in less loss of life than does war. Yet, as sanctions in Iraq, Haiti, and elsewhere have shown, they may contribute to death for many already living on the margins of subsistence, and they often have limited effectiveness (Lopez and Cortright 1995, 3–16; Eland 1995, 29–42).

The prevailing wisdom has been that economic sanctions, like military operations, are most effective when they impose heavy costs very quickly. However, in some cases a nearly opposite strategy may have merit (United States 1993). If one is attempting to extradite a handful of individuals who have been indicted for war crimes, for example, economic sanctions may be more likely to influence behavior positively if they seriously inconvenience only a relatively small elite located in the areas shielding an indictee and are maintained, if necessary, for a long time. Such an approach has a better chance of avoiding (1) severely negative consequences for a large number of people and (2) rally-round-the-flag phenomena for the government of the target state. United Nations authorities also can provide assurance of benefits to the surrounding society in the event the targeted misbehavior ends, allowing sanctions to be immediately lifted. The goal, of course, is to affect those wanted for crimes without harming the entire population. Sanctions that freeze assets and stop international travel of elites, for example, are not a way of bringing a society to its knees, but they can bring pressure on elites to quit shielding indictees, to allow extradition of the accused for a fair trial, or to discourage future crimes. The "smarter" and more precise sanctions become, the larger the step toward individual accountability.

No multilateral practice has contributed more to understanding the possibilities and pitfalls of establishing an effective UN civilian police force than the experience of UN peacekeeping. One corps of peacekeepers, the Blue Berets, have been unarmed and have performed largely as civilian police. They and the Blue Helmets have demonstrated that significant measures for dampening violence can be employed successfully when drawing on strengths such as the UN's international legitimacy; the willingness of contributing governments not only to supply soldiers but also to place them under the command of persons of another nationality, thereby subordinating nationality slightly for the benefit of the international community; the practice of constraining the use of force, limiting it to self-defense; the protection of innocent bystanders and the provision of humanitarian assistance to them where possible; and the maintenance of neutrality toward adversaries while on occasion also acting impartially to dissuade potential violators of a cease-fire.

Most of these conditions provide useful precedents and experience to demonstrate the feasibility and promise in a UN police force. Occasionally, peacekeepers themselves have engaged in a modest form of enforcement, even while acting under Chapter VI mandates, insofar as peacekeepers attempt to prevent individuals or small groups of people from violating a cease-fire that they have been deployed to uphold—even while maintaining neutrality toward the primary parties to the cease-fire. Negative factors in peacekeeping experience also have demonstrated the need for better training, for an ombudsman and grievance procedure for local people to bring complaints against UN personnel if their behavior is inappropriate, and for a more reliable form of financing.

Whereas the chief deficiency of military enforcement lies in its failure to nurture a culture of compliance because it legitimates collective violence and national partisanship, and whereas the primary deficiency of economic sanctions is its bluntness and normatively ambiguous impact, the main deficiency of peacekeeping is its failure to move beyond neutrality when necessary to act against gross violations of the norms of peace. More effective use of UN police offers possibilities for addressing each of these deficiencies, at least in part.

THE CONTRIBUTIONS OF UNITED NATIONS CIVILIAN POLICE TO A CULTURE OF COMPLIANCE

Because the UN cannot conduct combat well, because combat is not normatively desirable, and because economic sanctions and peacekeeping do not sufficiently pinpoint individual responsibility for misdeeds and call perpetrators to international accountability, the UN has good reason to explore an expanded role for UN police.

Early Recognition of the Need for a United Nations Constabulary

The need for a UN constabulary was recognized long ago but was never taken seriously by most governments. The first UN secretary-general, Trygvie Lie, recommended "the creation of a small United Nations Guard Force which could be recruited by the Secretary-General and placed at the disposal of the Security Council and the General Assembly." Lie continued, "Such a force would not be used as a substitute for the forces contemplated in Articles 42 and 43. It would not be a striking force, but purely a guard force." In addition, it could be used "as a constabulary in cities like Jerusalem and Trieste during the establishment of international regimes. It might also be called upon by the Security Council under Article 40 of the Charter, which provides for provisional measures to prevent the aggravation of a situation threatening peace" (Lie 1948, xvii–xviii).

Speaking in 1948, Lie said that "if [the guard force] had existed during the past year it would, I believe, have greatly increased the effectiveness of the work of the Security Council, and have saved many lives, particularly in Indonesia and Palestine" (ibid., xviii). In speaking on a similar theme fifteen years later, UN secretary-general U Thant, said, "I have no doubt that the world should eventually have an international police force which will be accepted as an integral and essential part of life in the same way as national police forces are accepted" (Thant 1963, 361). The well-known realist student of the international organization, Lincoln Bloomfield, concludes that the needed security framework "should . . . look more like law enforcement than war-fighting." A politically credible approach to collective security "will thus initially feature not armies, navies, and air forces but a step-by-step police process that mimics familiar domestic law enforcement . . ." (Bloomfield 1993, 201).[1]

A UN police and law-enforcement option is less likely to produce political backlash within the UN community or within the domestic society in which some officials are targets of investigations or arrests. It is not likely to provoke reckless counteractions, and it can be delivered with reasonable cost. It may not be immediately effective, but it can almost always be effective in part, and it is better than doing nothing. With this option, the UN stance against genocide can clearly exist before, during, and after a crisis, and if some persons are indicted for wrongdoing, they stand stigmatized before the world until they have appeared for trial to defend themselves. A UN coalition can continue to ask for investigations and trials until they occur. The police and law enforcement option also does not threaten vital interests of the target and thus decreases the prospect that a coalition will arise against the UN out of empathy for the wider society. All that is asked of the targeted individuals is that they obey the law.

Past UN Experience with Civilian Police

The United Nations of course has had experience with civilian police, because many peacekeeping missions have had small numbers of police participating in their operations. For example, the United Nations Civilian Police (UNCIVPOL) have been an important part of the United Nations Force in Cyprus (UNFICYP). A "constabulary ethic—the maintenance of order with the minimum of force"—was a principal guideline in preparing personnel for UNFICYP (Brown, Barker, and Burke 1984, 2). The civilian police unit within UNFICYP became "an outstanding success." The police subculture that civilians brought to the mission made UNCIVPOL better prepared than other types of personnel for interactions with the local police and citizenry. UNCIVPOL demonstrated that well-trained civilian police in peacekeeping operations could play a valuable role in dampening violence between hostile nationalities (ibid., 160, 166).

United Nations civilian police also set many new precedents in Namibia. The fifteen hundred United Nations civilian police monitors, nicknamed CIVPOL, closely monitored South African police units, defused incidents, and induced the local police administrators to perform in a way that made the elections there highly successful (UN Doc. S/20883 [October 6, 1989], 7–8). In addition, CIVPOL monitored political gatherings, observed voter registration and polling stations, and guarded ballot boxes, "together with local police." The United Nations Transition Assistance Group (UNTAG) used its police to conduct their own patrols to accompany the local police on their patrols. The UN police "curbed intimidation by local police and . . . maintained the cease-fire" (Fortna 1993, 365–71).

In the United Nations Transition Authority in Cambodia (UNTAC) thirty-six hundred civilian police were mandated not only to monitor but also to "supervise and control" the police of the existing Cambodian governing structures. This police experience was hampered by inadequate training, poor coordination, lack of experience in working together, inability to speak Khmer (more detrimental for effective functioning of police than of soldiers), lack of equipment, and lack of knowledge about driving police vehicles, all together making the operation, in Michael Doyle's characterization, "nothing short of quixotic" (1995, 48). Although CIVPOL was not prepared to carry out its ambitious mandate "to ensure that law and order are maintained" (United Nations Secretary-General 1992, para. 124), CIVPOL did give briefings on responsible policing to Cambodian police, and in at least one province, CIVPOL training "had a substantial impact and united all four [Cambodian political] factions." The training opportunities enabled CIVPOL to develop rapport with local police encouraged better communication with people at the local level. This in turn facilitated UN monitoring of human rights and "contributed to a general reduction in the most blatant forms of state intimidation" (Doyle 1995, 47–48).

Of special relevance to our search for nurturing enforcement through a culture of compliance is Doyle's report that the "single largest cause" of

UNTAC failures in the realm of public security "lay in the absence of an independent judicial framework" (ibid., 49). United Nations police had the authority to make arrests, and they acquired a facility to use as a UN prison: but the UN mission had no way to prosecute. Without the authority to establish a UN court or to take prisoners to an existing international tribunal, no system of legal order could come into being. This deficiency, which member governments did nothing to correct, easily discredits the genuine possibilities that could exist for using UN police more effectively and for deterring future misdeeds. The UNTAG special prosecutor, Mark Plunkett (1994, 65–78), recommended that any future UN peace-building operation include a "justice package" with carefully prepared agencies for prosecution, policing, and judicial proceedings. These should be established along with a mandate to train local people in the use of these and similar institutions. Appropriate UN training "can ensure that a UN operation leaves institutions behind that, with the proper domestic and international support, help carry forward a commitment to impartial justice and human rights" (quoted in Doyle 1995, 49).

To the extent that UNTAC achieved success, it was by communicating directly to the people about the meaning and importance of the election. Lieutenant General John Sanderson, UNTAC commander, said the strategy became to "bypass the propaganda of the Cambodian factions" and forge an "alliance with the Cambodian people" (ibid., 55). Toward this end the UN had its own radio broadcasting facilities with broadcasts received in part over 143,000 radios given by private Japanese donors. Despite continued violence and efforts to intimidate voters, 90 percent of Cambodian citizens turned out for their first national election.

After the UN mission left, the voters were vulnerable to the corrupt military forces, police, and other officials that had existed before the election was held. Yet a substantial degree of this could have been prevented if UN police had been available to remain in place after the election was over.

A rather amazing development in reestablishing the police in Somalia illustrates the enormous unrealized potential that lies in differentiating police from the military instrument in enforcement. A revealing study by the International Peace Academy demonstrates that "the military mind set" guiding the United Nations Unified Task Force (UNITAF) and continuing through the UN Operation in Somalia (UNOSOM) II committed many errors in what "should have essentially been a civilian operation, in large part because UNOSOM II was led by former and serving officials from the U.S. military establishment and the U.S. National Security Council." Indeed, "all civilian international efforts were subsumed by the military objectives of the U.S. and the UN. . . . By the time these military objectives changed in October 1993, UNOSOM II had become too discredited to be seen as an honest broker in the political process." For a time at least, the UN "had become too discredited to play an effective role in Somalia" (Jan 1996, 3–4). A more effective approach "would have been to help create civilian authorities in areas controlled by a unified clan and endorsed by the faction that served as the military arm of that clan. In this way, indigenous and authoritative clan-based civilian authorities could have been fostered" (Doyle 1995, 49).

After the "can-do" military forces had departed without success in restoring order, and despite years of fighting among heavily armed Somali clans, an indigenous police force has been gradually reconstituted with UN help to reestablish the rule of law in Somalia. To institute this process a political committee composed of members of the more powerful Somali clans met and decided that a security force was needed to deal with refugee problems but that clan military were not appropriate for that task. To create a new local police force, many former members of the Somali police, which had not functioned since 1991, were willing to put clan differences aside and serve their fellow citizens. The reconstituted police forces were the most effective where they were coordinated and supported by UNITAF (Sismanidis 1997, 10–11).

The Somali case demonstrates both the success of modest policing efforts where heavy-handed military operations had failed and the ability of UN civilian police to work cooperatively with local elders and community leaders to elicit "consent" for a UN involvement when meaningful consent had previously been lacking. This is an extremely important lesson, because the scope of UN enforcement can be enormously expanded at acceptable cost if a society consents to the UN presence. Without host consent, UN police can operate only at a distance and are far less likely to meet with success.

The experience of UN police in Bosnia illustrates the gap between mission purpose and the capabilities of the police. The International Police Task Force (IPTF) in Bosnia was mandated to "monitor, observe, and inspect law-enforcement activities; advise law-enforcement personnel; train law-enforcement personnel; assess threats to public order; advise on law-enforcement restructuring; facilitate assistance to law enforcement; and assist by accompanying law-enforcement personnel as they carry out their duties" (Sismanidis 1997, 9). With a deployed strength of thirteen hundred in a deeply fragmented and violent region, it is simply impossible for a small number of police to carry out such far-reaching functions. Even seventy thousand NATO soldiers were not asked to perform such extensive tasks.

The goal of attempting to ensure that local law-enforcement agencies act in accord with international human rights standards is laudable. It also is achievable, but only with sufficient numbers of UN police, adequate training, and good equipment. In the Sarajevo region, the Dayton accords called upon the UN police to establish "a sense of community confidence to minimize the exodus of Bosnian Serbs from the suburbs" as the region was transferred from Serbian to Bosnian Muslim control; to maintain ethnic balance and appropriate activities of the Bosnian Muslim–Croatian federation police; to discourage and control refugee influx in transition regions; and to coordinate collaborative efforts among local officials, IPTF, IFOR, the United Nations High Commissioner for Refugees (UNHCR), and other groups working at peace building. Although the UN police lacked the capabilities to maintain law and order, when problems arose in the transition areas many said the UN had once again failed to carry out its responsibilities. Yet the success of UN police in other difficult contexts suggests that they could have succeeded also in Sarajevo if they had been deployed in sufficient numbers and with appropriate preparation.

The Need for United Nations Civilian Police

The preceding historical examples suggest there are four important needs for a standing UN civilian police force. First is the need to provide an impartial, professional constabulary that is highly educated, well trained, well integrated and disciplined, well commanded, multinational, immediately available for deployment, and responsive only to the United Nations rather than to possibly confusing signals from national capitals. This force could be used to replace local police when they are fundamentally inadequate in implementing peace accords, executing peace building, or upholding international norms of peace and human rights. The need for an impartial UN constabulary to ensure civil order and security has been evident in locations such as Mostar, for example, where Croatian police officers opened fire on a peaceful Muslim procession on its way to a cemetery in February 1997. United Nations police filmed and identified Croatian police firing pistols into the fleeing crowd, including Ivan Hrkac, West Mostar's deputy police chief (Chris Hedges, "On Bosnia's Ethnic Fault Lines, It's Still Tense, but World Is Silent." *New York Times*, February 28, 1997, at A1.). If UN police had been available in larger numbers and had been continuously interacting with local police, it is unlikely that this incident would have occurred. The attack resulted in one death, the wounding of more than twenty, and further animosity between Croats and Muslims. Other reports indicated that Mostar's Muslim and Croat police leaders needed either to be more carefully monitored and retrained or to be replaced ("U.S. Presses Croatia on Lawlessness in Bosnia Town," Reuters report from Zagreb, February 27, 1997). If available, UN police could have stepped in to perform needed functions.

Second, in societies where law and order have broken down, UN police are needed to help reconstitute, screen, train, equip, and communicate with local police and to provide a feedback channel or complaint mechanism for citizens. United Nations police are needed to monitor new local police practices as the latter gradually establish a desirable code of conduct. As UN experience in Namibia, Cambodia, Somalia, Bosnia, Haiti, and El Salvador indicates, UN civilian police can prove invaluable in training local police units that have in the past lacked respect for human rights, especially of ethnic or religious minorities. The prospect for successful implementation of the Dayton accords, for example, would almost certainly have looked far brighter if UN police could have been provided in adequate numbers and with appropriate training. Bosnian president Alija Izetbegovic pleaded for expanded efforts to train local police ("Bosnian President: Catch War Criminals," United Press International, report from Washington, March 24, 1997).

Third, a standing UN police force is needed to assist the UN in systematic gathering of information for criminal investigations and to help international tribunals or truth commissions by providing specialized skills of investigation and surveillance, guarding prisoners, observing prison administration, and monitoring witness protection programs. Systematic investigation and reporting of alleged war crimes is important to deter future crimes, even if there is no immediate prospect of bringing the accused to trial (Meron 1993, 122–35). Because there is no statute of limitations for those accused of war crimes, the continuing stigma of indictment will be strengthened by systematic investigations and records. These will in turn be more likely to deter future misdeeds. The need to assist the International Criminal Tribunals for the former Yugoslavia and Rwanda was demonstrated, for example, when Dutch policemen needed protection to conduct forensic investigations to provide evidence for the trial of a Hutu militia leader accused of genocide in 1994, and when a woman and her entire family were killed before she was scheduled to testify against a former town mayor on trial for the massacre of two thousand people in 1994 (Hrvoje Hranjski, "Inadequate Protection Puts Rwanda Genocide Witness At Risk," Associated Press, report from Arusha, Tanzania, January 19, 1997, 1446). United Nations civilian police are urgently needed to safeguard the lives of prosecution witnesses if the international community is to take seriously the task of holding individuals accountable to international law.

A fourth need is to establish a special UN police unit and appropriate strategy to enforce, insofar as possible, the arrest warrants and decisions of the International Criminal Tribunals for the former Yugoslavia and Rwanda. For indicted war criminals to move about openly without facing arrest damages the credibility of the International Criminal Tribunal and is inconsistent with its mission not only to promote reconciliation but also to deter future lawbreakers by making it known that the international community will attempt to act against war crimes. Although U.S., Canadian, and European allied governments agreed that an enforcement force is needed, they could not agree on who should lead it or participate in it ("U.S. Considers Unit to Catch Bosnia War Criminals," Reuters report from Washington, January 27, 1997; Sullivan 1996, 21). This complication could have been more easily addressed had a permanent UN police force been available.

Benefits of Enforcement with United Nations Civilian Police

Past experience with international civilian police in training, monitoring, and enforcing activities demonstrates that enormous unrealized potential lies in making more effective use of such police, especially when external and local officers work together to uphold fair standards of enforcement. To be sure, many problems have arisen in the small number of past cases, but it is easy to see how corrective action could have produced much better results. Moreover, on many occasions international civilian police were needed and probably could have reduced human suffering, but they were simply unavailable or, if available, poorly trained and coordinated. By strengthening the quality, quantity, and availability of highly professional international civilian police, the international community could make gains in many areas: in reducing violence in societies about to erupt into violence or after cease-fires have been signed but not yet fully implemented, in improving the quality of local law enforcement where minorities fear victimization, in eliciting consent from national authorities hesitant about allowing an international presence on their soil, in assisting peacekeepers where they are deployed with ambiguity about host consent, in arresting indictees, and in deterring gross violations of international humanitarian law.

Providing adequate forces. A permanent UN police force could provide the larger number of well-trained police required to conduct more effective enforcement. In the past, none of the UN police operations has enjoyed the relatively large number of forces that are usually "regarded as indispensable to traditional law enforcement" (Brown, Barker, and Burke 1984, 1). After studying reasons for the failures in Somalia, U.S. officials reported that "the UN was essentially dysfunctional on the ground in Somalia under UNOSOM I because it did not have enough qualified personnel and resources" (United States 1993, 7–8). Many observers have concluded that the only solution is for the United Nations to develop and train its own civilian police (e.g., Brown, Barker, and Burke 1984, 59). The excellent Canadian study by the Ministry of Foreign Affairs and the Ministry of National Defense, *Towards a Rapid Reaction Capability for the United Nations*, notes that much needs to be done to remedy the recurring "shortage of civilian personnel with a full range of experience and expertise who could serve on relatively short notice." Because of problems in securing civilian police to serve in crisis situations, the study recommends that "Member States . . . help by training personnel to international standards and developing mechanisms to ensure availability" and that plans be pursued for establishing a standing police force (Canada 1995b, 49, 53). Although providing a standing, individually recruited police force would cost additional money, its successful operation, in terms of destruction avoided, would save many times its cost.[2]

Ensuring reliability. The most obvious advantage of a permanent, standing UN civilian police unit is its reliability. With such a force, the UN would not need to seek national contributions to peace operations, nor would it be forced "to await the lengthy domestic processes of each Member State before a critical mass of police forces is assembled." Moreover, a permanent force "could be trained to the high standards which the UN should demand of these units." Strikingly, the Canadian study concluded, "a UN rapid-reaction capability can be truly reliable only if it no longer depends on Member States of the UN for the supply of personnel for peace operations. If the UN is to build a rapid-reaction capability which is fully reliable, the challenge in years ahead will be to develop its own personnel, independent of state authority" (Canada 1995b, 59–60). The Canadian study favorably notes the statement of Nobel Laureate John C. Polanyi: "Fire departments and police forces do not always prevent fire or crime, yet they are now widely recognized as providing an essential service. Similarly, a rapid reaction capability may confront conditions beyond its capacity to control. This should not call into question its potential value to the international community. It is a civilized response to an urgent problem" (quoted in ibid., 60–61).

Improving the quality of enforcement. In some contexts civilian police are better able to perform enforcement duties than military personnel. In Somalia, for example, we already have noted the ability to connect with local people greatly increased after U.S. military personnel were withdrawn. Despite the greater utility of civilian approaches to conflict management, the UN civilian staff lacked water, computers, and basic office supplies. In Cambodia, UN police had no supplies or even furniture at first. In one province the *first* supply shipment arrived nine months after the operation began. In many districts there were only one-half the number of personnel estimated as necessary to handle the mission. The diverse UN police units could have done much more to dampen conflict if they had been prepared to work cooperatively or even to communicate with one another. Some police in UNTAC did not have a driver's license and could not speak either English or French, let alone Khmer, even though knowledge of English or French was a basic requirement. Some countries even sent personnel with little or no police experience.

In studying the effectiveness of UN civilian police and their unrealized potential for defusing volatile conflicts, it is easy to conclude that military forces have been the mainstay in peacekeeping primarily because military forces have personnel with free time on their hands and thus are readily available, whereas good police are always needed in their own municipalities (Canada 1995b, 53). Moreover, soldiers usually have supplies, logistical capability, and mobility and are disciplined to move as units. Military personnel are not necessarily chosen for peacekeeping because of a rational appraisal that they are in every respect the best people for the job. Many peacekeepers seldom engage in combat; they spend most of their time doing what well-trained police could do even better.

Eliciting Consent. The biggest difficulty the UN has faced in recent peace operations is the inability or unwillingness of governments to give meaningful consent to the presence and operation of UN peacekeepers and other personnel. If the government hosting peacekeepers is willing and able to keep local order, peacekeeping usually goes well. On the other hand, if the government cannot or will not provide internal order, peacekeepers find themselves needing to use the military instrument to fight antagonistic forces or to maintain local security and protect their own personnel.

To be sure, civilian police cannot solve all these problems. Nonetheless, the availability of UN police might in some instances elicit consent from a target government precisely because UN police could help maintain domestic order. When UN police are present and able to deliver needed services to the local population, human rights abuses and "ethnic cleansing" might never erupt or get out of hand. Readily available police, in such instances, are more useful than military forces because the host government is less likely to give consent for the latter to come, the latter would be less willing to go into high-risk areas, and they are, in any case, neither trained for nor eager to perform police duties on the local streets. Hence one of the valuable benefits of UN police is that in some instances they would help overcome the "consent" barrier in the minds of the host's decision makers, thus enabling enforcement to occur with host consent rather than without it. (In this gray area of operation, of course, once consent is given, the operation technically may be called pacific settlement rather than enforcement.) In any case, the prospect of the UN continuing to have meaningful consent is increased more by the deployment of effectively functioning police than by the somewhat aloof or even antagonistic presence of peacekeepers or external military forces. United Nations police at least open the door to turning the "us–them" relationship associated with external military occupation into an "us–us" relationship of police on the ground helping local communities sort out their problems. This symbolic and real transformation constitutes one of the UN's strongest assets and underutilized potential strengths.

To capitalize on this strength, the UN should prepare to offer a judicial package that includes not only police training, but also assistance in establishing professional penal and judicial systems. Arrests without the latter are no contribution to justice.

Assisting Peacekeeping. An effective UN police force can also help overcome the resistance of governments contributing troops for peacekeeping to supporting UN deployments in risky contexts. Members would be less likely to feel political reservations about deploying an individually recruited standing UN force. Because of their special training and contribution to keeping order in the host society, the deployment of UN civilian police could complement the deployment of UN *peacekeepers* and provide a safer context for their operations. Police would also aid other UN agencies involved in tasks of conflict resolution and peace building. Police can perform many more tasks than they have been asked in the past to carry, including some of the tasks that peacekeepers now carry out, and with more skill in relating to local people. Although peacekeepers are more heavily armed than police, this is not the most significant difference between them. As Brian Urquhart notes, "the principle of nonviolence sets the peacekeeping forces above the conflict they are dealing with; violation of the principle almost invariably leads to the peacekeepers becoming part of the conflict and therefore part of the problem" (Urquhart 1991, 7). This principle suggests that police, who ideally are trained to operate by the same principle in enforcing law locally, might be even more successful when carrying out functions that are more obviously useful to local people.

Arresting Indictees and Deterring War Crimes. A standing UN police force could be always prepared to make arrests of indictees wherever they gain entrance to a society in which alleged criminals reside or whenever indictees travel or lose the shielding effect of a pro-criminal sanctuary. Once the Security Council has authorized police enforcement and an international tribunal has authorized an arrest, any persons who oppose police efforts could be considered to be obstructing the Security Council's legally binding mandate and thus also be considered to be committing crimes against the peace. The possibility that people shielding indicted persons may place themselves also in lifelong fugitive status could aid the prospects for eventually making arrests.

United Nations police could also help inform and educate governments, local police, and others about the international obligation for individuals to honor the prohibition of genocide and the other norms of peace. The Security Council could require all military organizations throughout the world to instruct their soldiers in the obligation not to commit war crimes.

In societies where a government is obviously at odds with the norms of peace, a potentially useful UN enforcement tool exists in the possibility that the international community might weaken the hold of lawbreaking national officials and military commanders over their own soldiers and citizens. Because of their impartiality and focus on individual accountability, UN police may be better able than peacekeepers or military forces to emphasize that people need not support any of their own government's policies that are in violation of fundamental international norms. In addition to reducing the likelihood of local violence against UN personnel attempting to uphold the law, such a development would have a restraining effect on officials' misdeeds insofar as rulers could not be sure of their own citizens' loyalties should they attempt military aggression or severe repression. If soldiers throughout the world have been informed in advance of their international responsibility to avoid crimes against the peace, even if they are commanded by their superiors to commit them, they could in some cases seek to evade such orders.

As indicated previously, a different police strategy is needed for societies that are not accessible to UN police except through external surveillance and investigations. For these the international community should gather information during genocide or war to use in prosecuting people after the crisis has passed, even if the international community is unable to stop the violence in its midst. Eventually, with foreknowledge of serious investigative police work, some people would be deterred; with no statute of limitations, indictees would be minimally penalized even if not tried; still others might later face trials, especially when political tides and fortunes change in countries shielding indictees. In cases where the police attempt to arrest indicted persons, these actions can communicate that the entire society is not being targeted, a difference that often is obscured by military action and clarified by police enforcement. Unlike military operations, the police emphasis gives recognition to the reality of civil society even in the state where arrests are warranted. Most people living in a society where crimes have occurred benefit from arrest warrants because only the indicted may be targeted for arrest.

United Nations police also can offer positive inducements more effectively than military agents of enforcement. By being willing to participate in maintaining order, UN police can enable a leader to demonstrate that he or she seeks to prevent genocide by inviting in a UN police force to quell incidents pointing in the direction of genocide. It would become politically difficult for a reluctant government to oppose the introduction of UN police to monitor against, say, charges of genocide, because by opposing a UN police presence one seems to be giving license to commit genocide.

To enhance nonmilitary enforcement, it is imperative to establish the international criminal court now under discussion within the UN system.

Only a permanent court can signal that all alleged crimes, committed by people of any nationality, acting at any time in the future, will be under scrutiny. Anything less than a permanent, independent court and investigative capacity will give the impression that the international community wants only victor's justice or intends to penalize only a particular people acting in a specific conflict. This will not have the deterring effect needed to nurture a culture of compliance. If a permanent international criminal court is established and a UN prosecutor has the opportunity to bring charges against officials or their subordinates, regardless of nationality, because of alleged violations of the law against genocide or aggression, a subordinate could obtain reduced penalties by disclosing as much as possible about the deeds of superiors. (The stunning consequences of this dynamic have been demonstrated in 1996–97 in the proceedings of the South African Truth and Reconciliation Commission.) If this process implicates them, and if sufficient evidence confirms the allegations, indictments might proceed to higher-level officials. This risk to potential lawbreakers who do not open themselves to the possibility for cooperation with a UN prosecutor could encourage rulers to stop what they are doing that is illegal and begin to comply as soon as possible to improve their own record.

If an international criminal court indicts people, they could face some penalties, such as constraint on travel and foreign interactions, for the rest of their lives if they refuse to stand trial or confess their misdeeds. Confession within a certain length of time could ease or even remove those penalties and possibly more severe punishment if convicted. The prospect that lower-level persons may implicate higher officials can increase pressure for their good behavior. Superiors would begin to have a vested interest in maintaining a meritorious image, even if their government is not democratic, because of the prospect that they could face lifetime penalties, which would be irritating if not more seriously damaging, unless they faced trial once they had been indicted. The modest pretrial and preconviction penalties suggested here would presumably not matter to some leaders, but they could make a difference to others. For those not in leadership positions, the prospects of embarrassing investigations could motivate them to act more cautiously simply to avoid any possibility that an enforcement process could come home to haunt them merely because they endorsed killing unarmed civilians. Once some refuse to commit such misdeeds, others are put on notice that their behavior will stand out more clearly as normatively deficient because they violated international norms that others chose to respect. The keys to this dynamic process are a permanent international criminal court with general jurisdiction and permanent UN police powers impartially administered.

Deterrence is far from certain in specific cases, of course, but the deterring instruments could be quite strong even in situations in which police could not enter a society to make arrests. For those indicted for crimes, punitive action could include a lifelong stigma upon one's reputation for refusing to stand trial, lifelong freezing of all overseas assets, lifelong inability to travel and to have normal interactions with organizations located outside a shielding society, and lifelong fear that the shielding society may lose interest in forever shielding an indictee from a fair trial, especially at continuing cost to the shielding group. These penalties may seem small and not immediate enough to influence an official's behavior, and they would not always succeed. Yet if the international community would do its utmost to make clear that these penalties would be imposed and would be continued throughout the lifetime of the lawbreaker and any accomplices shielding indictees from a fair international trail, the deterring impact could be quite strong in the long run. Of course, the UN would be asking only for a fair trial, not for an admission of guilt, as a condition for ending secondary penalties.

HOLDING INDIVIDUALS ACCOUNTABLE: A GOLDEN OPPORTUNITY BEYOND COLLECTIVE SECURITY

Studies of intergroup hostilities show that genocide occurs because people attribute collective guilt to an out-group considered to be evil, inferior, or inhuman. Enforcement based on the instruments of collective security tends to reinforce collective prejudice and collective hysteria. Police responses, in contrast, can be focused on individual wrongdoers. The refusal of police to attack an entire nationality or group identity calls into question the human impulses underpinning genocide, thus making rationales for genocide less tenable and genocidal acts less likely. Indeed, most of the violent ideologies of the twentieth century "are chiefly about the redistribution of hatred," channeling it toward a collective identity. "Fascism, Nazism, nationalism, communism, and religious fundamentalism are about the punishment of those who are to blame" (du Preez 1994, 123).

Collective security responses to collective violence and attribution of guilt do not encourage the dismantling of bigotry. United Nations collective security operations in the form of Chapter VII military enforcement are far less likely than police enforcement to encourage "conflict transformation" (Lederach 1995) and the reduction of people's impulses to express hostility and attribute collective blame. Perhaps the single most important contribution UN civilian police can make is to help the international community turn the corner toward individualizing international legal responsibility.

Close scrutiny of the functions already performed by UN civilian police and the temporary war crimes tribunals confirms that progress in holding individuals accountable to international law could, given political will, proceed immediately. Although preoccupation with military enforcement persists, legal processes taking root in a culture of compliance need not be moribund. Just as the Nuremberg and Tokyo war crimes precedents, although flawed as victors' justice, were better than no precedents at all, so some police enforcement, in some conflicts, with some indictments and trials, will contribute more to human global governance than none at all.

In summing up the need for a more comprehensive approach to dealing with peacekeeping and enforcement, including the possibility of "establishing over the long term a permanent standing civilian police capability" and other UN forces for rapid response, the Canadian government study notes that "while these more visionary alternatives are controversial in current circumstances, they may well become the reality of the next century, should Member States determine that peace operations need to be done in a fundamentally new way" (Canada 1995b, 67, 71). Surely the experiences of "ethnic cleansing," genocide, and war in the 1990s and the echoes of victims' voices cry out for ushering in that fundamentally new way.

NOTES

1. For early discussion of the need for UN police, see Johansen and Mendlovitz (1980, 307–38).

2. The study of a United Nations Rapid Deployment Brigade (not a civilian police agency) by the Netherlands concluded that a unit of some five thousand persons might cost approximately $380 million annually. The Independent Working Group on the Future of the United Nations estimated a force of ten thousand (again not a civilian police force) might cost $500 million annually (Canada 1995b, 62).

III

Can Global Problems Be Governed?

10

Changing Norms in International Responses to Domestic Disorder

Alan Dowty and Gil Loescher

THE CHANGING IMPACT OF DOMESTIC DISORDER

Norms regarding legitimate international responses to internal disorder are clearly in a state of flux. Debate revolves around a number of key points of contention. What, for example, does customary international law say about intervention to prevent the spillover of such disorder into other states, and how do these legal standards apply as this impact multiplies? Does such intervention fall under the limitations of humanitarian intervention, whatever these may be, or can the United Nations Security Council invoke the enforcement powers of the UN Charter to legitimate broader action? And whatever the debate over principles, is such intervention becoming an increasingly accepted practice in the post–cold war order?

The framework for justifiable international military intervention suggested by Michael Walzer twenty years ago has served as a point of reference in subsequent debate. There are, Walzer argues, four instances in which "boundary crossings" are acceptable, in contradiction to the "legalist paradigm" of inviolable national sovereignty (Walzer 1977, 74–108). Two of these, preemption of a planned attack and counterintervention to neutralize a third state's intrusion, are arguably of greater importance under modern conditions but are continuations of traditional arguments and thus are not a focus of this chapter.

The third instance of justifiable intervention, to support a secession that has demonstrated its representative character, involves the very definition of the units that constitiue the political system. This is clearly more of an issue today with the proliferation of "failed states" and a greater acceptance of secession in practice (Soviet Union, Yugoslavia, Czechoslovakia,

Eritrea). Some democratic theorists see this as a consequence of the principle of self-determination itself: the sovereignty and legitimacy of any government need be respected, from within *or from without,* only if it is based on the consent of the governed. In other words, "states that abandon their principal *raison d'etre* —protection of citizens—in the interests of *raison d'état,* chip away at the legitimacy that insulates them from external interference" (Chipman 1992, 117; also see Teson 1988). Even traditional legal scholars have sometimes justified the infringement of national sovereignty on such grounds; for example, John Norton Moore argues that regional organizations might intervene in a state to promote self-determination because such action would be neutral and would be legitimated by broad consensus (Moore 1974, 3, 27).

Walzer's fourth ground for intervention was humanitarian: "when the violation of human rights . . . is so terrible that it makes talk of community or self-determination . . . seem cynical or irrelevant, that is, in cases of enslavement or massacre (Walzer 1977, 90). The argument for humanitarian intervention also has support in classic formulations of international law; Emerich de Vattel, for example, held that intervention was allowable, despite the principle of sovereignty, if "the persecution is carried to an intolerable degree, when it becomes a case of evident tyranny, against which all Nations may give help to an unfortunate people" (Vattel 1839, chap. IV, sec. 62).

Most relevant recent cases, however, are not "humanitarian intervention" according to the classic definition, a definition usually involving "unmixed" humanitarian motives and action *outside* the framework of United Nations Security Council authorization (Arend and Beck 1993). Most recent cases have mixed together state interests and humanitarianism and have been dealt with as "threats to peace and security" justifying Chapter VII enforcement action under the Charter. Recent history suggests the emergence of a fifth category of "mixed" cases in which domestic disorder spills over, or threatens to spill over, into other states, evoking a justifiable defensive response. Such cases often involve issues of self-determination as well, and they are typically mixed with humanitarian concerns. But the increased impact of domestic disorder is a force in its own right, reflecting two basic developments in international relations: the growing interdependence that is blurring national borders and the phenomenon of failed or collapsed states unable to exercise effective control within their borders.

The implications of growing interdependence have been studied in great depth in some areas but less so in the area of norms of international intervention. Clearly, however, as the distinction between "domestic" and "international" politics erodes, the legitimate scope of international authority will come to encompass issues once considered exclusively internal. In a sense, the internationalization of domestic disorder represents an extension to interstate relations of John Stuart Mill's basic principle of liberty among individuals: a state's freedom from external intervention is now understood to end when its domestic actions (or inactions) begin to impinge significantly on other states.

Interdependence also has consequences for the means of international intervention. Interdependence creates many more points of leverage for international bodies, whose actions have much greater impact within states. In particular, it serves to enlarge the nonmilitary methods of enforcement through such measures as economic sanctions and the generally growing cost of isolation from international institutions in financial, commercial, developmental, and other spheres of interaction. Events over the last few years have, for example, underlined the sensitivity of South Africa, former Eastern bloc states, and newly industrialized Asian states to their place in the international order.

Growing economic interdependence is also illustrated in such developments as claims of impacted states for compensation when they suffer economic losses because of their cooperation with international sanctions (in states dependent on trade with Iraq or Serbia, for example). Environmental issues are another clear case of cross-border impact, in which states are increasingly called to account for actions, or lack of actions, that inflict costs on other states.

Growing interdependence has a special edge when it comes to widespread disorder and violence in neighboring lands. The proliferating "war zones" within nations, where most contemporary armed conflicts are fought, seldom respect the sanctity of national borders. Traditionally, the claims of other states have centered on their own nationals and property that get caught in the war zone. This is clearly inadequate in most current cases.

Refugees have logically been the first focus of concern for impacted states. But the spillover from war zones goes well beyond this. There is the constant danger that the war will expand across existing borders, either generally or in sporadic intrusions. War zones can also readily serve as bases of operations or havens for groups whose hostility is directed toward the neighboring state; terrorism has thrived on these conditions. Lebanon has been the classic case, but more recently the Security Council has imposed sanctions on Sudan for, among other things, "giving shelter and sanctuaries to terrorist elements" (UN Doc. S/RES/1044 [January 31, 1996]). War zones are also sanctuaries for illicit trade in arms or drugs, which can inflict considerable harm on other states. The U.S. invasion of Panama, presumably undertaken to extradite General Manuel Noriega for involvement in drug trafficking, may not be the best case for international law, but the Security Council has involved itself in the internal Afghan scene on grounds that "the continuation of the conflict in Afghanistan provides a fertile ground for terrorism and drug trafficking which destabilize the region and beyond" (UN Doc. S/RES/1076 [October 22, 1996]). In general, the lawlessness of war zones brings with it numerous social plagues that threaten neighboring states, including crime, black markets, and prostitution.

Civil disorder is also a breeding ground for future threats. The military buildup in itself may create dangers for countries not equipped to defend their space. The danger that rogue regimes or rogue factions might gain access to weapons of mass destruction is one accompanying nightmare, described in at least one study as the major reason for countries in "zones of peace" to take an interest in affairs in "zones of turmoil" (Singer and Wildavsky 1993). As events in Afghanistan have demonstrated, protracted and bitter civil wars can leave a legacy of extremism and violent movements with which other nations will contend long after the event. If democratic regimes are a better guarantee of a future stable world order, as recent study tends to suggest, then the opposite may also hold, and the international community acquires a clear interest in the outcome of all civil wars (Franck 1990b; Hoffmann 1996). Even the demonstration effect of a civil conflict, with its impact on like-minded forces elsewhere, might motivate law-abiding states to intervene in order "to deter mimesis" (Farer 1991).

Finally, the question of "failed states" raises the question of whether sovereignty is a consideration at all when there is no generally recognized government exercising effective authority over a state's territory. The usual answers in the case of civic strife—foreign aid, consensual involvement of international governmental and nongovernmental organizations—tend to be useless in such circumstances. Furthermore, such situations show a distressing tendency to spread to neighboring regions (Helman and Ratner 1992–93). In such cases the absence of an invitation is hardly determinant; what we need are reasonable criteria for deciding when a state ceases to be a state, transferring to the international community not only the right but also the duty to intervene (Schorn 1995).

In the following sections of the chapter we make three specific arguments within this general framework: First, we argue that justifying international intervention on the grounds of the impact of domestic disorder on other states is a reasonable extension of customary law. Customary law neglected to deal with the issue not because principles of state responsibility were not applicable but because such impact was much more limited in the past. Second, we argue that as a threat to international peace and security, domestic disorder may also fall under Chapter VII of the UN Charter, legitimating enforcement action not subject to the limits of purely humanitarian intervention. (Of course it should be recalled that such intervention need not be military and can be subject to rules such as the requirement of authorization by the Security Council.)

Third, whatever the theoretical arguments, international intervention in response to domestic disorder, in various forms, has quietly become a *de facto* norm in state declaration and practice in recent years. In the second half of this chapter we take interventions in response to refugee flows as a major index of this change.

The Applicability of Customary Law

Customary international law has little to say about the spillover of domestic conflict because in the past this impact was sporadic and limited. Only in the twentieth century has this problem forced itself to the top of the international agenda. Traditional doctrines do, however, provide a reasonable basis for action against a state generating refugees. This was first pointed out in a little-noted article by R. Yewdall Jennings in 1939, in connection with the "refugee crisis" of that period (Jennings 1939). Jennings notes that "there is one aspect of the refugee problem to which the general and customary international law is relevant, and that is the consideration of the legality or illegality of the conduct of the state which creates a refugee population" (110).

Jennings' approach, like ours "has regard not so much to the ethics of domestic policy as to the repercussions of that policy on the material interests of third states" (111). Therefore, even in cases where a state may not be guilty of illegal acts, by inflicting costs on another state it creates grounds for the impacted state to resort to measures of *retorsion*, defined by Lassa Oppenheim as "retaliation for discourteous, or unkind, or unfair and inequitable acts by acts of the same or of a similar kind" (Oppenheim 1952, 134–35). Such acts of retaliation or reciprocation are commonly used to force states to alter their treatment of aliens or their trade practices; in the context of imposed refugee burdens, by analogy, *retorsion* would clearly seem to justify, at least, economic sanctions designed to impose on the country of origin a cost equivalent to that forced upon the host nation.

Jennings and other commentators go further, however, arguing that such actions are illegal. The illegality derives from the generally accepted doctrine of the abuse of rights, known in common law as *Sic utere tuo ut alienum non laedas* (Use your own property in such a manner as not to injure that of another). According to Oppenheim, this maxim "is applicable to relations of States no less than to those of individuals" and is "one of those general principles of law recognised by civilised States which the Permanent Court is bound to apply by virtue of Article 38 of its Statute" (Jennings 1939, 112; Oppenheim 1955; Brownlie 1979; Goodwin-Gill 1983).

The doctrine of abuse of rights, then, establishes the legal responsibility of the state of origin: "There is ample authority for the proposition that a state is obligated to avoid the generation across its borders of damage to other states" (Garvey 1988, 187). Numerous international treaties, declarations, and adjudications reflect this principle in various contexts. For example, in the Trail Smelter Arbitration the tribunal ruled that "no state has the right to use or permit the use of its territory in such a manner as to cause injury . . . in or to the territory of another or the properties or persons therein" (Trail Smelter Arbitral Tribunal 1941). Similarly, in the Corfu Channel case (1949), the International Court of Justice held that a state from whose territory transboundary damages were generated is responsible if it had knowledge of the harm and the opportunity to act, establishing "every State's obligation not to allow knowingly its territory to be used for acts contrary to the rights of other States" (Brownlie 1979, 355–56, 360). The 1972 Stockholm Declaration affirmed that "States have . . . the responsibility to ensure that activities within their area of jurisdiction or control do not cause damage to the environment of other States or of areas beyond the limits of territorial jurisdication" (UN Doc. A/CONF.48/14/Rev. 1 and Corr. 1, [1972] Principle 21). Jurists argue that state responsibility is "objective," that is, it does not depend on intent to harm, and that it can extend to actions of private citizens (such as insurgents or rioters) where a state has not acted to prevent injury (Oppenheim 1955; Brownlie 1979).

Recent international documents favor a broader definition of "state responsibility" that includes prevention as well as reparation. The final report of a UN study group, titled "International Cooperation to Avert New Flows of Refugees," for example, declares that "averting massive flows of refugees is a matter of serious concern to the international community as a whole"; such flows "carry adverse consequences for the economies of the countries of origin and entire regions, thus endangering international peace and security" (UN Doc. A/41/324, [May 13, 1986]). The link to "peace and security" is grounds for invoking Chapter VII of the UN Charter, which overrides claims of domestic jurisdiction. Similarly, the International Law Commission, in its "Draft Articles on State Responsibility," defined an international crime as "an internationally wrongful act which results from the breach by a State of an international obligation so essential for the protection of fundamental interests of the international community that its breach is recognized as a crime by that community as a whole." Included as examples of such crimes, justifying corrective action, are not only threats to peace and security but also "a serious breach on a widespread scale of an international obligation of essential importance for safeguarding the human being, such as those prohibiting slavery, genocide, *apartheid*" (Brownlie 1983).

But how does this expansion of "state responsibility" relate to the traditional principles of nonintervention and domestic jurisdiction? As Lori Fisler Damrosch has said, "the sphere of 'domestic jurisdiction' is a relative one that contracts as the sphere of activity governed by international law and other sources of obligation grows" (Damrosch 1993a, 95). Furthermore, it is well established in international law that a state cannot rely on the provisions of its own laws in defense against a claimed breach of international obligations; where the two conflict, international law takes precedence. It would follow, therefore, that as domestic chaos imposes massively increased burdens on other states, domestic jurisdiction will shrink.

Disorder as a Threat to Peace

The UN Security Council has increasingly defined not only refugee flows but also domestic disorder more generally as a threat to peace and security, thus opening the door to enforcement action under Chapter VII. In effect, a nation whose domestic turmoil threatens regional peace and security has internationalized its internal affairs, providing a cogent justification for policy makers elsewhere to act directly upon the source of the threat.

These arguments are accompanied by changing conceptions of "threats" and "security" in interstate relations. Certain internal acts and policies—especially those creating massive unrest—are increasingly regarded as threats to others, particularly by their neighbors. From this perspective, grievous human rights abuses are not an internal matter when neighboring states must bear the cost of repression. In recent years the Security Council itself has taken an increasingly inclusive view of "threats to peace" where actual hostilities remained limited largely to the territory of a single state. The UN Security Council's Summit Declaration of 1992 included "nonmilitary sources of instability in the economic, social, humanitarian, and ecological fields" as threats to international peace and security, while specifying "election monitoring, human rights verification, and the repatriation of refugees" as "integral parts of the Security Council's efforts to maintain international peace and security" (Text of Security Council Summit Declaration, *New York Times*, February 1, 1992, at A4).

After invoking Chapter VII enforcement powers in only two cases (South Africa and Rhodesia) during its first forty-five years of existence, the Security Council has invoked them frequently since 1990, and most of these cases involved civil disorder rather than classic international aggression by one state against another. These cases include:

Iraq 1991. The Security Council determined that repression within Iraq led to massive refugee flows and cross-border incursions "which threaten international peace and security (UN Doc. S/RES/688 [April 5, 1991]). (This case is discussed further below.)

Somalia 1992. The Security Council recognized that internal conflict had consequences for stability and peace in the region and that "continuation of this situation constitutes . . . a threat to international peace and security"

(UN Doc. S/RES/733 [January 23, 1992]; also see UN Doc S/RES/814 [March 26, 1993]). The importance of Somalia as a precedent lies, however, primarily in two other aspects of the UN intervention. This was "the first time the organization has intervened in the domestic affairs of a member state when that state has not presented a military threat to its neighbors" (Makinda 1993, 61). In addition, intervention had taken place without the "consent" of the target state, on grounds that there was no effective government in Somalia to give or withhold such consent.

Bosnia 1992. The UN's long involvement in this civil war began with the determination that "the situation in Bosnia and Hercegovina . . . constitutes a threat to international peace and security" (UN Doc. S/RES/757, [May 30, 1992]).

Croatia 1993. Referring to repeated violations of cease-fire obligations, the Security Council determined that "the situation thus created constitutes a threat to peace and security in the region" (UN Doc. S/RES/807 [February 19, 1993]). This has been reaffirmed as recently as January 1997 (UN Doc. S/RES/1093 [January 14, 1997]).

Liberia 1993. In commending the intervention of neighboring African states, the Security Council determined "that the deterioration of the situation in Liberia constitutes a threat to international peace and security, particularly in this region of West Africa" (UN Doc. S/RES/813 [March 26, 1993]).

Haiti 1993. The Security Council noted "the incidence of humanitarian crises . . . becoming or aggravating threats to international peace and security" and accordingly determined that "in these unique and exceptional circumstances, the continuation of this situation threatens international peace and security in the region" (UN Doc. S/RES/841 [June 16, 1993]).

Rwanda 1994. In authorizing French intervention during the final stages of genocide and civil war, the Security Council determined "that the magnitude of the humanitarian crisis in Rwanda constitutes a threat to peace and security in the region" (UN Doc. S/RES/929 [June 22, 1994]).

Zaire 1996. With the beginning of rebellion and a consequent threat to Rwandan Hutu refugees encamped in the country since 1994, the Security Council determined that "the present situation in eastern Zaire constitutes a threat to international peace and security in the region" (UN Doc. S/RES/1080 [November 15, 1996]).

Albania 1997. Widespread unrest in Albania led the Security Council to authorize a temporary multinational protection force, led by Italy, on grounds that "the present situation of crisis in Albania constitutes a threat to peace and security in the region" (UN Doc. S/RES/1101 [March 28, 1997]).

Kosovo 1998. With the renewal of unrest in Kosovo province, in Yugoslavia, the Security Council invoked an arms embargo on the Federal Republic of Yugoslavia in response to its military intervention in the province (UN Doc. S/RES/1160 [March 31, 1998]).

All these cases involve the implementation of Chapter VII enforcement powers of the United Nations. In other cases—Macedonia, Yemen, Burundi, and Afghanistan—the Security Council has also cited threats to regional peace and security, or to regional stability, as grounds for involvement in these nations, short of Chapter VII actions: calls for cease-fire, fact-finding or observer missions, and condemnations of violence and human rights violations (including, in the case of Afghanistan, denunciation of discrimination against girls and women that might lead to "possible repercussions on international relief and reconstruction programmes in Afghanistan").[1]

This new thinking ties in with changing ideas of national sovereignty. Although sovereignty is still regarded as a cornerstone of the international political and legal system, domestic matters previously shielded from outside interference have become open to comment and action. Because the most elementary justification for the modern state is its ability to provide reasonable security for its citizens, states that force these same citizens to flee call into question the very basis of their sovereignty. There is notably greater revulsion on the part of the international community toward using "sovereignty" to shield gross patterns of persecution and notably less hesitation in employing preemptive, as opposed to reactive, approaches to such problems.

Intervening in internal conflicts on the basis of a threat to peace and security, rather than on a purely humanitarian basis, also changes some of the considerations and conditions in execution. "Proportionality" would remain a condition, as in any sanctioned use of force, but the calculus would proceed on a different basis. Intervention would be aimed not just at the immediate relief of victims but also at rectification of the conditions that constitute a continuing threat to the peace of other states. Obviously such an "enforcement" mission could require broader changes, including, in the extreme case, removal of the offending government.

In addition, the "disinterest" often specified for humanitarian interventions is not possible, because intervention in this case is justified precisely *because of* the impact on other states. The fact that states are acting in their own interest is one reason to hope that such actions will be more effective than some actions have been in the past. A recent study of four interventions in refugee cases concluded that "cooperative governmental efforts to resolve problems of forced migration and other migration pressures will necessarily be based on states' interests, although informed by the same states' commitment to the protection of forced migrants" (Rogers and Copeland 1993, 117; also see Adelman 1992).

This leaves the issue of how interveners can be prevented from exploit-

ing such situations for particular gains unrelated to the situation that justified their action. The obvious answer would be to require multilateral legitimation and execution as much as possible; in a crude sense, "interest"
would provide the motive power for such justified interventions, multilateral mechanisms would provide the steering and control. It is reasonable
to assume that an authorized global or regional organization, acting on behalf of collective interests and values, would not be subject to the same suspicions and limits that would ordinarily attach to intervention by individual
states. In fact, considering the difficulty of achieving collective consensus,
the danger may be that there would be too little, rather than too much,
multilateral action: "The breadth of values, interests, and perspectives represented at the UN tends to limit even the Council to expeditious and decisive action only in exceptional cases, and then for ends considerably more
limited than promoters of liberal values might prefer" (Farer 1991, 331).

THE FLOW OF REFUGEES AS AN INDEX OF DISORDER

Refugees are a relatively new issue in interstate relations; with a few exceptions, forced migration in the past was not on a scale to cause noteworthy
concern on the part of host states. The term *refugee* itself was invented only
at the end of the seventeenth century, when French persecution of Protes-
tants (through revocation of the Edict of Nantes in 1685) forced some two
hundred thousand to three hundred thousand Huguenot *refugiés* into
flight. But on the whole, such movements were not substantial enough to
lead receiving states to protest.

Even when numbers were substantial, most premodern states did not feel
inclined to protest. Throughout the long history of expulsion and flight,
haven had usually been available because other states were willing, or even
eager, to admit the expelled population to their own territory. Population
was usually viewed as wealth, both in economic terms and as the foundation
of military power. The Jews who were expelled from various medieval European states as a foreign element, for example, were always able to find a
haven with other rulers who welcomed their skills as artisans and mer-
chants. The Ottoman sultan Bajezet, in opening the door to Jews expelled
from Spain in 1492, reputedly exclaimed, "Call ye this Ferdinand
'wise'—he who depopulates his own dominions in order to enrich mine?"
(quoted in Roth 1961, 252). It is only in the twentieth century, with the
closing of the open door in traditional lands of immigration (particularly
the New World) and an explosion in the numbers of the "unwanted," that
responsibility for the creation of refugees has become an issue of contention on the international agenda.

This has evoked the political self-interest, as well as humanitarian interests, of the receiving states, serving as the most tangible international linkage to domestic disorder. A large-scale movement of people across national borders, under duress, internationalizes what might otherwise be purely domestic issues related to the causes of that movement. This has become a norm, in theory and in practice, that is increasingly accepted as grounds for international action, including in some cases armed intervention, against the state generating the refugee flow (Loescher 1992, 1993). It is clear, in Guy Goodwin-Gill's words, that "established rules of international law nevertheless do permit the conclusion that states are bound by a general principle not to create refugee outflows and to co-operate with other states in the resolution of such problems as may emerge" (Goodwin-Gill 1983, 228). This suggests an obligation to remedy the cause of the outflow as well as reparation to the affected parties.

It is important to appreciate the burden that contemporary refugee flows typically impose on receiving states. The reality of this burden has forced a growing recognition of the way refugee issues link the internal and external realms. As Stanley Hoffmann has said, "there is no way of isolating oneself from the effects of gross violations abroad: they breed refugees, exiles, and dissidents who come knocking at our doors—and we must choose between bolting the doors, thus increasing misery and violence outside, and opening them, at some cost to our own well being" (Hoffmann 1981, 111). Leon Gordenker argues for the internationalization of refugee issues on grounds that measures short of violence "have an arguable legal and political basis as a form of self-help within a decentralized system" (Gordenker 1987, 207). The impact of a refugee flow on countries of refuge can be measured in direct and indirect economic costs, in negative social and cultural consequences, in threats to security both internally and externally, and in its broader impact on the fabric of global stability.

The international community, through the international refugee regime, already bears a portion of the cost for refugee relief and assistance. The resources devoted to humanitarian assistance have soared in the 1990s. In 1990, the United Nations High Commissioner for Refugees had a budget of $544 million and a staff of twenty-four hundred. In 1998, the budget had grown to more than $1.3 billion and the staff to five thousand. Moreover, several other UN agencies have increased their spending on emergencies. By the mid-1990s the World Food Program devoted about 80 percent of its resources to emergency food relief, and UNICEF (United Nations Children's Fund) directed about 25 percent of its expenditure toward humanitarian emergencies. In addition, in many NGOs, such as OXFAM or CARE, which traditionally considered themselves development agencies, emergency programs now form the bulk of their work as spending on humanitarian emergencies has increased while spending on official development assistance has decreased (OECD 1997).

But this is only part of the picture. Although developed countries contribute most of the funding for programs that assist refugees, the least developed countries host the overwhelming majority of the world's refugees. For example, twenty-one of the twenty-five nations with the highest ratio of refugees to population are among the very poorest countries of the world (United States Committee for Refugees 1997, 11). Thus the cost falls disproportionately on nations least able to afford such strain, where the presence of large impoverished refugee populations further burdens resources and perpetuates the poverty of the host nation. Refugees need water, food, fuel, and land, and the environmental impact in already marginal areas may be devastating. When they compete for jobs refugees drive wages down, and when they compete for scarce goods they create inflation (Rogers and Copeland 1993). They require social services beyond those provided by international agencies, putting further strain on domestic structures that may already have been inadequate.

As for the social and cultural impact, refugee movements often threaten intercommunal harmony and undermine major societal values by altering the ethnic, cultural, religious, and linguistic composition of host populations. In countries with racial, ethnic, religious, or other splits—that is, in most existing countries—a refugee influx can place great strain on the system. Mass influxes can endanger social and economic stability, particularly in countries in which ethnic rivalries may be virulent, the central government is weak and consensus on the legitimacy of the political system is lacking, and essential resources are limited. A large influx of refugees with ties to a particular domestic group can upset the internal balance and even threaten the existing system.

Refugees often become a political force in their host country, influencing its policies and particularly its relationship with the country of origin. In the United States, for example, refugee or immigrant communities have clearly influenced U.S. policy toward Cuba, China, Northern Ireland, Israel, Nicaragua, Poland, Vietnam, Mexico, and Cyprus, among others. Refugee communities may align themselves with opposition parties and use this leverage as pressure on ruling governments to advance their own interests, as Afghan refugee groups in Pakistan backed fundamentalist groups in that country.

Universally, societies fear that uncontrolled migration may swamp their existing cultural identity. Refugees typically seek to preserve their own cultural heritage and national identity in line with their dream of an eventual return to their homeland, thus complicating their integration into the host society. In Europe, the gulf between the cultural background of contemporary refugee groups and that of Europeans causes special concern. There are serious reservations about the ability of these groups to assimilate and about the willingness of Western publics to tolerate aliens in their midst.

These feelings, reinforced by racial and religious prejudices, pose difficult social and political problems for European governments. Xenophobic and racist attitudes are increasingly obvious among some segments of these populations, and racist attacks are increasing in every country hosting immigrant minorities. Anti-immigrant and antirefugee feeling is being exploited by extreme right-wing parties throughout Europe, a development that distorts the politics of these nations and in some cases (such as the former East Germany) impedes the process of democratization (Loescher 1992; Rogers and Copeland 1993; Weiner 1993).

Security concerns for the host state begin with the question of whether it can physically control the refugee population, which increasingly includes armed combatants. In Zaire, nothing was done to separate the armed Hutus from the main body of refugees, and the relief effort there was plagued from the beginning by the manipulation and diversion of aid to the very elements that had engineered the genocide and fueled the mass exodus. The militarization of refugee camps is not a new phenomenon. In the past, Afghan refugee leaders threatened to make their camps in Pakistan ungovernable if Pakistan made a deal with the government in Kabul. For more than a decade conflicting Cambodian exile groups maintained their headquarters in camps on Thai territory and posed serious problems for that government. In the Middle East, Arab political and military support for Palestinian refugees undermined some states' control of their own foreign and internal policies; in Lebanon, the presence of a large Palestinian population was a key factor in the eruption of civil war, the collapse of central government, and eventual domination by Syria. Fears regarding the loyalty of Palestinians in Kuwait led to their mass expulsion following the Gulf war (Weiner 1993).

Because refugees often remain in or near border areas, control of cross-border terrorism or smuggling may be especially difficult. Raids and guerrilla activity across the border may drag the host state into an existing conflict, and in fact this may be the deliberate strategy of armed exile groups. The offer of sanctuary to refugees may in itself invite military retaliation; in response to real or perceived threats of "refugee warrior communities," refugee camps have increasingly become military targets, as most recently seen in the former Zaire. In some cases host states have themselves armed or helped to arm refugee fighting groups as a weapon against the country of origin but then found themselves unable to control the consequences of having done so (particularly in the Middle East, the Horn of Africa, and Southeast Asia). In 1998, conflict in the border regions between Kosovo and Albania and Macedonia provided yet further evidence of how porous borders and population displacements shape the security situation.

More often, mass expulsions are used by the sending country to deliberately destabilize or embarrass strategic or political adversaries. Under such circumstances, expulsions are analogous to military invasions. Arab states that forced out their Jewish communities after Israeli independence in 1948 expected the massive influx to overwhelm the newly established state (whose population doubled in three years). Officials of Southeast Asian states claimed during the late 1970s that the massive Vietnamese expulsion of ethnic Chinese was a veiled attempt to create racial and economic problems in their countries and to infiltrate enemy agents into the ranks of its populace. More recently, China has begun to use the threat of massive outflows to discourage attacks on its human rights record; Wu Jianmin, China's delegate to the United Nations Human Rights Commission, declared on April 15, 1997, that the West had a powerful interest in maintaining China's stability: if even 1 percent of China's population were to flee, "the prosperity of East Asia would be destroyed overnight" ("China Defeats a UN Resolution Criticizing Its Rights Record," *New York Times*, April 16, 1997). Fidel Castro's expulsion of criminals and psychotics to the United States as a part of the 1980 Mariet boat lift was an even more obvious example of migration policy as a tool of foreign policy. Clearly, when refugees are being used as a weapon, the target state is within its rights in invoking the right of self-defense (Loescher 1992; Gordenker 1987; Weiner 1993).

Growing Resistance to Asylum

The broader impact of refugee flows is in part a result of the fact that asylum seekers are no longer limited to neighboring states. "Jet age" refugees now appear at the doorstep of distant nations, with a larger proportion of them finding their way to Western states in hope of better conditions. This comes, of course, on top of a steep rise in the number of illegal immigrants to the West from the Third World. In response, most northern states have concluded that preventing entry of asylum seekers by imposing visa requirements on the nationals of refugee-producing states, fining airlines for bringing refugees into their countries, and forcibly interdicting refugees at frontiers and in international waters is the best way to reduce both the numbers and the costs of asylum applications.

However, it is also significant that the trend toward excluding asylum seekers is spreading beyond the North to governments in the South. Alarmed by the economic, environmental, social, and security costs of hosting mass influxes of refugees, a number of governments across the world have taken steps to exclude asylum seekers from their territory and to ensure the rapid—and in some cases involuntary—repatriation of refugees. Faced with mass influxes and a greater share of the world's refugee burden, many governments in the South, which in the past had generally responded humanely to the needs of millions who were forced from their homelands, are now closing their doors to new arrivals. In many countries, refugees are perceived as a threat to the physical environment or security of the host state, especially when they include elements who are determined to use the asylum country as a base for political and military activities. In 1996, boatloads of Liberian refugees were stranded at sea for weeks until neighboring states reluctantly agreed to provide them refuge. Throughout the year, Tanzania, host to hundreds of thousands of refugees from neighboring countries, expelled and refused entry to thousands of asylum seekers and refugees fleeing violence in Burundi and Rwanda, and in late 1996 and early 1997 the Tanzanian army forcibly repatriated more than two hundred thousand Hutu refugees back to Rwanda.

Indeed, as some developing countries improve their administrative and military capacities, we can anticipate a hardening of borders and more-restrictive policies both toward the admission of refugees and toward their early repatriation. Consequently, there exist parallel asylum crises in the North and South. The result is a refugee crisis that threatens international relations generally, over and above its impact within particular states. Simply erecting new barriers in the North or the South will not make the problem go away, nor will it ensure a stable political base for international relations.

An angry, excluded world outside the West will almost inevitably create conditions in which extremist groups and governments will emerge and pose new security threats. The success of economic liberalism and political pluralism in the new democracies of Latin America, Eastern Europe, and the former Soviet Union is of decisive importance not only in averting future refugee and migrant flows but also in the security realm. Failure to stem the tide of poverty, violence, persecution, and other refugee-inducing factors will be costly in security terms. In countries where conditions are desperate, people will find ways to flee elsewhere. Dealing effectively with refugees both at home and abroad is a matter of self-interest for industrialized states and coincides with their search for long-term global and strategic stability.

What has changed perceptions of refugee issues in recent years, more than anything else, is the quantum leap in numbers. Based on figures from the United Nations High Commissioner for Refugees and the U.S. Committee for Refugees, in 1980 there were about 6 million refugees and 2 million internally displaced persons. Between 1980 and 1990, the number of refugees tripled to about 17 million refugees, and the number of internally displaced exploded to more than 22 million. According to the UNHCR, there were some 14.5 million refugees in 1997 (UNHCR 1997). Unlike the creation of refugees, internal displacement did not decline in the early 1990s, and by 1997 there were an estimated 23 million internally displaced.

These figures do not tell the whole story, however, as many victims of forced displacement do not figure in these statistics. These include migrants who have been expelled en masse from their countries of residence and people who have been uprooted by development projects, among others. Although it is difficult to provide accurate figures, there are probably more than 50 million people around the world who might be legimately described as displaced. This figure means that 1 of every 130 people on earth has been forced into flight. No continent now is immune from the problem of mass displacement. Refugee populations in excess of ten thousand can now be found in more than seventy countries across the world (UNHCR 1995).

Added to this growth in numbers of displaced people is the advent of global satellite communications. Television coverage of starving children in Somalia and butchery in Rwanda, of armed attacks on Kurds and Shiites in Iraq or Albanians in Kosovo, and of concentration camps in Bosnia have made citizens of industrialized nations increasingly aware of the human rights abuses leading to large-scale refugee movements. The very scale of the problem and the acceleration of demands overwhelm traditional refugee relief. Western publics become numbed by compassion fatigue, and Europe in particular faces a "dilemma of common aversion" in which any one state's efforts to reduce its own burden only increases the demands on others (Rogers and Copeland 1993). As a result, policies on international population movements need to be taken as seriously as trade policy or policy on other foreign and security issues. Policy makers must factor the complications of mass refugee movements, both actual and potential, into their basic policy planning.

Clearly, the past focus on charity—that is, on relief and assistance after the fact—is not adequate. Among other things, it is increasingly clear that charity alone often helps to perpetuate the injustice that caused the refugee flight, in that it relieves the sending country of pressure to correct the injustice. For example, during the 1980s it was claimed that "Guatemala's well-meaning neighbors inadvertently are making it easier for Guatemala's regime to deny its people. . . . They are providing a mechanism through which Guatemala's rulers can remove people who might press for reform. . . ." (Luper-Foy 1992, 52). Furthermore, the relief effort in emergency situations like Bosnia and Rwanda has been complicated by political factors; the UNHCR and other aid agencies increasingly operate in the midst of ongoing conflicts in which even the most humanitarian activities are perceived by one or more parties as a factor affecting the outcome of the confrontation. The emphasis internationally is therefore inevitably shifting "from humanitarian obligations to legal obligations of one state not to harm other states by imposing the burdens of unmanaged refugee flow" (Garvey 1988, 187).

Part of the response to this heavier burden has been greater stress on repatriation as the preferred outcome to refugee situations. In the past, integration in place or resettlement in third countries—the other two traditional solutions—were more common than repatriation, which requires a remedy to the original cause of flight. But given the jump in numbers and some favorable political developments (the end of the cold war, moderation of other conflicts, and a wave of democratization), repatriation has taken the lead in recent years. In Vietnam, Cambodia, Afghanistan, Sri Lanka, Burma, Ethiopia, Mozambique, Angola, Rwanda, Burundi, and elsewhere it has been established as the preferred solution. According to the UNHCR, more than ten million refugees have returned home since the beginning of the decade. A former director of the U.S. State Department Bureau of Refugee Programs clearly identified "development of integration programs in the country of origin for returning refugees" as the priority in the U.S. approach to the issue (Zimmerman 1993; Coles 1989).

Because repatriation of refugees is impossible without addressing the reasons for their flight, attention is also inevitably directed to addressing these problems before the event rather than waiting to correct the situation afterward. It can even be argued that "Red Cross ethics," dealing only with the aftermath, may even prolong the agony of a humanitarian disaster (Hoffmann 1996, 31). In any event the problem cannot be resolved simply by staving off refugee flows and forcing people to remain in untenable conditions. It has now become conventional wisdom among experts on refugee issues that future efforts must focus on the "root causes" of displacement *before* people are forced to flee and that international action should be preventive more than ameliorative (Loescher 1993; Farer 1991; Coles 1989; Zimmerman 1993; Hocké 1989; Dowty 1987).

This requires a closer look at the role of states themselves in causing mass exoduses. Certain kinds of government actions, ranging from decrees and overt use of force to more covert persecution, intimidation, discrimination and inducements of unwanted groups to leave, all generate refugee flows. Governments and their opponents now use population displacements for a variety of political and military purposes. Such strategies help armed groups gain or maintain control over people, territory, and other resources. They can be used to establish culturally or ethnically homogeneous societies, to perpetuate the dominance of one group over another, and to provide a means of removing groups of people whose loyalty to the state is questioned. Thus, in many situations, population displacement has been the very objective of wars.

INTERVENTION TO PREVENT REFUGEE FLOWS

International intervention related to refugee flows has in fact become common in state declaration and practice. Let us begin with those cases *most*

difficult to justify in theory: unilateral military interventions carried out
without the collective legitimation of the UN Security Council or other international bodies. There have been three such cases in recent years in
which "hideous repression within the target state, and consequent huge
refugee flows, would have seemed to provide a ready-made justification for
[intervention]" (Roberts 1993, 434).

The first case was India's intervention in East Pakistan (Bangladesh) in
1971, after an estimated ten million refugees poured into India as a result
of fighting sparked when the Pakistani government, which was dominated
by West Pakistan, annulled an election won by a party based in East Pakistan. The burden on India's economy was enormous, and India suspected
that the Pakistani government was trying to change the demographic balance between the two parts of the country by forcing massive numbers of
East Pakistanis into India. The second case was Vietnam's incursion into
Cambodia in late 1978, to overthrow the notorious Pol Pot regime, under
which large numbers of Cambodians had fled to Vietnam. Also in 1979,
Tanzania sent its forces into Uganda in support of Ugandan refugees based
in Tanzania. The Tanzanian forces sought to overthrow the Idi Amin regime and to repel Ugandan incursions into Tanzania.

Humanitarian intervention was not the major thrust of any of these actions. Although the burden of refugees in the Indian states of West Bengal,
Tripura, and Assam was clearly an important factor, India's objectives also
included the strengthening of its regional position *vis-à-vis* its traditional
rival, Pakistan. Similarly, Vietnam intervened in Cambodia for hegemonic
reasons and not to put an end to Pol Pot's genocide. Tanzania intervened
in self-defense, but its intervention was also influenced by the presence of
active Ugandan exiles in Dar es Salaam.

In all three cases the targeted regime was toppled; Bangladesh became
independent, Cambodia acquired a Vietnamese-sponsored government,
and in Uganda a previous regime was restored. In all three cases, refugees
(at least the original refugee group) were able to return home, relieving
the burden on the intervening state. Although all three interventions were
formally condemned as violations of national sovereignty, the condemnations were on the whole ritualistic and muted in light of the undeniable
fact that the interveners had halted widespread massacres and flight. However, the interventions in Bangladesh and Cambodia did provoke strong
countermeasures from global powers, who feared potential damage to
their interests in these regions. For example, in order to deter India from
attempting to extend its gains in the former East Pakistan by an attack on
West Pakistan, the Nixon administration moved the U.S. Sixth Fleet into
the Bay of Bengal. In Cambodia, the Chinese government, furious over the
loss of its close ally, the Khmer Rouge, to its historical archenemy, Vietnam,
sought to give Hanoi a "bloody nose" by an attack on northern Vietnam

in February 1979. Despite these events, it is significant that in all three cases, the international community made no move to restore the previous regime or even to continue recognizing it (except that many states recognized the successors of the Khmer Rouge because they opposed Vietnam's puppet regime in Phnom Penh).

In dealing with Bangladesh, in fact, the General Assembly did not flatly condemn India but dealt with the situation in all its aspects, including the return of refugees, and gave priority to condemnation of genocide over reaffirmation of the principle of sovereignty (Teson 1988; Weiner 1993). Subsequently the International Commission of Jurists, writing on the India–Pakistan case, set out four requirements for unilateral humanitarian intervention: (1) manifest guilt of the target government; (2) lack of practical peaceful means to correct the situation; (3) opportunity for the international community to act first; and (4) use of only necessary force, accounting to the international community, and withdrawal as soon as practical. Both the Indian and Tanzanian interventions did arguably meet these conditions, though the Vietnamese ultimately did not because of their prolonged presence in Cambodia (Schorn 1995).

Refugees were central in many of the cases listed above, in which the Security Council authorized Chapter VII action in a country's internal affairs. In the case of Haiti, UN Resolutions regarding the imposition of a mandatory trade embargo in June 1993 noted the massive displacement of the Haitian population brought about by the behavior of the military regime, called attention to the burden this displacement imposed on states in the area, and accordingly defined the situation as a threat to international peace and security, calling for action under Chapter VII (UN Doc. S/RES/841 [June 16, 1993], and S/RES/940 [July 31, 1994]). The U.S. government at this point was impelled to push for a quick resolution to the situation, in part, because of the continuing embarrassment and political difficulties of dealing with Haitian refugees and would-be refugees. In his public address on the eve of intervention, President Clinton stressed the need "to secure our borders and preserve stability in our hemisphere," adding more specifically,

> We have a particular interest in stopping brutality when it occurs so close to our shores. . . . As long as Cedras rules, Haitians will continue to seek sanctuary in our nation. This year, in less than two months, more than 21,000 Haitians were rescued at sea by our Coast Guard and Navy. Today more than 14,000 refugees are living at our naval base in Guantanamo. The American people have already spent $177 million to support them (Office of the Press Secretary 1994).

The refugee issue was also critical in Liberia. In late 1990 the Economic Community of West African States (ECOWAS) undertook a limited intervention in Liberia to try to restore order in the midst of civil war. Continued fighting threatened security in the region, both through creation of a huge refugee outflow into neighboring countries ill equipped to handle such influxes and through the risk of a direct spillover of fighting. In late 1992 the UN Security Council imposed an embargo on arms sales to the contending Liberian forces and supported ECOWAS's efforts to enforce a cease-fire.

But perhaps the most explicit and far-reaching precedent linking UN enforcement action under Chapter VII with prevention of a refugee crisis was Resolution 688, of April 5, 1991, on Iraqi Kurdistan. Following the end of the Gulf war, Iraqi suppression of widespread revolt in northern Kurdish areas had created fears that the entire Kurdish population would be uprooted—a particularly grave prospect for neighboring Turkey, with its own Kurdish minority unrest. Accordingly, the Security Council noted that it was "gravely concerned by the repression of the Iraqi civilian population in many parts of Iraq, including most recently in Kurdish populated areas, which led to a massive flow of refugees towards and across international frontiers and to cross-border incursions, which threaten international peace and security" (UN Doc. S/RES/688 [April 5, 1991]). Subsequently international forces were deployed to Kurdish areas to protect the population, Iraqi forces were (under pressure) withdrawn from the same areas, and a *de facto* autonomous Kurdish area came into being that allowed Kurdish refugees to return, at least, to safe havens in Iraqi Kurdish (not Turkish) territory.

It has been pointed out that this precedent was possible only in the aftermath of Iraq's military defeat, that the resolution attracted significant opposition (ten votes in favor, three opposed, and two abstentions including one permanent member, China), that there has been no commitment to finding a political solution to the Kurds' plight, and that there has been unilateral Turkish intervention in Iraqi Kurdistan during the period of UN operations there (Damrosch 1993a; Roberts 1993; White 1992). Nevertheless, the fact remained, as Adelman has put it, that

> a precedent had been set . . . for military intervention in the domestic affairs of a state for the purposes of protecting a minority population from the repression of its own government. . . . A new option to the traditional three solutions for refugees . . . had been created, that is, preventing the refugees from crossing an international border in the first place by 'humanitarian intervention,' creating safe havens protected by foreign military forces within the national homeland of the refugees (Adelman 1992, 62).

Of course, "intervention" does not necessarily mean armed intervention; various forms of "soft" intervention are considered legitimate even without authorization under Chapter VII. The fact that the UNHCR and other agencies now deal routinely with countries that produce refugees demonstrates an assumption that some forms of intervention are always permissible. Even in cases when Chapter VII has been or could be invoked, it is usually preferable to proceed by less forcible methods if possible. For example, the United Nations Transition Authority in Cambodia (UNTAC), while working under a peacekeeping mandate based in theory on the consent of all parties, nevertheless exercised vast authority during 1992–93 in implementing a peaceful settlement to that country's long civil war, including overseeing the successful repatriation of most of the refugees whose flight had been generated by that war. The Security Council does not face an all-or-nothing choice between full-scale military intervention or doing nothing at all. The table of "threats, injuries, and options for the international community" created by Robert Pastor puts threats, from "aggression" at the top and "economic development and social justice" issues at the bottom (with environmental degradation and refugee outflows falling in the middle), along one axis; on the other axis,the options dimension ranges from collective intervention through peacekeeping, economic sanctions, and verbal condemnation to total inaction (Pastor 1993).

Most UN activities relating to refugees are soft interventions, and their scope is continually being expanded. The UN resolution that established the Department of Humanitarian Affairs allows humanitarian aid to be provided with "the consent of the affected country" rather than at its request, as was the case in the past (UN Doc. A/RES/46–182, [December 19, 1991]). A more proactive approach has led to increased UNHCR involvement in countries of origin, collaboration with a wide range of actors from the political, development, and military arenas, and a number of innovative practices intended to ease the shipment of humanitarian relief and shield civilians against military attacks. The objective of such initiatives is twofold: to avert the onset of conditions that might force people to flee and to prepare for the repatriation and reintegration of previously uprooted populations. Many of these measures have been designed to strengthen the security of people within their homelands. Concepts such as "corridors of tranquillity," "zones of peace," "humanitarian cease-fires," and "safe havens" have been developed within the context of traditional peacekeeping, often as a form of intervention on behalf of refugees. Another recent innovation has been "cross-border, cross-mandate preventive zones" in which the UNHCR and other UN agencies divide the work along geographic lines with one agency assisting all of the uprooted people in a given area, thus circumventing some of the issues and limitations raised by borders (Drüke 1990). There is also increased recognition of the importance of establishing an early international presence of UN and NGO relief workers to permit international monitoring of the treatment of minorities and war-affected populations, in-country protection, and confidence building among warring factions.

Another important but underpublicized indication of greater international attention and action regarding refugee movements has been the proliferation of regional conferences and meetings during the past decade designed to stem refugee flows or promote the repatriation of refugees. In Europe numerous intergovernmental groups meet regularly to deal with migration issues, and European governments have formulated the Schengen and Dublin conventions to deal with population movements. International cooperation on refugees from Vietnam under UN auspices, culminating in an international conference and a comprehensive plan of action, attracted considerable attention and was important as a precedent in pressuring the country of origin to cooperate in a solution to the problem, ultimately including repatriation with international verification of nonprosecution and fair treatment (Rogers and Copeland 1993). Other regional conferences held on refugees in Southern Africa (SARRED [International Conferences on Assistance to Refugees in Africa], 1988), and Central America (CIREFCA [International Conference on Central American Refugees], 1989) paved the way for the resolution of conflicts and repatriation and reintegration of refugees during the 1990s. More recent collaborative and multilateral endeavors include the May 1996 Conference on Displacement in the Commonwealth of Independent States, organized jointly by UNHCR, the International Organization for Migration, and the Organization for Security and Cooperation in Europe. The objective of such efforts is to resolve refugee problems on a regional basis by strengthening the willingness and capacity of states to cooperate in managing population flows. These initiatives demonstrate the importance of developing regional systems for the management of conflicts and refugee crises. Neighboring states in conflict-prone regions are the most affected by refugee movements and thus have the greatest incentive to promote peace and the successful repatriation of refugees.

CONCLUSION

We have argued in this chaper, first, that justification of international intervention on the grounds of the impact of domestic disorder on other states is a reasonable extension of customary law; second, that as a threat to international peace and security, domestic disorder also falls under Chapter VII of the UN Charter, legitimating enforcement action not subject to the limits of purely humanitarian intervention; and third, that de facto international intervention in response to domestic disorder has become a norm in state declaration and practice in recent years.

The international community is in the process of establishing the principle that "the norm of the formal equality of states . . . can legitimately be dented when a state . . . behaves at home in a way that creates international disorder" (Hoffmann 1996, 21). Refugee movements are perhaps the clearest example of this shift. In Myron Weiner's words, "A country that forces its citizens to leave or creates conditions which induce them to leave has internationalized its internal actions. . . . If a people violate the boundaries of a neighboring country, then they and their government should expect others to intervene in their internal affairs" (Weiner 1993, 25, 26).

The case for intervention presented here stresses the actual impact on other states rather than general humanitarian arguments. In practice, of course, the issues are intertwined, and the combination of humanitarian concerns with the impact of disorder on others synergistically produces a stronger case for intervention in any particular historical case (Adelman 1992; Haass 1994).

This connection is not simply an accidental one in which humanitarian intervention is fortuitously justified by refugees or other transnational impacts. What is emerging is a clear and unassailable link between humanitarian concerns and legitimate international security issues. This link may in some cases provide justification for international action with positive humanitarian results where such justification might not otherwise exist, but it may also work in the other direction, to contain unwarranted interference on supposed humanitarian grounds.

This suggests the necessity of establishing a framework of general principles to guide the international community in deciding when a domestic situation, because of its potential to involve other states, warrants action by the Security Council or by regional organizations. Refugees are perhaps the most clear-cut expression of this potential, and they are an increasingly critical global problem by any measure. The global refugee problem is not going to disappear soon; in fact, it is assuming new dimensions that require a new and different approach tied to proactive foreign policies designed to respond to internal conflict. This will require, among other things, regulating international arms sales (especially small arms), promoting human rights and civil societies, and undertaking targeted interventions to forestall or mitigate violence and human rights abuses. Refugee problems are essentially born out of political conflict, and they directly engage the interests of states all over the world. More active intervention by the international community is in the long-term interest of all governments.

NOTES

1. For relevant resolutions see UN Doc. S/RES/795 (December 11, 1992) (Macedonia); UN Doc. S/RES/924 (June 1, 1994) (Yemen); UN Doc. S/RES/1040 (January 29, 1996) and UN Doc. S/RES/1072 (August 30, 1996) (Burundi); and UN Doc. S/RES/1076 (October 22, 1996) (Afghanistan).

11

Weapons Bans: Norms and Mechanisms of Global Governance

Richard Price

To speak of norms in world politics necessarily implies the existence of a social realm; in international relations this has been conceptualized variously with terms such as *international society, transnational relations, transnational networks,* and *global civil society.* These terms in turn imply the existence of socialization processes, processes that in essence constitute formations of global governance. Studies of international norms have often focused on socialization processes at the level of powerful states and political elites (Ikenberry and Kupchan 1990), and the field in general has tended to emphasize the notion of enforcement understood as a required interstate analogue to the role of domestic police in enforcing societal laws and norms. But in the absence of an effective and legally mandated supranational police force, it is alternative mechanisms of socialization that must be identified to assess the extent and efficacy of relations of global governance. In this chapter I investigate these mechanisms of socialization that occur in the genesis, development, and operation of a particular class of norms, namely, those proscribing the use of certain weapons in warfare. I identify the role of "grafting" and the constitution of utilities in generating weapons taboos as well as the dynamics facilitated by the absolute form of these norms, their institutionalization, the role of violations, their means of (re)enforcement and discipline, and the role of the state and civil society.

It is predominantly constructivist approaches to international relations (along with works in international law) that have focused upon the social importance of norms in world politics. The first generation of this work was carried on at a theoretical and metatheoretical level (Kratochwil 1984, 1989; Wendt 1992). More empirically oriented work explicitly drawing upon constructivist theoretical insights, as well as other work that is consistent with and can contribute to key constructivist ideas, has produced a range of empirical investigations regarding the genesis and functioning of norms of violence in world politics (Adler 1992; Katzenstein 1996b; Price 1997, 1998b; Tannenwald 1995; Thomson 1994). This chapter draws upon such empirical studies, particularly as they relate to norms that have developed around poison and poisoned weapons, chemical weapons, biological weapons, nuclear weapons, strategic defenses, antipersonnel (AP) land mines, and blinding laser weapons. The aim is to bring together theoretical insights about the role of norms as emphasized in the constructivist literature with a more systematic empirical accounting of the origins and roles of norms that goes beyond the idiosyncracies of specific cases. In the course of this investigation I draw attention to the implications of moving from a conceptualization of the social realm as an international society in which states are the actors, to the role of transnational or global civil society in which nonstate actors assume importance.

GRAFTING

Although numerous pathways for the genesis of new global norms have been identified (see Price 1998b), a singularly important social process in the origins of weapons taboos is the grafting of moral opprobrium from one category of technology onto another. An exemplar of this process is the way that chemical and biological weapons have often been associated with poison, a weapon believed to have been subject to an age-old prohibition across civilizations. This process of grafting also has been much in evidence in contemporary efforts to ban AP land mines. A ban has seemed far less outrageous a proposal to many members of international society than would otherwise be the case because of the existence of other viable weapons taboos—namely, those against the use of chemical and biological weapons—whose existence provides a background that makes it intelligible to countenance weapons bans.

Moreover, grafting has been employed as a self-conscious tool by those seeking a ban on AP mines. Proponents of a ban have sought to deconventionalize land mines and establish new international norms "which place AP mines in the same category as chemical and biological weapons, a category of weapons shunned by the world" (Landmine Update 1996, 1). Policy makers have echoed such sentiments: "Our goal should be to treat antipersonnel land mines with the same stigma as poison gas and other indiscriminate, inhumane weapons," according to U.S. senator Patrick Leahy (Leahy 1995, 5). Even members of national military establishments have voiced this position, including the following statement by a senior Pentagon policy maker: "We've all agreed we're going to have to get rid of land mines. We have to lump them together with chemical and biological weapons" (Fedarko 1996, 54).

One problem with directly grafting the aura of delegitimation surrounding chemical weapons to AP land mines is the fact that the perpetuation of the chemical weapons taboo owes much to continued unfamiliarity with gas. Soldiers and civilians alike have not had the unfortunate opportunity to resign themselves to the "reality" of gas as just another regrettable but unavoidable feature of warfare. That this avenue is obviously not open to the case of land mines has not gone unnoticed. Still, in the words of UN secretary-general Boutros Boutros-Ghali, an

> important avenue to pursue is placing mines in the same legal and ethical category as chemical and biological weapons in order to stigmatize them in the public imagination. The use of mines is so common that for those unfamiliar with their effects they may not invoke the horrific visions of chemical or biological warfare. Were their effects better known, land mines would undoubtedly shock the conscience of mankind—the same public reaction that led to the banning of chemical and biological weapons. (Boutros-Ghali 1994, 13)

An additional incarnation of this process of grafting is the situation of delegitimated weapons in a category of weapons of mass destruction. It has been argued that "landmines can be considered a weapon of mass destruction in slow motion. As a result, they should be perceived as being just as indiscriminate and inhumane as chemical weapons." (Human Rights Watch 1993, 1). Although the inclusion of chemical weapons and AP mines in a category of weapons of mass destruction has contributed to their illegitimacy, the existence of the grafting process should not be taken to impart a teleology to the development of weapon taboos, as if international society is destined to see an evolutionary growing of the category of delegitimated weapons. Grafting is not necessarily a good thing, and it can work in the opposite direction as well. The depiction of chemical and biological weapons as "poor man's bombs" and their inclusion as weapons of mass destruction has actually increased the allure of possessing them for some actors in the international system. This is because the possession of nuclear weapons confers status on its possessor, given the place of these weapons as a currency of international power. The universality of the delegitimation operation with respect to chemical weapons and perhaps biological weapons as well ultimately seems contingent upon a corresponding decrease in the allure of possessing nuclear weapons.

GENERATING UTILITIES

The realist and rationalist imagery of world politics as consisting of independent states that act upon their self-interests depicts an asocial realm devoid of relations of global governance. One of the most important mechanisms facilitating the development of norms that delegitimate weapons, however, has been the normative context in which the generation of utilities (of weapons' utility in particular), takes place. The realist expectation is that states will ban only weapons that are not militarily useful. The corollary of this claim is the supposition that weapons that have been subject to meaningful restraints must be militarily ineffective. Empirical analyses of the chemical and nuclear weapons taboos render this argument overly simplistic at best and erroneous at worst. For example, chemical weapons have been assessed at key moments by military establishments as having high military utility for certain situations, including their value had they been employed against the D-Day landings during World War II or against Japanese defenses in caves and tunnels in the Pacific arena.

Nonetheless, chemical weapons are sometimes claimed by scholars and policy makers to have little or no military utility as a way of explaining or justifying their abandonment. In fact, this is not entirely wrong for some states, in the sense that weapons that have been removed from standard military procurement, doctrine, and practice do in fact have questionable utility because as militaries are not prepared to utilize them and are not reliant upon them. The important theoretical point, however, is that such rationalist explanations for restraints on weapons are not entirely removed from the influence of post hoc rationalizations for limitations that have come about for other reasons. Constructivism highlights the role of norms in the definition of state security interests in a way that seeks to fill in the indeterminacy of rationalist models of utility (Price and Tannenwald 1996).

How has this process of generating utilities played out with respect to particular weapons? It has sometimes been remarked in the context of both World War II and the contemporary period that chemical weapons have not been a priority for great powers because other alternatives have been available. The point, however, is that no one would have bothered searching for alternatives and for reasons not to employ chemical weapons if they had been an utterly unremarkable and unpoliticized weapon. In preparations for World War II, the development of gas warfare capabilities, let alone their use, required an extra burden of proof that was not placed upon other weapons. In Germany, it was held that the production of gas on a large scale could be justified on military grounds only if a large-scale offensive use of poison gas were planned at the outset of a war, an eventuality that never happened. One of the major reasons given for German restraint in not using gas against the Allied landing at Normandy was the assessment that offensive and defensive preparations for gas were not adequate. What is interesting here is what comes to be defined as "adequate." At the time of the Normandy landing, Germany had a six-month supply of gas, including the Luftwaffe's half-million gas bombs and spray tanks, which could be used by aircraft. And yet, this was not deemed sufficient to wage chemical warfare (CW) (Price 1997).

In short, the criteria of sufficiency was not the same for chemical weapons as for other weapons. It was invariably assessed that "sufficient" preparations of gas were not available, whereas, by the standards of an unpoliticized weapon, rather large amounts of such arms often were on hand. In part this issued from a belief that one should have either an enormous supply of chemical weapons or none at all: a chemical attack had to be large scale in order to be effective, and constantly keeping on hand arsenals of a small number of chemical bombs would not be worthwhile. On the other hand, definitions of what counts as adequate are not simply objective calculations, and before and during the war such definitions were not immune from political and normative considerations.

In addition, because chemical weapons were not to be used and had not yet been used, assessments of their use could be made in terms of the relative advantage their employment would bring with respect to other weapons. Thus, rather than simply being employed without question as a standard auxiliary to high explosives and incendiaries in bombing raids or to augment other weapons in battlefield operations, the use of chemical weapons had to be *decisive* (often in and of itself), *and not just useful*, in order to justify their employment. By World War II, the burden of proof for the decisiveness of chemical warfare was incomparably—and as it turned out, prohibitively—high. This was partly the result of military assessments that gas warfare was not worth initiating unless it was decisive, because the net effect of the mutual employment of gas would just be a further logistical complication of the battlefield and would constitute the addition of extra burdens upon soldiers. The point, however, is that the same could be said of many weapons. The experience of the machine gun in the trench warfare of World War I particularly comes to mind. Machine guns greatly complicated military maneuvering on the battlefield, almost shutting it down while multiplying the slaughter, all to little or no end. No one thought as a result that machine guns might not be used.

Throughout history the fact that few other weapons have proven to be so "decisive" as to turn around a war did not hinder their employment, especially in their early and often less effective forms. There has been no shortage of candidates put forth as "war-winning" weapons throughout history, but few indeed have ever lived up to such expectations (see O'Connell 1989; van Creveld 1989; McNeill 1982; Raudzens 1990). Typical weapons today are regarded in unremarkable terms as meeting the standard of having utility; indeed, rarely is the question ever brought up. That is, the kind of politics wrought by weapons norms does not intrude. Rarely, however, have such weapons met the criterion of decisiveness that is so often required of chemical weapons. J. R. Hale's observations on the introduction of the first firearms serves to make the point of comparison:

> The effects of firearms were specific and dramatic: they raised problems of tactics, equipment, and supply; wars cost more, new methods of fortification had to be devised, but they had little effect on the fortunes of campaigns as a whole or on the balance of political power. . . . Firearms may have decided the issue of a single battle . . . but they cannot be said to have decided a war (Hale 1965, 114–15).

What counts as "suitable," "adequate," "useful," or "decisive" is highly context dependent, and in the case of chemical weapons, such assessments have been highly politicized. In World War II, an extraordinary burden of proof was demanded of chemical weapons that required not only that they be decisive in any given battle but also that gas supplies could be counted upon for uninterrupted future supply. The context in which the determination was made of what counted as suitable preparations for gas was therefore different from that for other weapons. The upshot of all this is that although chemical weapons were regarded as effective and even potentially decisive in some circumstances, the usual criterion of utility was not enough to gain acceptance of the weapon. It is thus that the accepted wisdom that "all useful weapons will be used in war" was retarded, along with its corollary that "restraint matters only for useless weapons." In the context of an international prohibitionary norm against gas, justifications for the use of chemical weapons required better reasons than the usual unsaid test of effectiveness and utility. The same can be said of strategic defenses: they must be proven to be not only useful but also effective and even foolproof to justify abrogating the Anti–Ballistic Missile (ABM) Treaty.

The effort to stigmatize the category of AP land mines has begun to have similar effects, and at an even more accelerated pace for many states than occurred in the case of chemical weapons. Many proponents of a ban, especially the International Committee of the Red Cross (ICRC), have been careful to position the issue of land mines in terms of searching for an earnest balance between legitimate military objectives and humanitarian concerns rather than risk being portrayed (and perhaps dismissed) by states as peace advocacy groups seeking world disarmament. Instead, the ICRC has sought to take on the military establishments of the world on the common ground of assessments of military utility and necessity. Although opponents of land mines like the ICRC have concluded that the humanitarian costs of AP mines outweigh their military utility, efforts to prevent their use by states initially met stern resistance on "the assumption that they are an essential weapon of high military value and that their military value outweighs their human cost" (ICRC 1996, 2). The ICRC therefore commissioned an analysis of the "military use and effectiveness of antipersonnel mines" to empirically assess the actual utility of mines in conflicts over the past fifty-five years. Written by a retired combat engineer of the British Army, the study's conclusions were unanimously agreed at a meeting of military experts convened by the ICRC and have since been endorsed by a number of additional military personnel. According to the report the evidence indicates that AP mines "have usually had little or no effect on the outcome of hostilities. No case was found in which the use of anti-personnel mines played a major role in determining the outcome of a conflict. At best, these weapons had a marginal tactical value under certain specific but demanding conditions" (ibid.).

Joined by prominent military voices questioning the utility of mines, the land mine campaign's constant raising of questions about the military utility of AP land mines legitimated the political space doubting the "necessity" of the weapon. This has provided political cover for decision makers morally persuaded to support the effort to ban mines. Contesting the utility of AP mines has also upped the ante of justification for using mines: the weapon must be not merely useful but necessary, irreplaceable, or even decisive.

The intrusion into or even displacement of the criterion of "effectiveness" or "utility" with a much more demanding criterion of "necessity" or "decisiveness" carries another potential effect. As special justifications become required for use, the search is undertaken for alternatives that may serve as less controversial substitutes, which may result in a gradual deemphasis in operations and increasingly less reliance on the ostracized weapon. This is the process of generating a "utility," and there is evidence that in their search for alternatives to mines in the face of their politicization by the International Campaign to Ban Landmines (ICBL), numerous states and their military establishments have begun or even accomplished precisely this movement (Price 1998b). In the United States, for example, a spokesman for the Pentagon has stated that doctrinal and tactical changes have been initiated "such that there will not be a requirement for" AP land mines (United States 1997). Although there has since been oscillation within the administration and the Pentagon between meeting or resisting the U.S. commitment to replace mines by 2006, such processes have already occurred at a vastly accelerated pace and in a more widespread fashion than occurred historically with other proscribed weapons.

Even where militaries have concluded that mines do have utility, a principal effect of the campaign has been to politicize AP mines such that political decisions intrude upon and sometimes even trump strictly military calculations. Thus, in South Africa the military was apparently unwilling to abandon AP mines; in the end, it was a political decision that overrode such resistance and produced a ban policy.[1] As of May 1998, 126 states have indicated a commitment to the position that the humanitarian costs of AP mines outweigh their military utility by signing the 1997 treaty banning AP mines.

THE DYNAMICS OF ABSOLUTE TABOOS

How much does the form of a global norm affect its efficacy? A crucial feature of weapons taboos for understanding their efficacy is the absolute character of these prohibitionary norms. Proscribing any use of a particular category of weapons technology stands opposed to the logic of military necessity that governs most restraints in warfare. This logic allows that means of warfare may be legitimately employed that are necessary for the success of military operations. The corollary of this principle is a prohibition on acts that are not strictly necessary, and thus actions that cause unnecessary suffering or superfluous injury, are forbidden. Although there certainly is evidence for compliance with such norms in the history of warfare, such restraints often have proved all too prone to bleeding in the heat of battle.

The successful stigmatization of any use of an entire category of weapons is a comparatively rare phenomenon, in large part because it runs contrary to the dominant modern understanding of technology. The contemporary practice of modernity is to view a given technology as a value-neutral instrument. It is neither moral nor immoral in itself; rather, the moral value of technology depends upon how it is used. The slogan, "Guns don't kill people, people do," embodies this powerful understanding that it is not technology but human beings who are to bear moral praise or condemnation. Absolute bans on weapons, in contrast, deny that there is any legitimate use of the proscribed technology. Rather than legitimating the use of a technology against military targets while attempting to deny their use against civilians, bans on poison, chemical weapons, radiological weapons, nuclear weapons, biological weapons, and AP mines deny legitimacy to any use of the technology in warfare.[2]

Although the historical record attests to the difficulty of attaining an absolute ban on a weapon, even incipient forms of such bans can stimulate processes that have palpable consequences. In the case of chemical weapons, even a nonratified treaty that sought only to prohibit the use of chemical weapons (the Washington Treaty of 1922) had the effect of retarding chemical preparations by Britain in the interwar period. The absolute norm embodied in the Geneva Protocol of 1925, which banned the use of gas, influenced preparations leading up to World War II and ultimately contributed to the nonuse of chemical weapons during that conflict by affecting the context of allocation decisions. Allocation priorities became a barrier for the use of chemical weapons not encountered by other weapons, and they became so largely by virtue of their situation in the context of a weapons-specific taboo that delegitimated the weapon as a whole. This stands in sharp contrast with the usual way in which restrictions were sought—namely, by limiting the way in which weapons were to be used, such as prohibiting the use of submarines against civilian shipping, *which would not affect preparations for the weapon itself because the weapon could be legitimately employed for a variety of other tasks.* To cite but one example of this process, during Britain's deliberations over chemical warfare preparations before World War II, the advocacy of full-scale capabilities by the Air Ministry and War Office gave way to the priorities established by the Treasury, for the reason that

> It would be illogical to reduce our offensive or defensive capacity in more important directions in order to include an ideal scale of provision for a weapon *which it is hoped will never be used.* Gas provision is therefore a direction in which some risk may legitimately be taken [italics added] (quoted in Harris 1980, 61).

The emergent ban on AP land mines has taken this form. The ICRC and members of the ICBL have argued, and many governments have agreed, that civilians will inevitably become victims of mines unless the weapon is banned altogether. Supporters of a ban thus pushed successfully for an absolute prohibition on AP land mines, which would make violations easily provable, rather than complex restrictions on how they are used (e.g., in marked and fenced minefields) and what types may be used (such as prohibiting only "dumb" mines while permitting "smart" mines that self-destruct or self-deactivate) (ICRC 1994, 136). Although the easy availability of AP mines presents difficulties for enforcement, a number of avenues exist by which the prohibitionary norm may come to have palpable effects (Price 1998a).

THE EFFECTS OF INSTITUTIONALIZATION

It would seem reasonable to suppose that the institutionalization of a norm represents a significant indicator of increasing robustness. This may indeed often be the case, though institutionalization by itself is not an adequate indicator of the efficacy of a norm; relatively informal norms (e.g., on the use of nuclear weapons) can be very powerful, and some institutionalized norms can be violated in widespread fashion (e.g., the norm on torture) or fade over time (e.g., the norm on colonization). The question thus arises: In exactly what ways and by what avenues does the process of institutionalization confer the potential for the increased efficacy of weapons taboos?

The formalization of a taboo in international law provides an institutional imprimatur condemning the use of the weapon in question as a violation of acceptable norms of violence. The effect of an institutionalized absolute ban is to remove from its place of privilege the comparative dimension of assessments of the qualities of the weapon that is usually enough to emasculate a ban. In debates concerning the desirability of a weapon, then, the burden of political proof may be reversed: instead of proponents of restraint having to show that one weapon is more cruel than others, opponents of restraint may be placed in a position of having to show that the weapon is not cruel.

This is one way by which the legal norms institutionalized in successive international forums have reinforced the broader moral odium with which chemical weapons are generally regarded. The existence of international treaty law has tended to serve as the taboo's own justification and confers a degree of legitimacy to the position that chemical weapons are odious, thereby foreclosing (though not rendering entirely impossible) the questioning of the designation of these weapons as inherently immoral. Once international treaty law was in place, the usual arguments that all weapons are cruel and are a regrettable but inevitable feature of international life were not enough to undo the prohibitive success of international agreement. The fact that all weapons are cruel is not reason to reject a prohibition against a particular weapon. The burden of proof required to undo the taboo has henceforth been to make the positive case that chemical weapons are a desirable invention. The effect over time of the institutionalization of a particular interpretation of the humanitarian qualities of this weapon has been to consolidate the humanitarian–moral core of the norm. The more the focus of debates shifts toward legal controversies and technicalities, the more removed from contestation becomes the question of moral desirability of a ban in the first place. The Chemical Weapons Convention (CWC) that entered into force in April 1997 represents a further move toward the routinization and thus deepening of the chemical weapons taboo as its implementation becomes increasingly bureaucratized.

Of course, in any given situation a variety of exogenous factors will be important in determining whether a weapon ban is eventually upheld or violated. Here I simply argue that the institutionalization of an absolute ban introduces an additional dynamic into the mix that potentially provides an additional source of strength for the norm, one that is not available in its absence. An important factor in whether or not the burden of proof is meaningfully reversed in such cases is the extent to which the institutionalization of the norm creates a political constituency. In the case of chemical weapons and ballistic missile defenses, important constituencies have included the state and civil society, in the form of political leaders who have been committed to the regimes, and, since the 1970s, epistemic communities of scientists and experts who have sought to ensure state fidelity to international commitments (Adler 1992; McElroy 1992; Müller 1993). Institutionalization creates an internationally legitimated opportunity for constituencies that provides an additional avenue for the efficacy of norms.

As suggested by the case of chemical weapons or strategic defenses, this feature can be of even more consequence for bans that anticipate new technological developments. Weapons bans that are attained before the weapons are actually developed and integrated into military practice have the advantage of altering the usual context of moral protests against novel instruments of warfare. Rather than incurring only an after-the-fact castigation by a surprised victim, a prohibition of a weapon before such uses involves a mutual pledge of self-denial. There is no guarantee that such bans are inherently more effective than bans sought after the regular employment of a weapon, but their proponents do have the advantage of being able to nip an emerging bud rather than having to remove an entangled weed.

Harald Müller has argued that the ABM Treaty has provided a different context for discussions about missile defenses in the United States and has thus retarded their development: "The sheer existence of a regime puts an 'extra' burden of proof on regime opponents because in discourses about proper behavior of states and other regime actors, the regime structure serves automatically as frame of reference" (Müller 1993, 383). The case of chemical weapons and the ABM Treaty's restriction on ballistic missile defenses illustrate an important dynamic set in motion with the institutionalization of an anticipatory ban: the creation of a legal and political constituency that, *ceteris paribus*, provides an additional source of leverage for retarding the employment of a proscribed means of war before it becomes standard military fare. A 1995 ban on the use of blinding laser weapons, although it is not an absolute ban per se, would be expected to bring such dynamics into play should the use of such weapons come under more serious consideration in the future.[3]

A final element important in the institutionalization of weapons taboos is their location within the realm of domestic law. The taboo against using poison was directed not only against its use in warfare but against its use in domestic society as well. Criminal codes have sometimes made special distinctions for killing with poison, reserving particular punishments for poisoners rather than simply treating all acts of murder alike (a statute of 1531 issued by Henry VII ordered that poisoners be boiled to death). With the enactment of domestic penal legislation as required by Article VII of the Chemical Weapons Convention, activities prohibited by the CWC are to be regarded as violations of domestic law.

Similarly, dozens of state parties to the Biological Weapons Convention (BWC) have enacted domestic legislation making it a crime to develop, produce, acquire, or transfer biological weapons. Such legislation is not mandated by the BWC, though Article IV does require states to "take any necessary measures to prohibit and prevent" actions in violation of the BWC anywhere under their jurisdiction. Thus, in 1995, FBI agents arrested a man in the United States who had been indicted for violating the domestic implementing legislation of the BWC for possessing the toxic agent ricin. Further restrictions on chemical and biological agents were enacted in 1996 through domestic terrorism legislation in the United States. Proposals have been made to try to establish the use, production, or acquisition of biological weapons as a crime under international law, which would involve prosecution by an international court. The establishment of an international criminal court would constitute a revolutionary development for global compliance with norms, including weapons taboos, though in practice it may well be that the convergence of domestic legislation proves more effective. The latter relies more directly on the isomorphized institutions of the state as the agent of transnational socialization, which amount to mechanisms of global governance by proxy.

The emergent ban on AP land mines has already manifested itself in the domestic legal context. In November 1996 a Cape Town–based man revealed he had sold mines to individuals to use for personal and property security in South Africa. This ran afoul of the moratorium on the manufacture and supplying of AP land mines that had been declared by the government of South Africa; the state argued that the Defence Act applied not only to government but to individuals as well (*Johannesburg Star*, November 5, 1996, 1).

In short, an important dimension of international norms is the criminalization of prohibited international practices in domestic implementing and penal legislation. Below an international criminal court, the internationally diffused or even mandated convergence of domestic legal norms, including the institutions to implement them, is an important dimension of the deepening of international society and an important source of the efficacy of norms. This socialization process is discernible both in its application to citizen-criminals within society and to pariah states within international society. In this way, the efficacy of norms of violence as a form of global governance is intimately linked to the power of the state and the state of the powerful.

DURABILITY AND VIOLATIONS

There is a widespread belief that social norms can be said to be robust only to the extent that actors abstain from violating them; the violation of a norm is indicative of its weakness. However, the theoretical literature on norms has argued that violations are not only important but may even be necessary for the continued efficacy of norms. Extrapolating from his understanding of how legal norms work, Steven Lee has taken this argument to its extreme, suggesting that the unacceptability of permitting even a single violation of the nuclear weapons taboo renders the norm inherently unstable. As he writes, "Paradoxically, the *success* of legal deterrence is dependent on its *failure* . . . because its success depends on the belief that the state is willing to carry out its threats, which depends on a history of threat executions" [italics added] (Lee 1993, 101). He argues that if a legal system were to succeed in reducing nonconforming instances of behavior to zero, over time the perception that the state is willing to carry out its threats would fade, and thus the norm would erode.

On this crucial issue there is some dissonance in the literature on norms. Lee argues that the longer the system goes on the more the fear of sanction fades, the more precarious the norm becomes, and the less likely it becomes that habits of compliance will be formed (ibid., 324–25). On the other hand, it has often been maintained from the perspective of international law that a continued tradition of nonviolation is a positive indicator of the robustness of a norm rather than cause for worry of its erosion. In short, some argue that a long tradition of strong adherence to a norm signals its strength, whereas others contend that too much success may actually portend the erosion of a norm. Which position is right?

Contra Lee, one could certainly argue that in the scenarios of robust norms he depicts, the practice of violations might not even occur to anyone. Such practices might literally become inconceivable as the norm becomes so taken for granted as a set of intersubjective beliefs that it is not consciously deliberated in terms of a cost–benefit calculation but instead structures social practice in a more profound way. This functioning of norms is a central insight of constructivist analyses and other traditions of interpretive social science. Norms can function in a variety of ways: they may serve as mere justifications or operate instrumentally in cost–benefit decisions, but they can also help define more broadly the context of understanding of a situation, within which the assigning of costs and benefits gains meaning in the first place. Thus, it might not occur to a Japanese bureaucrat to violate norms of consensual decision making because the alternative of competitive individualism just does not make sense in that cultural context.

On the other hand, it is clear that longevity in and of itself is insufficient as a condition for a powerful norm. This is not to argue that a tradition of abstinence from norm-transgressing behavior is not important; the empirical record demonstrates this is far from the case. But what are the processes through which duration transforms into strengthened norms of violence?

In the case of chemical weapons, a crucial source of the taboo has been their continued status as anachronistically novel instruments of war, especially in terms of their use against civilians. The special apprehension and fear that issues from the confrontation with sheer novelty in human life (what gas proponents have called "ignorance") has held in an almost anachronistic way because massive chemical attacks have not become a regular part of warfare that soldiers and civilians have grudgingly had to "get used to" as another despicable "inevitability" of war. Unfamiliarity has fed into uncertainty, which in turn has enhanced the symbolic status of chemical weapons.

Moreover, a generational tradition of the nonuse of CW in and of itself, regardless of the reasons, has become a crucial constituent of the moral discourse regarding chemical warfare and thus of the international norm proscribing the use of chemical weapons. This point can be illustrated with an illuminating episode from the period of the Iran–Iraq war. During U.S. Senate hearings over Iraq's use of chemical weapons in the early 1980s, it was remarked in one exchange that gas weapons surely were reprehensible since even Hitler did not use them against Allied armies or cities. No one present knew why Germany refrained from waging CW in World War II, but the salient fact remains: "We do know it did not happen" (United States 1990, 51).

This anecdote has implications for assessing the robustness of the taboo and understanding how norms work. A common suggestion for measuring the robustness of such norms is to ascertain whether particular cases of nonuse were the direct result of a belief that their use was illegal and immoral. Lee argues that an effective tradition of nonuse requires not only the fact of nonuse but also a normative element proscribing such use (Lee 1993, 324–25). In making this distinction between a rule and a mere regularity, Lee's position echoes that of many writing in the international law tradition who have long maintained that to conclude a legal norm exists, one must demonstrate not only that there was compliance with the norm but also that compliance was undertaken because of a belief that there was in fact a legal obligation. A genealogical approach emphasizing the role of contingency highlights the fact that events and circumstances of a less intentional character nevertheless can prove no less important in the development of a norm. Over time, the process of forgetting the origins and functions of such prohibitions—to the point of never having to question their authority, such as with the ban on poison—is an indicator of the strength of the norm.

Although these processes can be crucially important, mere duration and longevity of a norm by itself is ultimately not sufficient as an indicator of its robustness. Thus, in proffering "duration" as an indicator of the robustness of a norm, Jeffrey Legro is careful to define it not simply in terms of "how long the rules have been in effect" but also "how they weather challenges to their prohibitions" (Legro 1997, 34). As emphasized by constructivist analyses, what is important is how other agents respond to violations and, indeed, how they define deviant behavior in the first place. As Friedrich Kratochwil and John Ruggie argue, this means that

> Precisely because state behavior within regimes is interpreted by other states, the rationales and justifications for behavior which are proffered, together with pleas for understanding or admissions of guilt, as well as the responsiveness to such reasoning on the part of other states, all are absolutely critical component parts of any explanation involving the efficacy of norms. Indeed, such communicative dynamics may tell us far more about how robust a regime is than overt behavior alone (Kratochwil and Ruggie 1986, 768).

The case of chemical weapons provides an apposite illustration of these processes. The use of chemical weapons in a particular instance does not necessarily signal the simple death of the chemical weapons taboo, any more than the occurrence of a homicide indicates that there is not a generally robust general societal norm proscribing murder.

Thus, though the Italians in Ethiopia during 1935–36 and the Iraqis in the Iran–Iraq hostilities during the 1980s violated the norm prohibiting the use of chemical weapons, the fact that the Italians and Iraqis refused to admit their use is significant when viewed in historical perspective. These states engaged in a process of self-censorship that contributed to the sense of aberration concerning their practice of warfare. When the Iraqis could no longer deny the use of gas in the face of irrefutable evidence, they did not justify it (as the Germans had in World War I) as humane or even acceptable behavior in war. Indeed, the Iraqis went so far as to argue that they upheld the international norm prohibiting chemical warfare. One need not attribute any credence to such claims to agree that the Iraqis contributed to the anomalous status of chemical weapons; they did not seek to conventionalize the weapon.

Still, the question arises: Given such blatant violations, what can be said about the robustness of the norm? One way to gauge the efficacy of a norm is to assess how extreme a situation must be to justify its violation. The societal prohibition against murder is not generally regarded as having been invalidated in cases of killing in self-defense. The taboo against killing can be regarded as generally upheld even as it is violated from a strictly behavioral point of view, so long as the crossing of the threshold is understood as an extreme exception. On this score the chemical weapons norm can be seen as becoming more robust over time. It amounted to far less than a powerful inhibition on the Germans in World War II or on the Italians in Ethiopia; neither was driven to use gas only as a desperate defensive measure for their own survival. For the Iraqis, in contrast, initial resort to chemical weapons was taken as a desperate measure at a point when it appeared they might lose the war to Iran.

The establishment of such thresholds is a principal way that norms work in social life. Norms rarely render violations impossible but rather make them unlikely, by raising the threshold of what counts as a legitimate exception to the rule. Few people would feel the need to deliberate over the legitimacy of violating societal norms against murder in the event of a deadly attack on oneself; self-defense is a widely accepted exception to the injunction not to kill. The existence of such exceptions does not mean that the norm is otherwise not robust, however; it simply means that there is a very high threshold in accepting a violation as an exception and that those exceptions are not undertaken lightly.

The threshold against employing chemical weapons has become much steeper since World War I; indeed, so high has the threshold become that for most states gas could only be used as an act of utter desperation. Norms affect compliance by raising the threshold of violations of social practices, sometimes so high that certain forms of action are not even considered to be within the realm of intelligibility. The chemical weapons taboo does not have the latter unquestioned status, but it can be said to be a "settled" norm (following Frost 1996, 105) in the sense that violation of it requires extraordinary justification. To use chemical weapons is anything but an unpoliticized part of routine military doctrine and practice; it is, rather, a political decision requiring political intervention at the highest levels. The same, of course, can be said of biological and nuclear weapons. In conjunction with its absolute form, this means that the nuclear taboo presents enormous barriers to the use of even low-yield nuclear devices. The movement to ban AP land mines has already had the effect of politicizing the issue to such an extent that in many countries it is political elites at the highest levels, and not just military decision makers, who would be involved in decisions to violate the taboo.

As emphasized by Kratochwil and Ruggie, assessing the overall robustness of an international norm in light of a violation also involves taking into account the effect of subsequent practices by others to reinforce or further erode the norm. This is so because norms such as prohibitionary moral institutions are social—that is, shared—and not merely the property of any one individual actor. As such, their efficacy is contingent upon their continued and shared reproduction through social practices. Whether or not one can say that the taboo against chemical weapons, for example, has been strong or weak as an international phenomenon depends not just upon the practices of violators but also upon the reaction of the world community and whether the responses of its members have subsequently instantiated the norm as one that was crossed with mild or serious consequences. One indicator of the existence of a norm is the expectation of rebuke for deviating from existing practices (Krasner 1983, 9). Before their employment of chemical weapons, Iraqi leaders behaved as if they felt constrained by the existence of a norm prohibiting the use of CW and were apprehensive of the international reaction to its violation. Although Iraq thus appeared vulnerable to efforts to enforce the norm, its leaders were to find that the taboo did not have the robust backing that they had perhaps been willing to heed. If one indicator of the existence of a norm is the expectation of rebuke for violations, a further gauge of its strength is of course the extent to which violations are actually punished. According to this standard, the chemical weapons taboo has not qualified as an unquestioningly robust universal norm.

This failure to instantiate the norm in favor of short-term interests has had serious long-term consequences and points to the importance of the failure to muster even a discursive condemnation of aberrant practices. The lack of response by the international community, grounded in the expediency of forestalling Iranian victory, led to the Iraqi use of gas against Kurdish civilians. Moreover, tolerance of Iraqi chemical warfare came to haunt the Western powers themselves a short time afterward: just a few years later the coalition of Western allies faced explicit threats by Iraq of the use of chemical weapons during the Gulf war, an eventuality that never occurred but was feared and expected. Moreover, the tepid response to Iraq's chemical warfare convinced other states that their efforts to pursue a chemical capability would not be severely punished; thus a group of states led by Arab nations including Libya, Syria, Iraq, and Egypt have refused to join the CWC.

A Foucaultian approach goes further in explicating the nature of the communicative dynamics of violations essential for the operation of normalizing regimes. Violations provide the necessary opportunities to establish standards of what is natural, normal, and acceptable as opposed to what is avoidable, aberrant, illegitimate, deviant, or inconceivable. Prohibitionary norms do not merely restrain behavior; they also are productive, in that they constitute who we are: "We form our identities by conforming ourselves over time to tacitly understood norms and generally accepted practices" (Hoy 1989, 15). To use an example, during World War II a British proposal to prepare to use gas against a possible German invasion was withdrawn in the face of opposition such as that of Major General Henderson, who argued that "some of us would begin to wonder whether it really mattered which side won."[4]

Michel Foucault underlined the effectiveness of this internalized process of socialization by emphasizing the accomplishment that is entailed in self-discipline: sovereign power does not have to be exercised because subjects censor themselves. "A stupid despot may constrain his slaves with iron chains; but a true politician binds them even more strongly by the chain of their own ideas" (Foucault 1979, 102–3). Norms are performed as gauges of identity through self-discipline. Thus, "Disciplinary punishment is, in the main, isomorphic with obligation itself; it is not so much the vengeance of an outraged law as its repetition, its reduplicated insistence" (ibid., 180). The Chemical Weapons Convention provides the contemporary chemical weapons taboo with far-reaching disciplinary measures with which to invite and compel compliance. Beyond simple punishment, the surveillance functions to be taken up by the Organization for the Prohibition of Chemical Weapons are intended to create conforming international subjects by a variety of techniques that provide an international analogue to those outlined in Foucault's analysis of the operations of institutions of disciplinary power (ibid., 182–83).

Where do we locate these socialization processes, and what do the answers tell us about the depth of the global social realm? To put it differently: Who are the agents of normalization for norms of violence? Have the agents changed over time, and if so, what are the implications for the relations of global governance?

STATE DISCIPLINE AND WEAPONS OF THE WEAK

The state has obviously been at the forefront of such disciplinary measures. Poison was delegitimated in Renaissance and early modern Europe because it was perceived as a threat to the practice of warfare as a circumscribed and personalized contest of force by those in control of the most powerful means of force. In other words, if the political practice of war was to remain "the sport of kings," an institution that legitimated the right of the powerful to prevail, then techniques that might undermine that practice could not be tolerated. Poison threatened this social institution because of its easy accessibility and the inability to defend against it: it could prove to be an equalizer, a "weapon of the weak" that subverted the hierarchical relations of power.

The successful delegitimation of poison and poisoned weapons reveals the way in which war is a social institution, carefully circumscribed within specific bounds to maintain that institution as a mechanism of the contestation of legitimate domination. At the same time, the consolidation of the poison taboo is related to the increasing concentration of legitimated coercive means at the hands of the centralized sovereign state and the concomitant elimination of nonstate means of violence (see Thomson 1994). In short, a crucial delegitimation process involved in socializing potential wielders of violence has been the hierarchical ordering of relations of dom-

ination through the establishment of a currency that determines such relations, and the state has been very successful in this endeavor.

In interstate relations, certain forms of violence have been legitimated
as acceptable currencies for the contestation of power and status, whereas
others have not. Chemical weapons were originally perceived as an advantage for the technological military powers but over time have come to be
delegitimated as the "poor man's atomic bomb" as the taboo against gas
consolidated. Thus, biological and chemical weapons today are routinely
castigated as "weapons of the weak." On the other hand, the effort by some
states to portray chemical and biological weapons "weapons of mass destruction" has sought to make explicit the discriminatory nature of the international nonproliferation regime, which legitimates the continued possession of nuclear weapons as a source of status for some states.

The banning of AP land mines is pregnant with such disciplinary practices though they have yet to come to the fore. One strand of argumenta-
tion that is being played out in debates over the utility of AP land mines is
the notion that these weapons have become less relevant to modern ar-
mored warfare. Instead, it has been contended, AP mines are most useful
in civil and guerrilla conflicts because they are cheap and seen as effective
in harassing, containing, and terrorizing civilian populations. Human
Rights Watch has observed that a major reason for the rise of concern with
land mines is the proliferation of unconventional wars and the shift of
mines from a defensive battlefield weapon to an offensive weapon aimed
deliberately at civilians (Arms Project 1993, 9).

Although of decidedly secondary importance to this point, the portrayal
of land mines as especially effective in "unconventional" wars provides one
avenue by which most of the technologically advanced and powerful states
over time may be taught to view the prohibition of AP land mines as in
their interests. The reason is that "weapons of the weak," like poison in
Renaissance Europe and chemical weapons today, undermine the exclusive advantages of centralized high-technology state violence. The conde-
scending and delegitimating castigation of a means of warfare as an unfair
"equalizer" carries with it the power of the dominant wielders of violence
in the global system. As the cases of the delegitimation of poison and chemical weapons attest, such relations of domination can have much to do with
the ultimate success of a prohibitionary norm. Antipersonnel mines may
increasingly be understood as undercutting the centralized control over violence of technologically advanced states. Although it will no doubt be contested by some, it may be that the ban on AP land mines will increasingly
find a favorable hearing among the technologically advanced states, contributing to the prospects for enforcement.

CIVIL SOCIETY AND THE SOCIALIZATION OF STATES

A striking occurrence in the development of weapons taboos in this century has been the increasing involvement of civil society (as opposed to solely the state) as a source of new norms and as watchdogs for compliance with them. The first embodiment of the chemical weapons taboo was the Hague Declaration of 1899; the Hague Conferences that produced the declaration came about in the context of rising voices in European societies that questioned and challenged warfare as a natural, noble, and desirable endeavor. In the second half of the twentieth century, civil society has had moments of success in focusing widespread attention on nuclear weapons, though it has also encountered failures. The reduction in nuclear arsenals of the superpowers cannot be understood without taking into account the role of these social movements. More importantly, nuclear weapons have not been used in warfare since Hiroshima and Nagasaki, and the role of civil society in this development of an antinuclear norm ought not be completely dismissed. During the Korean War Eisenhower and John Foster Dulles wanted to remove "the moral problem and the inhibition on the use" of nuclear weapons and instead treat them "as simply another weapon in our arsenal" (Foot 1988–89, 94). They felt more constrained by public opinion than any other concern, however, and the nonuse of nuclear weapons during the Korean conflict was a crucial step in the generation of a norm of nonuse (Price and Tannenwald 1996, 138).

A particular stratum within civil society that has played an increasingly prominent role in delegitimating weapons and policing violations has been communities of scientific experts. Through forums including Pugwash and the Bulletin of the Atomic Scientists, these "epistemic communities" have been at the forefront of the movement to delegitimate nuclear weapons since World War II (see Adler 1992; Evangelista 1995). Particularly since Vietnam, a similar constituency has become prominent in politicizing chemical warfare and policing norm-violating practices (McElroy 1992).

The role of civil society in delegitimating weapons has never been more important than in the case of the campaign to ban AP mines. Through techniques such as issue generation, networking, grafting, and shaming, transnational civil society has persuaded decision makers to ban mines and prodded other states to succumb to social pressures of emulation (Price 1998b). Although such campaigns have existed since the antislavery campaign of the nineteenth century, several developments are worth noting: (1) the democratization of foreign policy and the blurring of state and society boundaries through the inclusion of NGO members on state delegations to treaty conferences; and (2) the rapidity and density of transnational networks facilitated by innovations in communications technologies such as the internet. The latter increases the space to challenge the autonomy of state security policy. As Ron Deibert notes of the revolution in communications technology he terms "hypermedia,"

> transparency in general has been raised in the hypermedia environment to such an extent that states themselves are caught in a surveillance web. . . . The hypermedia environment has *dispersed* and *decentralized* the centers of surveillance to a much wider domain. . . . Today, governments and politicians find themselves under an intense scrutiny by an ever-expanding 'pool of watchers' both 'internal' and 'external' to the state itself (Deibert 1997, 169–70).

In this sense, communications networks might actually facilitate the possibility of further international weapons prohibitions, as evidenced in the development of a Mines Watch surveillance system emerging for AP land mines. Such systems provide a confidence-building network of rapid information transmission from the local to the global, a cooperative state and civil society verification and surveillance system based on the ground that few recalcitrants could escape should they decide to cheat. *Network* (see Sikkink 1993 and Keck and Sikkink 1998) is indeed an apt term for the transnational society facilitated by the internet and the world wide web.

These activities by civil society are important because state security policy is widely held to present special obstacles of access and information to the influence of civil society in general and to transnational nonstate actors in particular. "Hypermedia" facilitates the erosion of the barrier of information through communities of experts who are outside of government and who are able to monitor states' compliance with or violation of desired norms of behavior. The experience on issues including strategic defenses, land mines, and nuclear and chemical weapons demonstrates that knowledge is not necessarily a debilitating handicap for nonstate actors; some of the foremost experts on these weapons systems are nonstate scientists active in the arms control community.

Such processes represent the deepening of the location of the norm as it gains adherence not only in international society but in transnational civil society: the state could be said to be more thoroughly "socialized" in this sense. These developments do not, however, necessarily equate with a robust norm of wide scope; transnational civil society is linked to the spaces created by the existence of democratic states, thus giving this emergent formation of global governance an uneven texture. Moreover, the use of AP mines by nonstate actors—often groups seeking self-determination—is a major present and future source of the land mines crisis. For this reason, however, it is all the more imperative that norms proscribing the use of mines be located in sites other than the exclusive terrain of political elites of world powers negotiating arms control agreements. Thus the importance of the ICBL in securing commitments from groups such as the Taliban regime in Afghanistan not to use AP mines.

CONCLUSION

A number of processes have been identified that are important in socializing international actors toward the acceptance of weapons taboos. The institutionalization of restraints on weapons, particularly in the form of absolute weapons taboos that proscribe any use of the technology, has the effect of creating opportunities to move the burden of proof from those who would establish restraints to those who would abandon them. This reversal of burdens of proof is facilitated by the grafting of taboos from one proscribed category of weapons to another, much as arguments against apartheid drew successfully upon the case against related practices such as slavery and colonization.

State security interests with respect to its utility can be redefined over time as a delegitimated weapon becomes increasingly marginalized and the search for less politicized alternatives is undertaken. This can occur as a consequence of transnational civil society taking the initiative to teach states what can be seen as in their interests. The use of a weapon can also come to be marginalized through the politics of identity and discipline involved in violations of norms. Here too, the role of both the state and nonstate actors are important elements in the converging restraint of state practices of violence. For norms to operate as thresholds there must be a constituency prepared to instantiate the norms by defining aberrant behavior, and civil society has increasingly sought an active voice in the disciplinary mechanisms of international society.

NOTES

1. Interviews with South African government officials, Pretoria, February 24, 1997, and with Noel Stott and Penny McKenzie of the South African Campaign to Ban Landmines, Maputo, February 27, 1997.

2. Nuclear weapons represent a peculiar case insofar as their possession has conferred status as world power. In that sense they have retained a use in deterrence despite the existence of a robust absolute taboo against their employment in warfare.

3. The Fourth Protocol of the Convention on Conventional Weapons (CCW), which was adopted on October 2, 1995, at the review conference of parties to the CCW, provides that "it is prohibited to employ laser weapons specifically designed, as their sole combat function, or as one of their combat functions, to cause permanent blindness to unenhanced vision."

4. Memo of June 16, 1940, Public Records Office (Kew, United Kingdom), file WO/193/732.

References

Aaron, Henry J., Ralph C. Bryant, Susan M. Collins, and Robert Z. Lawrence. 1995. "Preface to the Studies on Integrating National Economies." In *Taxation in an Integrating World*, by Vito Tanzi. Washington, D.C.: Brookings Institution, vi–xxiv.

Acheson, Dean. 1966. "Canada: 'Stern Daughter of the Voice of God.'" In *Neighbors Taken for Granted: Canada and the United States*, ed. Livingston T. Merchant. New York: Praeger, 134–47.

———. 1969. *Present at the Creation: My Years in the State Department*. New York: Norton.

Adelman, Howard. 1992. "The Ethics of Humanitarian Intervention: The Case of the Kurdish Refugees." *Public Affairs Quarterly* 6 (January): 61–87.

Adler, Emanuel. 1992. "The Emergence of Cooperation: National Epistemic Communities and the International Evolution of the Idea of Nuclear Arms Control." *International Organization* 46, no. 2:101–45.

Advisory Commission on Intergovernmental Relations (ACIR). 1981. *Regional Growth: Interstate Tax Competition*. Washington, D.C.: GPO.

Alnasrawri, Abbas. 1993. *The Economy of Iraq: Oil, Wars, Destruction of Development, and Prospects, 1950–2010*. Westport, Conn.: Greenwood.

Al-Sowayel, Dina, and Sean Bolks. 1998. "How Long Do Sanctions Last? Examining the Sanctioning Process Through Duration." Department of Political Science, Rice University. Unpublished manuscript.

American Friends Service Committee. 1993. *Dollars or Bombs: The Search for Justice through International Sanctions*. Philadelphia, Pa.: American Friends Service Committee.

Anderson, Kym. 1995. Review of *Greening the GATT: Trade, Environment and the Future*, by Daniel Esty. *Journal of International Economics* 39:389–92.

Arend, Anthony Clark, and Robert J. Beck. 1993. *International Law and the Use of Force: Beyond the UN Charter Paradigm*. London: Routledge.

Arms Project of Human Rights Watch and Physicians for Human Rights. 1993. *Landmines: A Deadly Legacy*. New York: Human Rights Watch.

Aronson, Jonathan D., and Peter F. Cowhey. 1989. *When Countries Talk: International Trade in Telecommunications Services*. Cambridge, Mass: Ballinger.

"An Assault on Nuclear Arms." 1991. *U.S. News and World Report*. October 7, 24–28.

Axelrod, Robert. 1986. "An Evolutionary Approach to Norms." *American Political Science Review* 80, no. 4:1095–1111.

245

————. 1994. *The Evolution of Cooperation*. New York: Basic Books.

Axelrod, Robert, and Robert O. Keohane. 1986. "Achieving Cooperation under Anarchy: Strategies and Institutions." In *Cooperation under Anarchy*, ed. Kenneth A. Oye. Princeton: Princeton University Press, 226–54.

Baldwin, David A. 1971. "The Power of Positive Sanctions." *World Politics* 24, no. 1:25.

————. 1985. *Economic Statecraft*. Princeton: Princeton University Press.

Barnett, Michael N. 1995. "The United Nations and Global Security: The Norm Is Mightier than the Sword." *Ethics and International Affairs* 9:37–54.

————. 1996. "The Politics of Indifference at the United Nations and Genocide in Bosnia and Rwanda." In *This Time We Knew It: Western Responses to Genocide in Bosnia*, ed. Thomas Cushman and Stjepan C. Mestrovic. New York: New York University Press, 128–62.

Barringer, Richard E. 1972. *War: Patterns of Conflict*. Cambridge: Massachusetts Institute of Technology Press.

Berdal, Mats R. 1996. "Disarmament and Demobilisation after Civil Wars." *Adelphi Paper* 303. London: International Institute of Strategic Studies.

Blackhurst, Richard, and Arvind Subramanian. 1992. "Promoting Multilateral Cooperation on the Environment." In *The Greening of World Trade Issues*, ed. Kym Anderson and Richard Blackhurst. London: Harvester Wheatsheaf, 247–68.

Bloomfield, Lincoln P. 1993. "Collective Security and U.S. Interests." In *Collective Security in a Changing World*, ed. Thomas G. Weiss. Boulder: Lynne Rienner, 203–19.

Bloomfield, Lincoln P., and Amelia C. Leiss. 1969. *Controlling Small Wars: A Strategy for the 1970s*. New York: Knopf.

Bordo, Michael D., and Barry Eichengreen, eds. 1993. *A Retrospective on the Bretton Woods System*. Chicago: University of Chicago Press.

Borjas, George J. 1987. "Self-Selection and the Earnings of Immigrants." *American Economic Review* 77, no. 4:531–53.

Boutros-Ghali, Boutros. 1992. *An Agenda for Peace—Preventive Diplomacy, Peacemaking, and Peace-keeping: Report of the Secretary General Pursuant to the Statement Adopted by the Summit Meeting of the Security Council on 31 January 1992*. New York: United Nations.

————. 1994. "The Land Mine Crisis: A Humanitarian Disaster." *Foreign Affairs* 73, no. 5:8–13.

————. 1995. *An Agenda for Peace, 1995*. New York: United Nations.

Brody, Reed. 1995. "The United Nations and Human Rights in El Salvador's 'Negotiated Revolution.' " *Harvard Human Rights Journal* 8, no. 2:153–78.

Brown, Gavin, Barry Barker, and Terry Burke. 1984. *Police as Peace-Keepers*. Victoria B.C.: UNCIVPOL.

Brownlie, Ian. 1979. *Principles of Public International Law*. 3d ed. New York: Oxford University Press.

————. 1983. *State Responsibility*. Part 1. New York: Oxford University Press.

Buchanan, Patrick. 1998. *Great Betrayal. How American Sovereignty and Social Justice Are Being Sacrificed to the Gods of the Global Economy*. Boston: Little, Brown.

Buck, Lori, Nicole Gallant, and Kim Richard Nossal. 1998. "Sanctions as a Gendered Instrument of Statecraft: The Case of Iraq." *Review of International Studies* 24:69–84.

Bull, Hedley. 1977. *The Anarchical Society. A Study of Order in World Politics*. New York: Columbia University Press.

Buzan, Barry. 1993. "From International System to International Society: Structural Realism and Regime Theory Meet the English School." *International Organization* 47, no. 3:327–52.

Cafruny, A. W. 1987. *Ruling the Waves: The Political Economy of International Shipping, 1945–1985*. Berkeley: University of California Press.

Canada. Secretary of State for International Affairs. 1970. *Foreign Policy for Canadians*. Ottawa: Queen's Printer for Canada.

Canada, Department of Foreign Affairs and International Trade. 1994. *"Pro-Active Sanctions: A New/Old Approach to Non-Violent Measures."* DFAIT Policy Staff Paper 94/17. Ottawa.

Canada. 1995a. *Canada in the World: Government Statement*. Ottawa: Canada Communication Group Publishing.

Canada. Ministry of Foreign Affairs and Ministry of National Defense. 1995b. *"Towards a Rapid Reaction Capability for the United Nations."* Ottawa. Department of Foreign Affairs and International Trade.

Canada 21 Council. 1994. *Canada 21: Canada and Common Security in the Twenty-First-Century*. Toronto: University of Toronto Centre for International Studies.

Carment, David. 1994. "The Ethnic Dimension in World Politics: Theory, Policy, and Early Warning." *Third World Quarterly* 15, no. 4:551–82.

Center for Economic and Social Rights. 1996. *Unsanctioned Suffering: A Human Rights Assessment of United Nations Sanctions on Iraq*. New York: Center for Economic and Social Rights.

Cerny, Philip G. 1993. "Plurilateralism: Structural Differentiation and Functional Conflict in the Post–Cold War World Order." *Millennium* 22, no. 1:27–51.

———. 1996. "The Paradox of the Competition State: Structure, Agency, and the Logic of Globalization." Paper presented at the joint meeting of the Japan Association of International Relations and the International Studies Association, September, Makuhari, Japan.

Chayes, Abram, and Antonia Handler Chayes. 1991. "Compliance without Enforcement: State Behavior under Regulatory Treatises." *Negotiation* 7 (July): 311–30.

———. 1993. "On Compliance." *International Organization* 47, no. 2:363–89.

———. 1995. *The New Sovereignty: Compliance with International Regulatory Agreements*. Cambridge: Harvard University Press.

Checkel, Jeffrey T. 1997. "International Norms and Domestic Politics: Bridging the Rationalist–Constructivist Divide." *European Journal of International Relations* 3, no. 4:473–95.

Chipman, John. 1992. "The Future of Strategic Studies: Beyond Even Grand Strategy." *Survival* 34: 1 (Spring): 109–131.

Chiswick, Barry R. 1991. Review of *Friends or Strangers*, by George Borjas. *Journal of Economic Literature* 29 (June): 627–29.

Cline, William R. 1995. *International Debt Reexamined*. Washington, D.C.: Institute for International Economics.

Codding, George A., Jr. 1964. *The Universal Postal Union: Coordinator of the International Mails.* New York: New York University Press.

Codding, G. A., Jr., and A. M. Rutkowski. 1982. *The International Telecommunications Union in a Changing World.* Dedham, Mass.: Artech House.

Cohen, Benjamin J. 1998. *The Geography of Money.* Ithaca: Cornell University Press.

Coleman, James S. 1990. *Foundations of Social Theory.* Cambridge, Mass.: Harvard University Press, Belknap Press.

Coles, Gervaise. 1989. "Approaching the Refugee Problem Today." In *Refugees and International Relations,* ed. Gil Loescher and Laila Monahan. New York: Oxford University Press, 373–410.

Commission on Global Governance. 1995. *Our Global Neighbourhood: Report of the Commission on Global Governance.* Oxford: Oxford University Press.

Conlon, Paul. 1995. "The UN's Questionable Sanctions Practices." *Aussenpolitik* 45, no. 4:327–38.

Cooper, Richard N. 1989. "International Cooperation in Public Health as a Prologue to Macroeconomic Cooperation." In *Can Nations Agree?* Washington, D.C.: Brookings Institution, 178–254.

Cordesman, Anthony H., and Ahmed S. Hashim. 1997. *Iraq: Sanctions and Beyond.* Boulder: Westview.

Cortell, Andrew P., and James W. Davis. 1996. "How Do International Institutions Matter? The Domestic Impact of International Rules and Norms." *International Studies Quarterly* 40, no. 4:451–78.

Cortright, David, ed. 1997. *The Price of Peace: Incentives and International Conflict Prevention.* Boulder: Rowman and Littlefield.

Cortright, David, and George A. Lopez. 1998. "Carrots, Sticks, and Cooperation: Economic Tools of Statecraft." In *Causes and Strategies for Preventive Action,* ed. Barnett Rubin. New York Council on Foreign Relations and Twentieth Century Fund Press, 113–34.

———. eds. 1995. *Economic Sanctions: Panacea or Peacebuilding in a Post–Cold War World?* Boulder: Westview.

Crawford, Neta C. 1997. "The Humanitarian Consequences of Sanctioning South Africa: A Preliminary Assessment." In *Political Gain and Civilian Pain: The Humanitarian Impacts of Economic Sanctions,* ed. Thomas G. Weiss, David Cortright, George A. Lopez, and Larry Minear. Lanham, Md.: Rowman and Littlefield.

Crawford, Neta C., and Audie Klotz, eds. 1999. *How Sanctions Work: South Africa in Comparative Perspective.* London: Macmillan.

Crumm, Eileen. 1995. "The Value of Economic Incentives in International Politics." *Journal of Peace Research* 32, no. 3:313–30.

Cuthbertson, Brian. 1977. *Canadian Military Independence in the Age of the Superpowers.* Toronto: Fitzhenry and Whiteside.

Dam, Kenneth W. 1982. *The Rules of the Game: Reform and Evolution in the International Monetary System.* Chicago: University of Chicago Press.

Damrosch, Lori Fisler. 1993a. "Changing Conceptions of Intervention in International Law." In *Emerging Norms of Justified Intervention,* ed. Laura W. Reed and Carl Kaysen. Cambridge, Mass.: American Academy of Arts and Sciences, 91–110.

———. 1993b. "The Civilian Impact of Economic Sanctions." In *Enforcing Restraint:*

Collective Intervention in Internal Conflict, ed. Lori Damrosch. New York: Council on Foreign Relations, 274–315.

Davis, Jennifer. 1995. "Sanctions and Apartheid: The Economic Challenge to Discrimination." In *Economic Sanctions: Panacea or Peacebuilding in a Post–Cold War World?,* ed. David Cortright and George Lopez. Boulder: Westview, 173–86.

Deibert, Ronald. 1997. *Parchment, Printing, and Hypermedia: Communication in World Order Transformation.* New York: Columbia University Press.

Dempsey, Paul Stephen. 1994. *Law and Foreign Policy in International Aviation.* Dobbs Ferry, N.Y.: Transnational.

Dicken, Peter. 1992. *Global Shift.* 2d ed. New York: Guilford.

Diehl, Paul E. 1993. *International Peacekeeping.* Baltimore: Johns Hopkins University Press.

Doern, G. Bruce, and Brian W. Tomlin. 1991. *Faith and Fear: The Free Trade Story.* Toronto: Stoddart.

Doganis, Rigas. 1991. *Flying Off Course: The Economics of International Airlines.* London: Allen and Unwin.

Donagan, Alan. 1977. *The Theory of Morality.* Chicago: University of Chicago Press.

Downs, George W., and David M. Rocke. 1995. *Optimal Imperfection: Domestic Uncertainty and Institutions of International Relations.* Princeton: Princeton University Press.

Downs, George W., David M. Rocke, and Peter N. Barsoon. 1996. "Is the Good News about Compliance Good News about Cooperation?" *International Organization* 50, no. 3:379–406.

Dowty, Alan. 1987. *Closed Borders: The Contemporary Assault on Freedom of Movement.* New Haven: Yale University Press.

———. 1994. "Sanctioning Iraq: The Limits of the New World Order." *Washington Quarterly* 17, no. 3:179–98.

Doxey, Margaret P. 1987. *International Sanctions in Contemporary Perspective.* New York: St. Martin's.

———. 1996. *International Sanctions in Contemporary Perspective,* 2d ed. London: Macmillan.

———. 1997. *United Nations Sanctions: Current Policy Issues.* Halifax, N.S.: Dalhousie University Centre for Foreign Policy Studies.

Doyle, Michael W. 1995. *UN Peacekeeping in Cambodia: UNTAC's Civil Mandate.* Boulder: Lynne Rienner.

Drake, William J., ed. 1995. *The New Information Infrastructure: Strategies for U.S. Policy.* New York: Twentieth Century Fund Press.

Drüke, Luise. 1990. *Preventing Action for Refugee Producing Situations.* Frankfurt: Peter Lang.

Duffield, John S. 1992. "International Regimes and Alliance Behavior: Explaining NATO Conventional Force Levels." *International Organization* 46, no. 4:819–55.

du Preez, Peter. 1994. *Genocide: The Psychology of Mass Murder.* New York: Boyars/Bowerdean.

Easton, David. 1953. *The Political System: An Inquiry into the State of Political Science.* New York: Knopf.

Eayrs, James. 1972. *In Defence of Canada: Peacemaking and Deterrence.* Toronto: University of Toronto Press.

———. 1980. *In Defence of Canada: Growing Up Allied.* Toronto: University of Toronto Press.

Eden, Lorraine, and Fen O. Hampson. 1997. "Clubs Are Trump: The Formation of International Regimes in the Absence of a Hegemon." In *Contemporary Capitalism: The Embeddedness of Institutions,* ed. J. Rogers Hollingsworth and Robert Boyer. Cambridge: Cambridge University Press, 361–94.

Edgerton, Robert B. 1985. *Rules, Exceptions, and Social Behavior.* Berkeley: University of California Press.

Eland, Ivan. 1995. "Economic Sanctions as Tools of Foreign Policy." In *Economic Sanctions: Panacea or Peacebuilding in a Post–Cold War World?,* ed. David Cortright and George A. Lopez. Boulder: Westview, 29–42.

Elliot, Kimberly Ann. 1993. Remarks at Conference on Economic Sanctions and International Relations, University of Notre Dame, Notre Dame, Ind., April.

Enders, Alice, and Amelia Porges. 1992. "Successful Conventions and Conventional Success: Saving the Ozone Layer." In *The Greening of World Trade Issues,* ed. Kym Anderson and Richard Blackhurst. London: Harvester Wheatsheaf, 130–44.

Esty, Daniel C. 1994. *Greening the GATT: Trade, Environment, and the Future.* Washington, D.C.: Institute for International Economics.

Evangelista, Matthew. 1995. "Transnational Relations, Domestic Structures, and Security Policy in the USSR and Russia." In *Bringing Transnational Relations Back In,* ed. Thomas Risse-Kappen. Cambridge: Cambridge University Press, 146–88.

Falk, Richard. 1995. *On Humane Governance: Towards a New Global Politics.* University Park: Pennsylvania State University Press.

Farer, Tom J. 1991. "An Inquiry into the Legitimacy of Humanitarian Intervention." In *Law and Force in the New International Order,* ed. Lori Fisler Damrosch and David J. Scheffer. Boulder: Westview, 185–201.

Farthing, Bruce. 1987. *International Shipping: An Introduction to the Policies, Politics, and Institutions of the Maritime World.* London: Lloyd's of London Press.

Fearon, James D. 1998. "Bargaining, Enforcement, and International Cooperation." *International Organization* 52, no. 2:269–305.

Fedarko, Kevin. 1996. "Land Mines: Cheap, Deadly, and Cruel." *Time,* May 13, 20.

Feldstein, Martin S. 1992. "The Budget and Trade Deficits Aren't Really Twins." *Challenge* (March–April): 60–63.

Fidler, David P. 1997. "Return of the Fourth Horseman: Emerging Infectious Diseases and International Law." *Minnesota Law Review* 81: 771–867.

Finkelstein, Lawrence S. 1995. "What Is Global Governance?" *Global Governance* 1, no. 3:367–72.

Finlayson, Jock A., and Mark W. Zacher. 1981. "The GATT and the Regulation of Trade Barriers: Regime Dynamics and Functions." *International Organization* 35, no. 4:561–602.

Finnemore, Martha. 1996. "Constructing Norms of Humanitarian Intervention." In *The Culture of National Security: Norms and Identity in World Politics,* ed. Peter J. Katzenstein. New York: Columbia University Press, 153–85.

Fisher, Roger. 1969. *International Conflict for Beginners.* New York: Harper and Row, 119–24.

Florini, Ann. 1996. "The Evolution of International Norms." *International Studies Quarterly* 40, no. 3:363–89.

Foot, Rosemary. 1988–1989. "Nuclear Coercion and the Ending of the Korean Conflict." *International Security* 13, no 3:92–112

Foran, Virginia I., and Leonard S. Spector. 1997. "The Application of Incentives to Nuclear Proliferation." In *The Price of Peace: Incentives and International Conflict Prevention*, ed. David Cortright. Boulder: Rowman and Littlefield, 21–53.

Forsberg, Tuomas. 1996. "The Efficacy of Rewarding Conflict Strategies: Positive Sanctions as Face Savers, Payments, and Signals." Paper presented at the annual meeting of the International Studies Association, April 16–20, San Diego.

Fortna, Virginia Page. 1993. "United Nations Transition Assistance Group in Namibia." In *The Evolution of UN Peacekeeping*, ed. William J. Durch. New York: St. Martin's, 353–75.

Foucault, Michel. 1979. *Discipline and Punish.* New York: Vintage Books.

Foulkes, Charles. 1966. "The Complications of Continental Defense." In *Neighbors Taken for Granted: Canada and the United States*, ed. Livingston T. Merchant. New York: Praeger, 101–33.

Fournier, Julie. 1995. *Les conflits de nationalités en Europe centrale et orientale: Une analyse comparative des cas tchécoslovaque et yougoslave.* Master's thesis, Université Laval, Quebec City.

Franck, Thomas M. 1990a. *The Power of Legitimacy among Nations.* Oxford: Oxford University Press.

———. 1990b. "Secret Warfare: Policy Options for a Modern Legal and Institutional Context." Paper presented at the Conference on Policy Alternatives to Deal with Secret Warfare: International Law, U.S. Institute of Peace, March 16–17. Washington, D.C.

Frankel, Jeffrey A. 1992. "Measuring International Capital Mobility: A Review." *American Economic Review* 82, no. 2:197–202.

Frost, Mervyn. 1996. *Ethics in International Relations: A Constitutive Theory.* Cambridge: Cambridge University Press.

Gaddis, John Lewis. 1987. *The Long Peace: Inquiries into the History of the Cold War.* Oxford: Oxford University Press.

Gallarotti, Giulio M. 1991. "The Limits of International Organization: Systematic Failure in the Management of International Relations." *International Organization* 45, no. 2:183–220.

Galtung, Johan. 1967. "On the Effects of International Economic Sanctions, with Examples from the Case of Rhodesia." *World Politics* 19, no. 4:378–416.

———. 1983. "On the Effects of International Sanctions." In *Dilemmas of Economic Coercion: Sanctions and World Politics*, ed. Miroslav Nincic and Peter Wallensteen. New York: Praeger, 26–27.

Gamson, William, and Andre Modigliani. 1971. *Untangling the Cold War.* Boston: Little, Brown.

Garrett, Laurie. 1994. *The Coming Plague.* New York: Farrar, Straus, and Giroux.

Garvey, Jack I. 1988. "The New Asylum Seekers: Addressing Their Origin." In *The New Asylum Seekers: Refugee Law in the 1980s*, ed. David Martin. Boston: Martinus Nijhoff, 181–94.

George, Alexander L. 1991. *Forceful Persuasion: Coercive Diplomacy as an Alternative to War.* Washington, D.C.: United States Institute of Peace Press.

George, Alexander L., Philip J. Farley, and Alexander Dahlin, eds. 1988. *U.S.–Soviet Security Cooperation: Achievements, Failures, Lessons*. New York: Oxford University Press.

George, Alexander L., David K. Hall, and William R. Simons. 1971. *The Limits of Coercive Diplomacy: Laos–Cuba–Vietnam*. Boston: Little, Brown.

George, Alexander L., and Richard Smoke. 1974. *Deterrence in American Foreign Policy: Theory and Practice*. New York: Columbia University Press.

Glazebrook, G. P. de T. 1947. "The Middle Powers in the United Nations System." *International Organization* 1, no. 2:307–15.

Globerman, Steven, and Aidan Vining. 1983. "Bilateral Cultural Free Trade: The U.S.–Canadian Case." In *Canadian–U.S. Interdependence in the Cultural Industries: Proceedings of a Conference Held at Columbia University, New York, November 2, 1994*, ed. Fred Thompson. New York: Canadian Studies Program, Columbia University.

Goertz, Gary, and Paul F. Diehl. 1992. "Toward a Theory of International Norms: Some Conceptual and Measurement Issues." *Journal of Conflict Resolution* 36, no. 4:634–64.

Gold, Edgar. 1981. *Maritime Transport: The Evolution of International Shipping Law*. Lexington, Mass.: Lexington Books.

Goodman, Neville. 1971. *International Health Organizations and Their Work*. Edinburgh, Scotland: Churchill Livingstone: Aylesbury.

Goodwin-Gill, Guy S. 1983. *The Refugee in International Law*. New York: Oxford University Press.

Gordenker, Leon. 1987. *Refugees in International Politics*. New York: Columbia University Press.

Goulet, Denis. 1989. *Incentives for Development: The Key to Equity*. New York: Horizons Press.

Graubart, Jonathan. 1989. "What's News: A Progressive Framework for Evaluating the International Debate over the News." *California Law Review* 77, no. 9:629–63.

Haass, Richard N. 1990. *Conflicts Unending: The United States and Regional Disputes*. New Haven: Yale University Press.

———. 1994. *Intervention: The Use of American Military Force in the Post–Cold War World*. Washington, D.C.: Carnegie Endowment for International Peace.

Hahn, Robert W., and Kenneth R. Richards. 1989. "The Internationalization of Environmental Regulation." *Harvard International Law Journal* 30, no. 2:421–46.

Hale, J. R. 1965. "Gunpowder and the Renaissance: An Essay in the History of Ideas." In *From the Renaissance to the Counter-Reformation*, ed. Charles Carter. New York: Random House, 113–44.

Hampson, Fen Osler. 1996. *Nurturing Peace: Why Peace Settlements Succeed or Fail*, Washington, D.C.: United States Institute of Peace Press.

Harris, Paul. 1980. "British Preparations for Offensive Chemical Warfare, 1935–1939." *Journal of the Royal United Services Institute for Defence Studies* 125, no. 2:56–62.

Hart, Michael, with Bill Dymond and Colin Robertson. 1994. *Decision at Midnight: Inside the Canada–U.S. Free-Trade Negotiations*. Vancouver: University of British Columbia Press.

Hart, Robert A., Jr. 1996. "Economic Sanctions and Democracy: Toward a Theory of Democratic Conflict Behavior." Paper presented at the annual meeting of the International Studies Association, April 16–20, San Diego.

Harvard Center for Population and Development Studies. 1993. *Sanctions in Haiti: Crisis in Humanitarian Action.* Cambridge: Harvard University Program on Human Security.

Harvard Center for Public Health. 1991. *Health and Welfare in Iraq after the Gulf Crisis.* Cambridge: Harvard Center for Public Health.

Hasenclever, Andreas, Peter Mayer, and Volker Rittberger. 1997. *Theories of International Regimes.* Cambridge: Cambridge University Press.

Held, David. 1997. "Democracy and Globalization." *Global Governance 3,* no. 3:251–67.

Helman, Gerald B., and Steven R. Ratner. 1992–1993. "Saving Failed States." *Foreign Policy,* no. 89:3–20.

Hillen, John F. III. 1994. "Policing the New World Order: The Operational Utility of a Permanent U.N. Army." *Strategic Review* 22, no. 2:54–62.

Hilliker, John. 1990. *Canada's Department of External Affairs. Vol. 1, The Early Years, 1909–1946.* Montreal: McGill–Queen's University Press.

Hoagland, Jim. 1993. "The Sanctions Bromide." *Washington Post,* November 12.

Hocké, Jean-Pierre. 1989. "Beyond Humanitarianism: The Need for Political Will to Resolve Today's Refugee Problem." In *Refugees and International Relations,* ed. Gil Loescher and Laila Monahan. New York: Oxford University Press, 37–48.

Hoekman, Bernard, and Michel Kostecki. 1995. *The Political Economy of the World Trading System: From GATT to WTO.* Oxford: Oxford University Press.

Hoffmann, Stanley. 1981. *Duties beyond Borders: On the Limits and Possibilities of Ethical International Politics.* Syracuse: Syracuse University Press.

———. 1996. *The Ethics and Politics of Humanitarian Intervention.* Notre Dame: University of Notre Dame Press.

Holm, Hans-Henrik, and Georg Sorensen, eds. 1995. *Whose World Order?: Uneven Globalization and the End of the Cold War.* Boulder: Westview.

Holmes, John W. 1979. *The Shaping of Peace: Canada and the Search for World Order, 1943–1957.* Vol. 1. Toronto: University of Toronto Press.

———. 1982. *The Shaping of Peace: Canada and the Search for World Order. 1943–1957.* Vol. 2. Toronto: University of Toronto Press.

Holsti, Kalevi J. 1991. *Peace and War: Armed Conflicts and International Order, 1648–1989.* Cambridge: Cambridge University Press.

Hoskins, Eric. 1997. "The Humanitarian Impacts of Economic Sanctions and War in Iraq." In *Political Gain and Civilian Pain: The Humanitarian Impacts of Economic Sanctions,* ed. Thomas G. Weiss, David Cortright, George A. Lopez, and Larry Minear. Lanham, Md.: Rowman and Littlefield, 91–147.

Hoy, David Couzens. 1989. Introduction to *Foucault: A Critical Reader,* ed. David Couzens Hoy. Oxford: Basil Blackwell, 1–25.

Hufbauer, Gary Clyde (assisted by Joanna M. Van Rooij). 1992. *U.S. Taxation of International Income: Blue Print for Reform.* Washington, D.C.: Institute for International Economics.

Hufbauer, Gary Clyde, Jeffrey J. Schott, and Kimberley Ann Elliott. 1985. *Economic Sanctions Reconsidered: History and Current Policy.* Washington, D.C.: Institute for International Economics.

————. 1990. *Economic Sanctions Reconsidered: History and Current Policy.* 2d ed. Washington, D.C.: Institute for International Economics.

Human Rights Watch. 1993. "Major New Report Calls for Global Ban on Landmines." <gopher://gopher.igc.apc.org:5000/00/int/hrw/arms/1> (November 7).

Ikenberry, G. John, and Charles Kupchan. 1990. "Socialization and Hegemonic Power." *International Organization* 44, no. 3:283–315.

International Committee of the Red Cross (ICRC). 1994. "Report of the International Committee of the Red Cross for the Review Conference of the 1980 United Nations Convention." *International Review of the Red Cross* 299:123–82.

————. 1996. "Anti-personnel Landmines—Friend or Foe?: A Study of the Military Use and Effectiveness of Anti-personnel Mines." http://www.icrc.org/icrcnews/48da.htm (March 28).

Jackson, John. 1989. *The World Trading System.* Cambridge: MIT Press.

Jackson, Robert. 1993. *Quasi-States: Sovereignty, International Relations, and the Third World.* Cambridge: Cambridge University Press.

Jackson, Robert H., and Mark W. Zacher. 1997. *"The Territorial Covenant: International Society and the Stabilization of Boundaries."* Working Paper no. 15, Institute of International Relations, University of British Columbia, Vancouver.

Jan, Ameen. 1996. "Peacebuilding in Somalia." International Peace Academy Policy Briefing Series: New York.

Jennings, R. Yewdall. 1939. "Some International Law Aspects of the Refugee Question." *British Year Book of International Law* 20:98–114.

Jensen, Lloyd. 1984. "Negotiating Strategic Arms Control, 1969–1979." *Journal of Conflict Resolution* 28, no. 4:535–59.

Jepperson, Ronald L., Alexander Wendt, and Peter J. Katzenstein. 1996. "Norms, Identity, and Culture in National Security." In *The Culture of National Security: Norms and Identity in World Politics,* ed. Peter J. Katzenstein. New York: Columbia University Press, 33–75.

Jervis, Robert. 1989. *The Meaning of the Nuclear Revolution.* Ithaca: Cornell University Press.

Job, Brian, ed. 1992. *The Insecurity Dilemma: National Security of Third World States.* Boulder: Lynne Rienner.

Johansen, Robert. 1996. "The Future of United Nations Peacekeeping and Enforcement: A Framework for Policymaking." *Global Governance* 2, no. 3:299–333.

Johansen, Robert, and Saul Mendlovitz. 1980. "The Role of Enforcement of Law in the Establishment of a New International Order: A Proposal for a Transnational Police Force." *Alternatives* 6, no. 2:307–38.

Jonsson, Christer. 1987. *International Aviation and the Politics of Regime Change.* New York: St. Martin's.

Kaempfer, William H., and Anton D. Lowenberg. 1995. "The Problems and the Promise of Sanctions." In *Economic Sanctions: Panacea or Peacebuilding in a Post–Cold War World?,* ed. David Cortright and George Lopez. Boulder: Westview, 61–72.

Karl, Terry Lynn. 1992. "El Salvador's Negotiated Revolution." *Foreign Affairs* 71, no. 2:147–64.

Karns, Margaret P., and Karen A. Mingst. 1990. *The United States and Multilateral Institutions: Patterns of Changing Instrumentality and Influence.* Boston: Unwin Hyman.

Katzenstein, Peter J. 1996a. *Cultural Norms and National Security: Police and Military in Postwar Japan.* Ithaca: Cornell University Press.

———, ed. 1996b. *The Culture of National Security: Norms and Identity in World Politics.* New York: Columbia University Press.

Keating, Tom. 1993. *Canada and World Order: The Multilateralist Tradition in Canadian Foreign Policy.* Toronto: McClelland and Stewart.

Keck, Margaret, and Kathryn Sikkink. 1998. *Activists beyond Borders: Advocacy Networks in International Politics.* Ithaca: Cornell University Press.

Kegley, Charles W., and Gregory Raymond. 1994. *Multipolar Peace?: Great-Power Politics in the Twenty-First Century.* New York: St. Martin's.

Keohane, Robert O. 1984. *After Hegemony: Cooperation and Discord in the World Political Economy.* Princeton: Princeton University Press.

Kier, Elizabeth, and Jonathan Mercer. 1996. "Setting Precedents in Anarchy. Military Intervention and Weapons of Mass Destruction." *International Security* 20, no. 4:77–106.

Kirgis, Frederic L., Jr. 1995. "The United Nations at Fifty: The Security Council's First Fifty Years." *American Journal of International Law* 89, no. 3:506–39.

Klevorik, Alvin K. 1996. "Reflections on the Race to the Bottom." In *Fair Trade and Harmonization: Prerequisites for Free Trade?* Vol. 1., ed. Jagdish Bhagwati and Robert E. Hudec. Cambridge: MIT Press, 459–68.

Klotz, Audie. 1995a. *Norms in International Relations: The Struggle against Apartheid.* Ithaca: Cornell University Press.

———. 1995b. "Norms Reconstituting Interests: Global Racial Equality and U.S. Sanctions against South Africa." *International Organization* 49, no. 3:451–78.

Kocs, Stephen A. 1994. "Explaining the Strategic Behavior of States: International Law as System Structure." *International Studies Quarterly* 38, no. 4:535–46.

Kowert, Paul, and Jeffrey Legro. 1996. "Norms, Identity, and Their Limits: A Theoretical Reprise." In *The Culture of National Security: Norms and Identity in World Politics,* ed. Peter J. Katzenstein. New York: Columbia University Press.

Krasner, Stephen. 1983. "Structural Causes and Regime Consequences: Regimes as Intervening Variables." In *International Regimes,* ed. Stephen Krasner. Ithaca: Cornell University Press, 1–21.

Kratochwil, Friedrich. 1984. "The Force of Prescriptions." *International Organization* 38, no. 4:685–708.

———. 1989. *Rules, Norms, and Decisions: On the Conditions of Practical and Legal Reasoning in International Relations and Domestic Affairs.* Cambridge: Cambridge University Press.

Kratochwil, Friedrich, and John Ruggie. 1986. "International Organization: A State of the Art on the Art of the State." *International Organization,* no. 40:753–75.

Krueger, Anne O. 1997. "Trade Policy and Economic Development: How We Learn." *American Economic Review* 87, no. 1:1–22.

Krugman, Paul R. 1995. *"Technology, Trade, and Factor Prices."* Working Paper no. 5355, National Bureau of Economic Research, Cambridge, Mass.

———. 1997. "What Should Trade Negotiators Negotiate About?" *Journal of Economic Literature* 35 (March): 113–20.

Kudrle, Robert T. 1999. "Globalization and the Politics of the Future," in Jeffrey Hart and Aseem Prakash, eds., *Globalization and Governance*. New York: Routledge.

Kudrle, Robert T., and Theodore Marmor. 1980. "The Development of the North American Welfare State." In *The Development of Welfare States in Europe and North America*, ed. Peter Flora and Arnold Heidenheimer. New Brunswick, N.J.: Transaction Books.

Landmine Update, Canada. 1996. <http://www.web.apc.org> (April 25).

Lawrence, Robert Z. 1996. "Workers and Economists II: Resist the Binge." *Foreign Affairs* 75, no. 4:170–73.

Leahy, Patrick. 1995. "Hidden Killers: Solving the Global Land Mine Crisis." *America* 172 (June 17): 21.

Lederach, John Paul. 1995. *Preparing for Peace: Conflict Transformation across Cultures*. Syracuse: Syracuse University Press.

Lee, Steven. 1993. *Morality, Prudence, and Nuclear Weapons*. Cambridge: Cambridge University Press.

Legault, Albert, John Sigler, Janice Stein, and Blema Steinberg, eds. 1979. *L'Analyse comparative des conflits*. Quebec City: Centre québécois de relations internationales.

Legro, Jeffrey. 1997. "Which Norms Matter?: Revisiting the 'Failure' of Internationalism." *International Organization* 51, no. 1:31–63.

Leive, David M. 1976. *International Regulatory Regimes: Case Studies in Health, Meteorology, and Food*. Lexington, Mass: Lexington Books.

Leng, Russell. 1993. "Influence Techniques among Nations." In *Behavior, Society, and International Conflict*, vol. 3, ed. Philip E. Tetlock, Oxford: Oxford University Press, 115.

Levinson, Arik. 1996. "Environmental Regulations and Industry Location: International and Domestic Evidence." In *Fair Trade and Harmonization: Prerequisites for Free Trade?* Vol. 1, ed. Jagdish Bhagwati and Robert E. Hudec. Cambridge: MIT Press, 429–58.

Lewis, Peter M. 1998. "Nigeria: The Challenge of Preventive Action." In *Cases and Strategies for Preventive Action*, ed. Barrett R. Rubin. New York: Twentieth Century Fund Press, 93–112.

Lie, Trygvie. 1948. *Annual Report of the Secretary-General on the Work of the Organization, 1 July 1947–30 June 1948*. General Assembly Official Records: Third Session Supplement no. 1 (A/565). Lake Success, N.Y.: United Nations.

Lindsay, James M. 1986. "Trade Sanctions as Policy Instruments: A Re-examination." *International Studies Quarterly* 30, no. 2:153–73.

Lipschutz, Ronnie. 1992. "Reconstructing World Politics: The Emergence of Global Civil Society." *Millennium* 21, no. 3:389–420.

———. 1997. "From Place to Planet: Local Knowledge and Global Environmental Governance." *Global Governance* 3, no. 1:83–102.

Lipson, Charles. 1984. "International Cooperation in Security and Economic Affairs." *World Politics* 37, no. 1:1–23.

Littwak, Edward M. 1995. "Toward Post-Heroic Warfare." *Foreign Affairs* 74, no. 3:117–18.

Loescher, Gil. 1992. "Refugee Movements and International Security." *Adelphi Paper*, London: International Institute of Strategic Studies, no. 268.

————. 1993. *Beyond Charity: International Cooperation and the Global Refugee Crisis.* New York: Oxford University Press.

Long, William J. 1996a. *Economic Incentives and Bilateral Cooperation.* Ann Arbor: University of Michigan Press.

————. 1996b. "Trade and Technology Incentives and Bilateral Cooperation." *International Studies Quarterly* 40, no. 1:77–106.

Lopez, George A., and David Cortright. 1995. "Economic Sanctions in Contemporary Global Relations." In *Economic Sanctions: Panacea or Peacebuilding in a Post–Cold War World?*, ed. David Cortright and George A. Lopez. Boulder: Westview, 3–16.

————. 1998. "Trouble in the Gulf: Pain and Promise." *Bulletin of the Atomic Scientists* (May–June): 39–43.

Lund, Michael S. 1996. "Burundi's Failed Transition to Legitimate Politics, 1993–1996: Could International Conflict Management Have Done Better?" Paper presented at the Third Annual Conference on Preventive Action, Council of Foreign Relations, December 12, New York.

Luper-Foy, Steven. 1992. "Intervention and Guatemalan Refugees." *Public Affairs Quarterly* 6 (January): 45–60.

McElroy, Robert. 1992. *Morality and American Foreign Policy.* Princeton: Princeton University Press.

M'Gonigle, R. Michael, and Mark W. Zacher. 1979. *Pollution, Politics, and International Law: Tankers at Sea.* Berkeley: University of California Press.

McKenna, Peter. 1995. *Canada and the OAS: From Dilettante to Full Partner.* Ottawa: Carleton University Press.

McLin, Jon B. 1967. *Canada's Changing Defense Policy, 1957–1963: The Problems of a Middle Power in Alliance.* Baltimore: Johns Hopkins University Press.

McNeill, William. 1982. *The Pursuit of Power.* Chicago: University of Chicago Press.

Makinda, Samuel M. 1993. *Seeking Peace from Chaos: Humanitarian Intervention in Somalia.* Boulder: Lynne Rienner.

Malone, David, and John G. Cockell. 1996. *The Security Council in the 1990s: Lessons and Priorities.* Ottawa: Department of Foreign Affairs and International Trade.

Mansfield, Edward. 1995. "International Institutions and Economic Sanctions." *World Politics* 47, no. 4:575–605.

Markakis, John, and Katsuyoshi Fukui. 1994. *Ethnicity and Conflict in the Horn of Africa.* Athens: Ohio University Press.

Martin, Lisa. 1993. "Credibility, Costs, and Institutions." *World Politics* 45, no. 3:406–32.

Matte, Nicholas M. 1981. *Treatise on Air/Aeronautical Law.* Toronto: Carswell.

Matthews, Robert O. 1989. *International Conflict and Conflict Management.* 2d ed. Scarborough, Ont.: Prentice-Hall Canada.

Mearsheimer, John J. 1995. "The False Promise of International Institutions." *International Security* 19, no. 3:5–49.

Meron, Theodor. 1993. "The Case for War Crimes Trials in Yugoslavia." *Foreign Affairs* 72, no. 3:122–35.

Milner, Helen. 1988. *Resisting Protectionism.* Princeton: Princeton University Press.

Minear, Larry, David Cortright, Julia Wagler, George A. Lopez, and Thomas G.

Weiss. 1998. *Toward More Humane and Effective Sanctions Management: Enhancing the Capacity of the United Nations System.* Occasional Paper 31, Watson Institute, Brown University.

Mitchell, Ronald B. 1998. "Sources of Transparency. Information Systems in International Regimes." *International Studies Quarterly* 42, no. 1:109–30.

Mittelman, James H. 1996. "The Dynamics of Globalization." In *Globalization. Critical Reflections*, ed. James H. Mittelman. Boulder: Lynne Rienner, 1–19.

Moore, John Norton. 1974. "Towards an Applied Theory for the Regulation of Intervention." In *Law and Civil War in the Modern World*, ed. John Norton Moore. Baltimore: Johns Hopkins University Press.

Morgan, T. Clifton. 1993. "Democracy and War: Reflections on the Literature." *International Interactions* 18:197–203.

Morgan, T. Clifton, and Valerie L. Schwebach. 1997. "Fools Suffer Gladly: The Use of Economic Sanctions in International Crises." *International Studies Quarterly* 41, no. 1:27–50.

Morgenthau, Hans. 1962. "A Political Theory of Foreign Aid." *American Political Science Review* 56 (June):301–09.

Morrison, Alex. 1995. "Canada and Peacekeeping: A Time for Reanalysis?" In *Canada's International Security Policy*, ed. David B. Dewitt and David Leyton-Brown. Scarborough, Ont.: Prentice-Hall Canada.

Mueller, John. 1989. *Retreat from Doomsday: The Obsolescence of Major War.* New York: Basic Books.

Müller, Harald. 1993. "The Internalization of Principles, Norms and Rules by Governments: The Case of Security Regimes." In *Regime Theory in International Relations*, ed. Volker Rittberger. Oxford: Oxford University Press, 361–88.

Murray, Shoon Kathleen, Louis Klarevas, and Thomas Hartley. 1997. "Are Policymakers Misreading Public Views toward the United Nations?" Paper presented at the annual meeting of the International Studies Association, March, Toronto.

Nadelman, Ethan A. 1990. "Global Prohibition Regimes: The Evolution of Norms in International Society." *International Organization* 44, no. 4:479–526.

Nelson, Joan M., and Stephanie J. Eglinton. 1993. *Global Goals, Contentious Means: Issues of Multiple Aid Conditionality.* Washington, D.C.: Overseas Development Council.

Niou, Emerson M. S., and Peter C. Ordeshook. 1994. " 'Less Filling, Tastes Great': The Realist–Neoliberal Debate." *World Politics* 46, no. 2:209–34.

North, Douglas C. 1990. *Institutions, Institutional Change, and Economic Performance.* Cambridge: Cambridge University Press.

Nossal, Kim Richard. 1989. "International Sanctions as International Punishment." *International Organization* 43, no. 2:301–22.

———. 1993b. "The Limits of Linking Aid and Trade to Human Rights." In *Cross Currents: International Relations in the Post–Cold War Era*, ed. Mark Charlton and Elizabeth Riddell-Dixon. Toronto: Nelson Canada, 443–50.

———. 1993a. "The Democratization of Canadian Foreign Policy?" *Canadian Foreign Policy* 1, no. 3:95–104.

———. 1995. "The Democratization of Canadian Foreign Policy: The Elusive Ideal." In *Democracy and Foreign Policy: Canada among Nations, 1995*, ed. by Maxwell A. Cameron and Maureen Appel Molot. Ottawa: Carleton University Press, 29–43.

———. 1999. "International Sanctions as Instruments of Global Governance?" *Global Society* 13, no. 2.

Nossal, Kim Richard, and Carolynn Vivian. 1997. "A Brief Madness: Australia and the Resumption of Nuclear Testing." Canberra Papers 121. Australian National University, Canberra.

"Nuclear Weapons: Going, Going." 1991. *Economist.* October 12, 54.

Oakland, William H., and William A. Testa. 1996. "State Local Business Taxation and the Benefits Principle." *Economic Perspective* 20, no. 1:2–19.

O'Connell, Robert. 1989. *Of Arms and Men.* Oxford: Oxford University Press.

Office of the Press Secretary. 1994. *Selected Remarks Prepared for Delivery by President William Jefferson Clinton on U.S. Policy toward Haiti,* September 15.

Olson, Mancur. 1965. *The Logic of Collective Action.* Cambridge: Harvard University Press.

Onuf, Nicholas G. 1989. *World of Our Making: Rules and Rule in Social Theory and International Relations.* Columbia: University of South Carolina Press.

Onuf, Nicholas G., and Frank F. Klink. 1989. "Anarchy, Authority, and Rule." *International Studies Quarterly* 33, no. 2:149–73.

Oppenheim, Lassa. 1952. *International Law: A Treatise.* Vol. 2, *Disputes, War, and Neutrality.* 7th ed., ed. H. Lauterpacht. New York: David McKay.

———. 1955. *International Law: A Treatise.* Vol. 1, *Peace.* 8th ed., ed. H. Lauterpacht. New York: Longmans, Green.

Organization of Economic Cooperation and Development (OECD). 1997. *Development Cooperation Report, 1996.* Paris: OECD.

Osgood, Charles E. 1962. *An Alternative to War or Surrender.* Urbana: University of Illinois Press.

Pape, Robert. 1997. "Why Economic Sanctions Do Not Work." *International Security* 22, no. 1:90–136.

Pastor, Robert. 1993. "Forward to the Beginning: Widening the Scope for Global Collective Action." In *Emerging Norms of Justified Intervention,* ed. Laura W. Reed and Carl Kaysen. Cambridge, Mass.: American Academy of Arts and Sciences, 133–47.

Patchen, Martin. 1988. *Resolving Disputes between Nations: Coercion or Conciliation?* Durham: Duke University Press.

Pearson, Geoffrey A. H. 1993. *Seize the Day: Lester B. Pearson and Crisis Diplomacy.* Ottawa: Carleton University Press.

Pearson, Lester B. 1972. *Mike: The Memoirs of the Rt. Hon. Lester B. Pearson.* Vol. 1, *1897–1948.* Toronto: University of Toronto Press.

———. 1973. *Mike: The Memoirs of the Rt. Hon. Lester B. Pearson.* Vol. 2, *1948–1957.* Toronto: University of Toronto Press.

Petrazzini, Ben. 1996. *Global Telecom Talks: A Trillion Dollar Deal.* Washington, D.C.: Institute for International Economics.

Plumptre, A. F. W. 1977. *Three Decades of Decision: Canada and the World Monetary System, 1944–1975.* Toronto: McClelland and Stewart.

Plunkett, Mark. 1994. "Law and Order; Institution Building: The Establishment of the Rule of Law in Post Conflict Peacebuilding." In *International Peacekeeping: Building on the Cambodian Experience,* ed. Hugh Smith. Canberra: Australian Defence Studies Centre, 65–78.

Powell, Robert. 1993. "Absolute and Relative Gains in International Relations Theory." In *Neorealism and Neoliberalism: The Contemporary Debate,* ed. David A. Baldwin. New York: Columbia University Press, 209–33.

———. 1998b. "Reversing the Gun Sights: Transnational Civil Society Targets Land Mines." *International Organization* 52, no. 3:613–44.

Price, Richard. 1997. *The Chemical Weapons Taboo.* Ithaca: Cornell University Press.

———. 1998a. "International Norms and the Mines Taboo: Pulls towards Compliance." *Canadian Foreign Policy* 5, no. 3:105–23.

Price, Richard, and Nina Tannenwald. 1996. "Norms and Deterrence: The Nuclear and Chemical Weapons Taboos." In *Culture of National Security,* ed. Peter J. Katzenstein. New York: Columbia University Press, 114–52.

Price, Robert. 1991. *The Apartheid State in Crisis: Political Transformation in South Africa, 1975–1990.* Oxford: Oxford University Press.

Quigley, John. 1996. "The 'Privatization' of Security Council Enforcement Action: A Threat to Multilateralism." *Michigan Journal of International Law* 17 (Winter): 249–83.

Raudzens, George. 1990. "War-Winning Weapons: The Measurement of Technological Determinism in Military History." *The Journal of Military History* 54, no. 4:403–33.

Ray, James Lee. 1995. *Democracy and International Conflict: An Evaluation of the Democratic Peace Proposition.* Columbia: University of South Carolina Press.

Reid, Escott. 1977. *Time of Fear and Hope: The Making of the North Atlantic Treaty, 1947–1949.* Toronto: McClelland and Stewart.

———. 1983. *On Duty: A Canadian at the Making of the United Nations, 1945–1946.* Toronto: McClelland and Stewart.

Reinicke, Wolfgang H. 1997. "Global Public Policy." *Foreign Affairs* 76, no. 6:127–38.

———. 1998. *Global Public Policy: Governing without Government?* Washington, D.C.: Brookings Institution.

Reisman, W. Michael. 1993. "The Constitutional Crisis in the United Nations." *American Journal of International Law* 87, no. 1:83–100.

Richman, Alvin. 1993. "American Support for International Involvement." *Public Opinion Quarterly* 57:264–76.

———. 1996. "American Support for International Involvement: General and Specific Components of Post–Cold War Changes." *Public Opinion Quarterly* 60:305–21.

Ritchie, Gordon. 1997. *Wrestling with the Elephant: The Inside Story of the Canada–U.S. Trade Wars.* Toronto: Macfarlane, Walter, and Ross.

Roberts, Adam. 1993. "Humanitarian War: Military Intervention and Human Rights." *International Affairs* 69 (July): 429–49.

———. 1996. "Humanitarian Action in War." *Adelphi Paper* 305. London: International Institute of Strategic Studies.

Robinson, H. Basil. 1989. *Diefenbaker's World: A Populist in Foreign Affairs.* Toronto: University of Toronto Press.

Rodrik, Dani. 1997a. *Has Globalization Gone Too Far?* Washington, D.C.: Institute for International Economics.

———. 1997b. "Sense and Nonsense in the Globalization Debate." *Foreign Policy* 107 (Summer): 19–37.

Rogers, Rosemarie, and Emily Copeland. 1993. *Forced Migration: Policy Issues in the Post–Cold War World.* Medford, Mass. Fletcher School of Law and Diplomacy, Tufts University.

Rose, R. 1991. "What Is Lesson Drawing?" *Journal of Public Policy* 11:3–30.

———. 1993. *Lesson-Drawing in Public Policy.* Chatham, N.J.: Chatham House.

Rosecrance, Richard. 1987. *The Rise of the Trading State.* New York: Basic Books.

Rosenau, James N. 1990. *Turbulence in World Politics: A Theory of Change and Continuity.* London: Harvester Wheatsheaf.

———. 1992. "Governance, Order, and Change in World Politics." In *Governance without Government: Order and Change in World Politics,* ed. James N. Rosenau and E. O. Czempiel. Cambridge: Cambridge University Press, 1–29.

———. 1995. "Governance in the Twenty-First Century." *Global Governance* 1, no. 1:13–43.

Rosenau, James N., and F. O. Czempiel, eds. 1992. *Governance without Government: Order and Change in World Politics.* Cambridge: Cambridge Unviersity Press.

Roth, Cecil. 1961. *History of the Jews.* New York: Shocken.

Russett, Bruce. 1993. *Grasping the Democratic Peace.* Princeton: Princeton University Press.

Sandler, Todd. 1997. *Global Challenges: An Approach to Environmental, Political, and Economic Problems.* Cambridge: Cambridge University Press.

Sassen, Saskia. 1996. *Losing Control: Sovereignty in an Age of Globalization.* New York: Columbia University Press.

Saul, John Ralston. 1994. "Culture and Foreign Policy." In *Report of the Special Joint Committee of the Senate and of the House of Commons Reviewing Canadian Foreign Policy—Canada's Foreign Policy: Position Papers.* Ottawa: Canada Communications Group Publishing.

Savage, James D. 1989. *The Politics of International Telecommunications Regulation.* Boulder: Westview.

Schelling, Thomas. 1980. *The Strategy of Conflict.* 2d ed. Cambridge: Harvard University Press.

Scholte, Jan Aart. 1996. "Beyond the Buzzword: Towards a Critical Theory of Globalization." In *Globalization: Theory and Practice,* ed. Eleonore Kofman and Gillian Youngs. New York: Pinter, 43–57.

Schorn, Tim. 1995. "United Nations Intervention in Crises of Authority and Failed States: A New Basis in Theory and Practice." Ph.D. diss., University of Notre Dame.

Schott, Jeffrey J. 1994. *The Uruguay Round: An Assessment.* Washington, D.C.: Institute for International Economics.

Schroeder, Paul W. 1994. "The New World Order: A Historical Perspective." *Washington Quarterly* 17, no. 2:25–46.

Schumpeter, Joseph A. 1943. *Capitalism, Socialism, and Democracy.* London: Unwin University Books.

Searle, John R. 1995. *The Construction of Social Reality*. New York: Free Press.

Sikkink, Kathryn. 1993. "Human Rights, Principled Issue-Networks, and Sovereignty in Latin America." *International Organization* 47, no. 3:411–41.

Simpson, John, and Darryl Howlett, eds. 1995. *The Future of the Non-Proliferation Treaty*. New York: Macmillan.

Sinclair, Timothy J. 1997. "Global Governance and the International Political Economy of the Commonplace." Paper presented at the annual meeting of the International Studies Association, March 18–22, Toronto.

Singer, Max, and Aaron Wildavsky. 1993. *The Real World Order*. Chatham, N.J.: Chatham House.

Sismanidis, Roxane D. 1997. *UN Police Functions in Peace Operations*. Washington, D.C.: United States Institute of Peace.

Skolnikoff, Eugene B. 1990. "The Policy Deadlock on Global Warming." *Foreign Policy* 79: 77–93.

Slaughter, Matthew, and Phillip Swagel. 1997. "Does Globalization Lower Wages and Export Jobs?" Economic Issues no. 11, International Monetary Fund, Washington D.C.

Slemrod, Joel. 1990. "Tax Principles in an International Economy." In *World Tax Reform: Cases Studies of Developed and Developing Countries,* ed. Michael J. Boskin and Charles E. McLure Jr. San Francisco: Institute for Contemporary Studies Press, 11–23.

Smith, Anthony. 1995. "The Natives Are Restless," *Media Studies Journal* 9, no. 4:1–5.

Smith, Arnold Cantwell, with Clyde Sanger. 1981. *Stitches in Time: The Commonwealth in World Politics*. Don Mills, Ont.: General Publishing.

Solingen, Etel. 1995. "The New Multilateralism and Nonproliferation: Bringing in Domestic Politics." *Global Governance* 1, no. 2:205–27.

Spaak, Paul-Henri. 1959. *Why NATO?*, Baltimore: Penguin Books.

Spero, Joan Edelman. 1982. "Information: The Policy Void." *Foreign Policy* 48 (Fall): 139–56.

Spybey, Tony. 1996. *Globalization and World Society*. Cambridge, U.K.: Polity Press.

Stairs, Denis. 1974. *The Diplomacy of Constraint: Canada, the Korean War, and the United States*. Toronto: University of Toronto Press.

———. 1995. "The Public Politics of the Canadian Defence and Foreign Policy Reviews." *Canadian Foreign Policy* 3, no. 1:91–116.

Stirling, Patricia. 1996. "The Use of Trade Sanctions as an Enforcement Mechanisms for Basic Human Rights: A Proposal for Addition to the World Trade Organization." *American University Journal of International Law and Policy* 11, no. 1:1–46.

Stremlau, John. 1996. *Sharpening International Sanctions: Toward a Stronger Role for the United Nations*. Carnegie Commission on Preventing Deadly Conflict. New York: Carnegie Corporation of New York.

Stueck, William. 1995. *The Korean War: An International History*. Princeton: Princeton University Press.

Sullivan, Stacy. 1996. "Bosnia's Most Wanted Mostly Accessible." *Washington Post,* November 27.

Tacsan, Joaquin. 1992. *The Dynamics of International Law in Conflict Resolution*. The Hague: Martinus Nijhoff.

Takach, George. 1990. "Moving the Embassy to Jerusalem, 1979." In *Canadian Foreign Policy: Selected Cases,* ed. Don Munton and John Kirton. Scarborough, Ont.: Prentice-Hall Canada, 273–85.

Tannenwald, Nina. 1995. *Dogs That Don't Bark: The United States, the Role of Norms, and the Non-Use of Nuclear Weapons in the Post–World War Two Era.* Ph.D. diss., Cornell University.

Teeple, Gary. 1995. *Globalization and the Decline of Social Reform.* Toronto: Garamond Press.

Telser, L. G. 1980. "A Theory of Self-Enforcing Agreements." *Journal of Business* 53, no. 1:27–44.

Teson, Fernando. 1988. *Humanitarian Intervention: An Inquiry into Law and Morality.* Dobbs Ferry, N.Y.: Transnational.

Thakur, Ramesh. 1986. "A Dispute of Many Colours: France, New Zealand, and the 'Rainbow Warrior' Affair." *World Today* 42 (December): 209–14.

Thant, U. 1963. "A United Nations Stand-by Peace Force." In *Public Papers of the Secretaries-General of the United Nations,* ed. Andrew W. Cordier and Max Harrelson. New York: Columbia University Press, 363–65.

Thomson, Janice E. 1993. "Norms in International Relations: A Conceptual Analysis." *International Journal of Group Tensions* 23, no. 1:67–83.

———. 1994. *Mercenaries, Pirates, and Sovereigns.* Princeton: Princeton University Press.

Tow, William T. 1993. "Contending Security Approaches in the Asia-Pacific Region." *Security Studies* 3 (Autumn): 75–116.

Trail Smelter Arbitral Tribunal. Trail Smelter Arbitration *(U.S. v. Canada).* 1941. *Reports of International Arbitral Awards* 3:1905.

Tuathail, Gearoid O., Andrew Herod, and Susan M. Roberts. 1997. "Negotiating Unruly Problematics." In *An Unruly World? Globalization, Governance, and Geography,* ed. Andrew Herod, Susan M. Roberts, and Gearoid O. Tuathail. New York: Routledge, 1–24.

Tunstall, Jeremy. 1995. "Are the Media Still American?" *Media Studies Journal* 9, no. 4:7–16.

United Nations. 1995. *The United Nations and Nuclear Non-Proliferation: The United Nations Blue Books Series.* Vol. 3. New York: United Nations.

———. 1996. *Report of the Copenhagen Roundtable on United Nations Sanctions in the Case of the Former Yugoslavia,* S/1996/776.

United Nations High Commissioner for Refugees (UNHCR). 1995. *The State of the World's Refugees: In Search of Solutions.* New York: Oxford University Press.

———. 1997. *Statistics.* Geneva: UNHCR.

United Nations Secretary-General. 1992. *Report of the Secretary-General,* February 19, S/23613.

United States. General Accounting Office. 1992. *Economic Sanctions: Effectiveness as Tools of Foreign Policy.* Washington, D.C: GPO.

———. 1993. U.S. Senate, Committee on Foreign Relations. *U.N. Peacekeeping: Observations on Mandates and Operational Capability.* Statement of Frank C. Conahan, Assistant Comptroller General, National Security and International Affairs Division, GAO 1.5/2: T-NSIAD-93–15.

————. 1994. *International Trade: Issues Regarding Imposition of an Oil Embargo against Nigeria*, report prepared for the chairman, Subcommittee on Africa, Committee on Foreign Affairs, U.S. House of Representatives, 103rd Congress, 2nd session, November. GAO/GGD-95-24, 12.

United States. Office of the Assistant Secretary of Defense (Public Affairs). 1997. Background Briefing on Landmine Policy. <http://www.dtic.mil/defenselink/news/Jan97/x011797_x0117ldm.html> (January 23).

United States. Senate. 1990. *United States Policy toward Iraq: Human Rights, Weapons Proliferation, and International Law: Hearing before the Committee on Foreign Relations*. 101st Cong., 2d sess., June 15.

United States Committee for Refugees. 1997. *World Refugee Survey*. Washington, D.C.: United States Committee for Refugees.

Urquhart, Brian. 1991. Foreword to *United Nations Peacekeeping and the Non-Use of Force*, by F. T. Liu. International Peace Academy Occasional Paper Series. Boulder: Lynne Rienner, 6–8.

van Bergeijk, Peter. 1994. *Economic Diplomacy, Trade, and Commercial Policy: Positive and Negative Sanctions in a New World Order*. Aldershot, U.K.: Edward Elgar, 12.

van Creveld, Martin. 1989. *Technology and War*. New York: Free Press.

Van Harpen, Robin L. 1995. "Mama, Don't Let Your Babies Grow Up to Be Cowboys: Reconciling Trade and Cultural Independence." *Minnesota Journal of Global Trade* 4:165–94.

Vattel, Emerich de. 1839. *Law of Nations, or The Principles of Natural Law*. Philadelphia: T. & J. W. Johnson.

Väyrynen, Raimo. 1969. "A Case Study of Sanctions: Finland–the Soviet Union in 1958–1959." *Cooperation and Conflict* 5, no. 3:205–33.

————. 1991. "To Settle or to Transform? Perspectives on the Resolution of National and International Conflicts." In *New Directions in Conflict Theory: Conflict Resolution and Conflict Transformation*, ed. Raimo Väyrynen. Newbury Park, Calif.: Sage Publications, 1–25.

————. 1997a. "Economic Incentives and the Bosnian Peace Process." In *The Price of Peace: Incentives and International Conflict Prevention*, ed. David Cortwright. Lanham, Md.: Rowman and Littlefield, 155–79.

————. 1997b. "International Stability and Risky States: The Enforcement of Norms." In *Risky States*, ed. Gerald Schneider and Patricia Weitsman. London: Macmillan, 37–59.

Velzeboer, Marijke. 1996. "Globalization and the Internet: Opening a Window for Grassroots Producers." *Grassroots Development* 20, no. 2:12–17.

Vogler, John. 1992. "Regimes and the Global Commons: Space, Atmosphere, and Oceans." In *Global Politics: Globalization and the Nation-State*, ed. Anthony G. McGrew, and Paul G. Lewis. Cambridge, U.K.: Polity Press.

Walter, Andrew. 1991. *World Power and World Money: The Role of Hegemony and International Monetary Order*. Hemel Hempstead, U.K.: Harvester Wheatsheaf.

Walzer, Michael. 1977. *Just and Unjust Wars: A Moral Argument with Historical Illustrations*. New York: Basic Books.

Weiner, Myron. 1993. "Security, Stability, and International Migration." Introduction to *International Migration and Security*, ed. M. Weiner. Boulder: Westview, 11–19.

————. 1995. *The Global Migration Crisis: Challenge to States and to Human Rights.* New York: HarperCollins.

————. 1996. "Nations without Borders: The Gifts of Folk Gone Abroad." *Foreign Affairs* 75, no. 2:129–34.

Weiss, Thomas G., David Cortright, George A. Lopez, and Larry Minear, eds. 1997. *Political Gain and Civilian Pain: The Humanitarian Impacts of Economic Sanctions.* Lanham, Md.: Rowman and Littlefield.

Weiss, Thomas G., and Leon Gordenker. 1996. *NGOs, the UN, and Global Governance.* Boulder: Lynn Rienner.

Wendt, Alexander. 1992. "Anarchy Is What States Make of It: The Social Construction of Power Politics." *International Organization* 46, no. 2:391–425.

Wertheimer, Alan. 1987. *Coercion.* Princeton: Princeton University Press.

Whalley, J., and R. Wigle. 1991. "The International Incidence of Carbon Taxes." In *Economic Policy Responses to Global Warming,* ed. R. Dornbusch and J. Poterba. Cambridge: MIT Press.

White, N. D. 1992. *Keeping the Peace: The United Nations and the Maintenance of International Peace and Security.* New York: Manchester University Press.

Who will Reconnect with the People: Republicans, Democrats, or . . . none of the above? Americans Talk Issues, no. 28. 1995. St. Augustine, Fl.: Americans Talk Issues Foundation.

Wilson, John Douglas. 1996. "Capital Mobility and Environmental Standards: Is There a Theoretical Basis for a Race to the Bottom?" In *Fair Trade and Harmonization: Prerequisites for Free Trade?* Vol. 1, ed. Jagdish Bhagwati and Robert E. Hudec. Cambridge: MIT Press, 393–428.

Winters, L. Allan. 1992. "The Trade and Welfare Effects of Greenhouse Gas Abatement." In *The Greening of World Trade Issues,* ed. Kym Anderson and Richard Blackhurst. London: Harvester Wheatsheaf.

Wittkopf, Eugene R. 1996. "What Americans Really Think about Foreign Policy." *Washington Quarterly* 19, no. 3:91–106.

Wolfers, Arnold. 1962. "Power and Influence: The Means of Foreign Policy." In *Discord and Collaboration: Essays on International Politics,* by Arnold Wolfers. Baltimore: Johns Hopkins University Press, 107–8.

World Health Organization (WHO). 1998. *International Health Regulations: First Annotated Edition.* Geneva: WHO.

Yarborough, Beth V., and Robert M. Yarborough. 1986. "Reciprocity, Bilateralism, and Economic 'Hostages': Self-Enforcing Agreements in International Trade." *International Studies Quarterly* 30, no. 1:7–21.

————. 1992. *Cooperation and Governance in International Trade: The Strategic Organizational Approach.* Princeton: Princeton University Press.

Young, Oran R. 1979. *Compliance and Public Authority: A Theory with International Applications.* Baltimore: Johns Hopkins University Press.

————. 1989. *International Cooperation: Building Regimes for Natural Resources and the Environment.* Ithaca: Cornell University Press.

————. 1992. "The Effectiveness of International Institutions: Hard Cases and Critical Variables." In *Governance without Government: Order and Change in World Politics,* ed. James N. Rosenau and Ernst-Otto. Zempiel. Cambridge: Cambridge University Press, 160–94.

———. 1994. *International Governance: Protecting the Environment in a Stateless Society.* Ithaca: Cornell University Press.

———. 1997. "Global Governance: Toward a Theory of Decentralized World Order." In *Global Governance: Drawing Insights from the Environmental Experience*, ed. Oran R. Young. Cambridge: MIT Press, 273–99.

Zacher, Mark W. 1979. *International Conflicts and Collective Security, 1946–1977.* New York: Praeger.

Zacher, Mark W., with Brent A. Sutton. 1996. *Governing Global Networks: International Regimes for Transportation and Communications.* Cambridge: Cambridge University Press.

Zartman, William I. 1985. *Ripe for Resolution: Conflict and Intervention in Africa.* Oxford: Oxford University Press.

———. 1986. "Ripening Conflict, Ripe Moment: Formula and Mediation." In *Perspectives on Negotiation*, ed. Diane B. Bendahmane and John W. McDonald Jr. Washington, D.C.: Foreign Service Institute, Department of State.

———, ed. 1995. *Collapsed States: The Disintegration and Restoration of Legitimate Authority.* Boulder: Lynne Rienner.

Zartman, William I., and Maureen Berman. 1982. *The Principal Negotiator.* New Haven: Yale University Press.

Zimmerman, Warren. 1993. Statement before the Subcommittee on Foreign Operations of the Senate Appropriations Committee, June 30. *Department of State Dispatch*, July 12.

Zürn, Michael. 1995. "The Challenge of Globalization and Individualization: A View from Europe." In *Whose World Order?: Uneven Globalization and the End of the Cold War.*, ed. Hans-Henrik Holm and Georg Sorensen. Boulder: Westview, 137–63.

———. 1998. *Regieren jenseits des Nationalstaates. Globalisierung und Denationalisierung als Chance.* Frankfurt am Main: Suhrkamp.

Index

About the Contributors

David Cortright is president of the Fourth Freedom Forum in Goshen, Indiana, and a research fellow at the Joan B. Kroc Institute for International Peace Studies at the University of Notre Dame. He is the recipient of a 1990 research and writing award for peace and international cooperation from the John D. and Catherine T. MacArthur Foundation. Cortright has authored and edited several books, including *The Price of Peace: Incentives and International Conflict Prevention* (Rowman & Littlefield, 1997) and, with George Lopez, *Economic Sanctions: Panacea or Peacebuilding in a Post–Cold War World?* (Westview, 1995).

Alan Dowty is professor of government and international relations and fellow at the Joan B. Kroc Institute for International Peace Studies at the University of Notre Dame, where he has taught since 1975. Before that, he was on the faculty of the Hebrew University in Jerusalem for twelve years, during which time he also served as executive director of the Leonard Davis Institute for International Relations and as chairman of the Department of International Relations. Among his books are *The Limits of American Isolation* (New York University Press, 1971); *Middle East Crisis* (University of California Press, 1984), which won the Quincy Wright Award of the International Studies Association; *Closed Borders: The Contemporary Assault on Freedom of Movement* (Yale University Press, 1987), which was originaly written as a Twentieth Century Fund report; and *The Jewish State: A Century Later* (University of California Press, 1998).

Robert C. Johansen is professor of government and international studies at the University of Notre Dame and Acting Regan Director of the Joan B. Kroc Institute for International Peace Studies. He is author of *The National Interest and the Human Interest: An Analysis of U.S. Foreign Policy* (Princeton University Press, 1980) and coeditor of *The Constitutional Foundations of World Peace* (State University of New York Press, 1993) and has published articles on security issues in *World Politics, Journal of Peace Research, Security*

281

Dialogue, Global Governance, Third World Quarterly, Journal of International Affairs, Mershon International Studies Review, Political Studies, and more popular periodicals such as *Atlantic, Harper's,* and the *Nation.* He is the founding editor in chief of *World Policy Journal* and past president of the World Policy Institute. He has held visiting appointments at the Center for International Studies at Princeton University and the Center for International Affairs and the Center for the Study of World Religions at Harvard University. He earned his doctorate at Columbia University.

Robert T. Kudrle is professor of public affairs at the Hubert H. Humphrey Institute of Public Affairs, University of Minnesota, where he has also served as associate dean for research and director of the Orville and Jane Freeman Center for International Economic Policy. Professor Kudrle is past coeditor of *International Studies Quarterly* and has published widely on industrial organization, public policy toward business, international economic policy, and the political economy of social services. Much of his recent research concerns economic relations among the industrialized countries. He has consulted for many national and international agencies, including the Antitrust Division of the U.S. Department of the Justice, the Internal Revenue Service, the Overseas Private Investment Corporation, the Agency for International Development, the Canadian Department of Consumer and Corporate Affairs, and the United Nations Centre on Transnational Corporations. Professor Kudrle holds a bachelor's degree from Harvard College (government), a master's degree from Oxford University (economics), and a doctorate from Harvard University (economics).

Albert Legault is full professor in the Department of Political Science at Laval University (Quebec). He is also director of L'Institut Québécois des Hautes Études Internationales (IQHÉI). From 1973 to 1980 and from 1994 to 1995, he was director general of the Québec Center for International Relations (CQRI). Professor Legault earned his master's degree at the University of Chicago and his doctorate at the University of Geneva, and he has received an honorary doctorate from the University of Paris at Versailles. He has directed the publication of more than twenty works, including *Les Conflits dans le Monde,* an annual publication of the IQHÉI, as well as works concerning strategy and arms control. In 1994, he was awarded a prize by ACFAS (Association Canadienne Française pour l'Avancement des Sciences) for his contribution to the study of international relations, and in 1995 he received the Innis-Gérin medal of the Royal Society of Canada, of which he has been a member since 1977. In March 1997, he produced a report for the prime minister of Canada entitled "Bringing the Canadian Armed Forces into the Twenty-First Century." In June 1997, professor Legault was awarded a NATO fellowship.

Gilburt Loescher is a fellow of the Joan B. Kroc Institute for International Peace Studies and professor of government and international studies at the University of Notre Dame. He has held visiting research appointments at the Centers of International Studies at Princeton and the London School of Economics, at Oxford, and at the International Institute for Strategic Studies in London. His major publications include *Calculated Kindness: Refugees and America's Half-Open Door* (Free Press, 1986); *Beyond Charity: International Cooperation and the Global Refugee Crisis* (Oxford University Press, 1993); *Refugees and International Relations* (Oxford University Press, 1989); and *The Moral Nation: Humanitarianism and U.S. Foreign Policy* (University of Notre Dame Press, 1989); *Human Rights and American Foreign Policy* (University of Notre Dame Press, 1979). He has regularly served as an adviser to the United Nations High Commissioner for Refugees and the Ford Foundation and he has served on the Board of Directors of Amnesty International USA.

George A. Lopez is a fellow at the Joan B. Kroc Institute for International Peace Studies and professor of government and international studies at the University of Notre Dame. Lopez's research interests focus primarily on the problems of state violence and coercion, especially economic sanctions, and gross violations of human rights. His work has been published in *Chitty's Law Journal, Human Rights Quarterly,* the *Bulletin of the Atomic Scientists, International Studies Quarterly, Fletcher Forum,* and the *International Journal of Human Rights.* With David Cortright he has contributed to and edited *Economic Sanctions: Panacea or Peacebuilding in a Post–Cold War World?* (Westview, 1995) and with Thomas Weiss, Cortright, and Larry Minear, *Political Gain and Civilian Pain: Assessing the Humanitarian Impact of Economic Sanctions* (Rowman and Littlefield, 1997).

Karen A. Mingst is professor of political science and chair of the department of political science at the University of Kentucky. She is the author, coauthor, and coeditor of a number of books, including *Essentials of International Relations* (W.W. Norton, 1998), *The United Nations in the Post–Cold War Era* (Westview, 1995), *Teaching International Affairs with Cases: Cross-National Perspectives* (1997), *The United States and Multilateral Institutions: Patterns of Changing Instrumentality and Influence* (Unwin Hyman, 1990), and *Politics and the African Development Bank* (University Press of Kentucky, 1990). Under a grant from the United States Institute of Peace, she is currently writing *State Participation in Multilateral Peacekeeping: A Comparative Analysis.*

Kim Richard Nossal is a professor in the Department of Political Science at McMaster University. Schooled in Melbourne, Beijing, Toronto, and Hong Kong, he received his bachelor's, master's, and doctoral degrees from the

University of Toronto. He joined McMaster University in 1976 and served as chair of the political science department from 1992 to 1996. From 1992 to 1997 he was editor of *International Journal*, the quarterly of the Canadian Institute of International Affairs. His books and monographs include *The Patterns of World Politics* (Prentice Hall Allyn and Bacon, 1998), *The Politics of Canadian Foreign Policy*, 3d ed. (Prentice-Hall, 1997), *Rain Dancing: Sanctions in Canadian and Australian Foreign Policy* (University of Toronto Press, 1994), and *The Beijing Massacre: Australian Responses* (Australian Foreign Policy Publications Programme, Australian National University, 1993).

Richard Price has been an assistant professor of political science at the University of Minnesota since 1994. His published works include *The Chemical Weapons Taboo* (Cornell University Press, 1997) and articles in *International Organization, Review of International Studies,* and the *European Journal of International Relations.*

Denis Stairs is a former president of the Canadian Political Science Association and a fellow of the Royal Society of Canada. Currently McCulloch Professor in Political Science at Dalhousie University in Halifax, Nova Scotia, he was the founding director of Dalhousie's Centre for Foreign Policy Studies from 1970 to 1975 and has served as chair of his department and as the University's vice-president (academic and research). He specializes in Canadian foreign and defense policy, and in Canada–United States relations.

Raimo Väyrynen is professor of government and international studies at the University of Notre Dame. From 1993 to 1998 he served as the Regan Director of the Joan B. Kroc Institute for International Peace Studies and he continues as a senior fellow of the Institute. He was professor of international relations from 1978 to 1998 and dean of the faculty for social sciences from 1990 to 1993 at the University of Helsinki. He has chaired the Finnish Political Science Association, the Finnish Social Science Research Council, and the Nordic Committee on International Relations and has been a member of the Council of the United Nations University, the Nordic Council of Social Sciences, and the Committee for Social Sciences of the European Science Foundation. He has held visiting positions at Princeton University, Harvard University, MIT, and the University of Minnesota. Väyrynen has published extensively on the theory of international relations, international security and disarmament, international political economy, and peace and conflict studies. His most recent books are *Military Industrialization and Economic Development* (Dartmouth, 1992), a biography of Urho Kekkonen (Weilin and Soos, 1994), and *Global Transformation:*

Economics, Politics, and Culture (The Finnish National Fund for Research and Development, 1997).

Mark W. Zacher is professor of political science and acting director of the Institute of International Relations at the University of British Columbia. He was director of the Institute of International Relations from 1971 to 1991. Zacher is a specialist in international regimes and organizations. He is the author of *Dag Hammarksjold's United Nations* (Columbia University Press, 1970) and *International Conflicts and Collective Security, 1946–1977* (Praeger, 1979). He is the coauthor of *Pollution, Politics, and International Law: Tankers at Sea* (University of California Press, 1979), *Managing International Markets: Developing Countries and the Commodity Trade Regime* (Columbia University Press, 1988), and *Governing Global Networks: International Regimes for Transportation and Communications* (Cambridge University Press, 1996).